GREAT BATTLES
AND THEIR
GREAT GENERALS

Also by Harry Roskolenko

Novels:

BLACK IS A MAN
LAN-LAN

Autobiography:

WHEN I WAS LAST ON CHERRY STREET
THE TERRORIZED
THE TIME THAT WAS THEN

Poetry:

SEQUENCE ON VIOLENCE
I WENT INTO THE COUNTRY
A SECOND SUMMARY, *illustrated by Sidney Nolan*
NOTES FROM A JOURNEY, *illustrated by Sidney Nolan*
PARIS POEMS, *illustrated by Zao Wou-Ki*
AMERICAN CIVILIZATION, *illustrated by John Olsen, Clifton Pugh,
Albert Tucker*

Travel:

POET ON A SCOOTER
WHITE MAN, GO!

Anthology:

SOLO: GREAT ADVENTURES ALONE
GREAT BATTLES AND THEIR GREAT GENERALS

GREAT BATTLES
AND THEIR
GREAT GENERALS

EDITED BY

Harry Roskolenko

ᕰᕱP

A Playboy Press Book

Published simultaneously in the United States and Canada by Playboy Press, Chicago, Illinois. Printed in the United States of America. Library of Congress Catalog Card Number: 73–91655. First edition. ISBN 87223–395–2.

PLAYBOY and Rabbit Head design are trademarks of Playboy, 919 North Michigan Avenue, Chicago, Illinois 60611 (U.S.A.), Reg. U.S. Pat. Off., marca registrada, marque déposée.

To Louise—and peaceful pursuits

CONTENTS

FOREWORD

War is hell, an abomination, a waste—all of the things, in fact, that have been said about it down through the ages. Yet, war is also the most moving and demanding of human experiences, an inspiration to the genius of such different men as Shakespeare, Goya and Hemingway. It exerts upon even the noblest a malign attraction. Robert E. Lee told his staff before Fredericksburg that it was well war was so terrible, lest men become too fond of it.

Wars have marked history's great divides. They have shaped the world in which we live, just as they have shaped man's destiny since the Stone Age. The reason, as Karl Von Clausewitz wrote, is that war "is not merely a political act, but also a political instrument, a continuation of political relations, a carrying out of the same by other means." Man is a political animal, and the ultimate solution to his political differences has been war.

Since history began, philosophers have dreamt of war's abolition. Wars have been fought to end war. It is with us still.

The realist must accept war and the threat of war because he understands that peace depends only on the stability of existing political and economic conditions. The long peace from Waterloo to the Marne was possible because conditions in Europe, then the center of the world, remained relatively stable. The rise of the German Empire altered this situation, and war came.

The conditions under which the Western world has lived since 1945 are changing with alarming rapidity. America's military primacy is becoming a thing of the past. Ideological rivalries remain fierce if temporarily latent. A new struggle for raw materials, particularly oil, is in its first phase.

Great Battles and Their Great Generals is a guide to humanity's most awesome experience. Only fools would neglect its lessons. Harry Roskolenko has collected the accounts of 13 of the greatest battles of history and presented them along with some penetrating comments on the commanders involved.

These are all major battles from Cannae in 216 B.C. to Inchon in Korea more than 2000 years later. The size of a battle in terms of the number of combatants, however, is not the only criterion of importance. Small actions, often ignored by history, may have decisive effects on the minds of commanders, which is where, ultimately, battles are won and lost. The British tank break-through on August 8, 1918, struck the phlegmatic Ludendorff as "the black day for the German Army" and seriously affected his will to fight even though it was a relatively minor battle on a vast front.

A battle's influence on history is another criterion. Hastings, for example, brought the Normans, unity and strong government to England. The French Revolutionary Army's triumph over the Allies at Valmy in 1792 seduced France into the triumphs and tragedies of the Napoleonic wars. The Battle of Britain in 1940 ended Hitler's chances of winning the war in the West.

A reader having any acquaintance with war will be struck by the difference between these accounts and his own experience in battle. No historian can convey the confusion, terror and excite-ment of combat. For those we must go to the novelists. I never understood the true greatness of Ernest Hemingway's account of the retreat from Caporetto in *A Farewell to Arms* until, as a young man, I was part of the retreat of the British and French armies to the Channel coast in May of 1940.

The art of war has not progressed steadily through the ages from crude fumblings to expert and polished campaigns. The Battle of Cannae, the first in this book, was a masterpiece. Gener-als ever since have tried to reproduce it. Of all the battles in this book it was the most conclusive. Not only was Cannae a model battle, it was a battle won by a brisk disregard of the rules. Hanni-bal, attacking with numerically inferior forces, took the supreme risk of enveloping both Roman flanks. Genius, in war as else-where, breaks the rules and succeeds. Both accounts of Cannae, one by Alfred von Schlieffen, the German master planner of World War I, and the other by the American, Theodore Ayrault Dodge, are concise, direct, incisive.

With the fall of the Roman Empire, war, in Europe at any rate, degenerated into mob scenes in which first the shock of armored cavalry and then the missile—in this case the English cloth-yard arrow—were decisive. Tactics languished, generalship was rare.

We must guard too, against confusing historical accounts with the bloody reality. In history, battles are orderly; blocks of troops move mechanically to their appointed positions; attacks take place when planned. But we know that there were delays, that some troops behaved badly, that commanders lost their nerve and sweated into their sword hilts. What Clausewitz called "the friction of war" is inescapable.

The defeat of the Spanish Armada by the English in 1588 was a singular event. Here was a battle that had a tremendous immediate effect on Europe and that also exerted an enormous influence on the development of arms and strategy. Cannae, to be sure, was a famous victory, but in the end the Romans won the Punic Wars. The armada's defeat, however, ended Spain's long domination of Europe and cleared the way for the rise of the French and British empires.

Winston Churchill's dictum that nothing is so uncertain as a battle at sea is confirmed by the records of this hazardous, confusing battle. When it was over the world had been taught two lessons. The first was that command of the sea can be attained only by what Mahan called "the fleet in being." The second was that the day of galleys bearing soldiers into battle against other ships was over, blown into the past by the English cannon firing at what was, in those days, long range on the great, unwieldy floating castles of Spain.

Drake, Hawkins and the others who harried the Spaniards up the Channel did not have to attend staff schools to get the message. The "affair of the Armada" was not only the first harsh application of the potential of sea power but the seedbed for naval strategy and tactics. From 1588 until the advent of the fleet aircraft carrier, naval tactics remained essentially the same. Ships were faster, guns heavier and more accurate, but Drake would have been at home on Nelson's *Victory* at Trafalgar or with Dewey on the *Olympia* at Manilla Bay.

The Battle of Saratoga in 1777 is justly included in this book. This was an important battle, but it is pertinent to recall that it came at the end of nearly two years' fighting between the Americans and the British. There had been dozens of small actions on land and on Lake Champlain. The British were almost always successful in these, yet each victory cost them dearly in men, material and, what is always of vital importance in war, time. So when Arnold and Morgan slashed into the British at Saratoga, their commanders, notably Burgoyne, were already psychologically prepared for defeat and capitulation. Reading firsthand accounts of the campaign—diaries, letters and the like—I have been impressed, too, by how much the size of the land, and the fierceness of the climate affected the battleworthiness of the British and their Hessian mercenaries.

Many of the accounts in this book illustrate the fact that chance plays a large and often decisive part in battle. Gettysburg was the most important battle of the Civil War; after that, every road led to Appomattox. But it can be argued that neither Lee nor Meade meant to fight there, that the two armies blundered into each other. The Army of Northern Virginia, remember, was blinded by the absence of Stuart and his cavalry. We can only conclude, too, from the fine account in this book and in others that Lee, the supreme tactician, momentarily lost his touch. But more of Lee later.

When I was a young war correspondent, the old soldiers of World War I emphasized that the decisive battle of *their* war, the Battle of the Marne, was fought very early in the conflict. The accounts of this battle provided by Mr. Roskolenko are by Marshal Joffre, Georges Blond and Joseph Delteil, and even the marshal substantiates the idea that the Marne, in military terms, was not a battle comparable to Waterloo or Shiloh. It was instead a series of isolated, incoherent actions fought by the French and, belatedly, the British against the Germans who, flushed with victory, had made the irretrievable mistake of exposing their right flank. Although the number of men engaged was very large, the losses from combat were small. It was in the earlier Battle of the Frontiers, in which German machine guns extinguished the French doctrine of the offensive, that the real losses were suffered.

Mr. Delteil's report on the transport of a French division from Paris by taxi is fine, exciting reading. This is the stuff of myths and legends. The division was driven out of Paris in taxis as part of General Gallieni's sortie against the German flank. The brutal truth, however, is that the sortie was far from an unqualified success. Certainly it was not the decisive point in the battle. Mr. Delteil to the contrary, it took several hours to sort out the division when it reached the front. Only then could it attack.

The "break" in the Battle of the Marne developed after Von Kluck, commanding the First Army, called back two corps and created a 30-mile gap between his army and Von Bulow's Second Army. Von Bulow, sensitive to the danger, withdrew his right flank. Into the gap thus created marched the British Expeditionary Force. Its advance after fighting, which by the standards of the day was light, prompted a general German withdrawal and the decisive "battle" was over.

No one, certainly not Joffre, Foch or Gallieni, won it. Von Kluck probably lost it. The Marne campaign is a good example of how Clausewitz's "friction of war" affects generals on the same side. The German army commanders were schooled and skillful. They were also jealous of each other and hostile to the directives of the Great General Staff. It is symptomatic of that staff's ultimate authority that the order to retreat from the Marne was given not by any of the army commanders or by Von Moltke, the commander in chief, but by a staff officer, Colonel Hentsch.

The Alamein battle is an example of the manner in which great battles may be decided before they begin. In late August of 1942 Rommel, then at the height of his fame, tried to turn the left flank of the British position at Alam el Halfa. In this almost forgotten battle the Afrika Korps failed against a new general, Montgomery, and new tactics; the British let the Germans come to them and then shot them up from well-concealed positions. The Axis losses in tanks were very heavy. The short-sighted German High Command in Berlin denied Rommel the replacements he needed. Thus, when the British offensive opened at Alamein, he did not have the resources necessary for a successful defense or a counteroffense.

Stalingrad, which with Alamein and Midway made the defeat of the Axis ultimately certain, was a Hitlerian blunder of fantastic proportions. Had the demonic genius in Berlin been willing to retreat, much of Paulus's army might have been saved and the Russians cheated of their most important victory.

In any event, a great many factors combined to defeat the

Germans. One of these, not usually mentioned, is the character of the terrain. I was struck, when touring the battlefield in 1946, by the deep ravines that cut through the western plain outside Stalingrad and continue on through the city to the west bank of the Volga. These ravines made it virtually impossible for the Germans to mount enveloping attacks against the Soviet defenders. They had to slug it out face-to-face against troops who day by day became more numerous, confident and better armed.

The landing in Normandy in 1944 was a classic example of what the military call the "set piece" battle—an attack upon a known, static position. Fortunately for the Allies, Field Marshal Montgomery who commanded excelled at that type of battle. After the war both General Eisenhower and General Walter Bedell Smith, his chief of staff, told me that no one but Montgomery could have planned and won the battle.

The accounts of D day make it all sound deceptively simple, and in a sense it was. You soften them up with bombardment by sea and air. You drop parachute troops, Americans here, British there. Then, under cover of bombardment, you come storming across the beaches. In essence it worked that way. But of all battles it seemed to have the highest proportion of uncertainty and confusion, of imbalance and agonizing delay. Fortunately this was not all on the Allied side. The excerpt from Cornelius Ryan's great book shows the Germans smitten with doubts, prey to wishful thinking and, above all, lethally slow in recognizing the invasion for what it was. It says much for the courage and resilience of the Germans that they sustained this salient defeat and yet fought on for another 11 months.

The battles described in this book involved some of the greatest commanders in history. The accounts of their generalship raises the question: What makes a great general?

From these accounts and from my memories of the commanders I saw at close range in World War II—Eisenhower, Bradley, Patton, Clark, Alexander, Montgomery, Auchinleck, Brooke, to name a few—I am prompted to offer my views on what makes a great general.

The first quality is coolness in action. This was more difficult to maintain in the days of Blenheim, Waterloo and Gettysburg, when generals were at the front. Marlborough's marvelous handling of his troops on the spot at Blenheim, Wellington's cold, correct calculations at the height of battle are examples. And, although General Eisenhower was well removed from personal risk, his decision to take advantage of a few hours of reasonably calm weather and invade must be accounted remarkable. Though a large and able staff was available and reports on every aspect of the Allied and German preparations were in hand, nonetheless Eisenhower himself had to review in his mind the enormous number of factors that argued for and against his decision. Although even then an agonizingly inarticulate speaker, his mind was capacious, orderly and retentive. This was exercise of command of the highest order

How can Lee's performance at Gettysburg be reconciled with his greatness on other battlefields? The reader may get the impression from this book, as I did, that the Confederate leader was overconfident after his successes against the hapless Hooker and other Union generals. The Union Army was there, he commanded the finest infantry this country had ever seen and with one blow he could win. Emotion won over cool intellect, so the long gray lines went forward—to be smashed.

The great Virginian's performance at Gettysburg resembles in many respects that of Napoleon at Waterloo. Each broke their best troops in headlong assaults on armies that they underestimated and that were commanded by generals who were not awed by their adversaries' reputations. Meade, of course, was no Wellington, but on those July days and later, under Grant, he showed coolness and perception in command.

The greatest generals see wars in simplistic terms. Grant is an example. He paid little attention to the "On to Richmond" campaign waged by northern editorialists and politicians. The job was to beat Lee; stop maneuvering for Richmond or to defend Washington and go after the Army of Northern Virginia.

By World War I the size of battles had grown so great that a Foch or a Ludendorff could do no more than draw up the general plan and wait upon results. From 1914 onwards in Europe, the real tacticians were the army and corps commanders, men like Collins in the First U.S. Army and Horrocks in the British Second in World War II.

Rommel, at his most successful, falls into this category. The

Afrika Korps and his front were small enough to foster personal command. He was at his best then. Later, when he commanded in Normandy, his control was less certain, his touch less sure.

Simplicity of approach, coolness of mind, a thorough understanding of the logistical problem, the sort of understanding Wellington demonstrated on a hundred battlefields, are all important. But there is an additional quality. Churchill called it "that innate, instinctive revolt against acquiescing to the will of the enemy."

Different generals express it in different ways. Patton was profanely, bombastically aggressive. But Alexander on the beaches of Dunkirk was as determined and as aggressive, supremely confident that the Germans would not defeat the British on the beaches.

Patton was a strange man. I cannot accept entirely Ernest Hemingway's comment that he was "a lucky Custer." He had great aptitude for exploitation and pursuit. Once his Third Army was moving, Patton directed it with tireless energy and a keen insight into the enemy's weaknesses. But the military historians of the future may conclude that he lacked that essential ingredient of coolness of head and heart.

Generals are men subject to man's weaknesses. Some are drunks, some are wenchers; I knew one successful French commander who was an ardent and obvious homosexual. Some are ambitious and show it. Some, like Bradley and Alexander, are content to do their duty. More than most mortals, generals are prey to hazard. Battles, even wars, can be—have been—lost for want of a horseshoe nail, or because of a sudden rainstorm, or a lost order. "In war," Polybius wrote, "we must always leave room for strokes of fortune, and accidents that cannot be foreseen."

We know that war is an insane evil. Yet, accepting that, believing that politics must be directed toward war's final prohibition, we cannot blind ourselves to its contribution to the human story. The spearmen at Cannae, the valiant Spaniards of the armada, Morgan's sharpshooters at Saratoga, the thin red line at Waterloo all added something to the experience of the race, something misguided and terrible, but with lessons of fortitude and bravery.

DREW MIDDLETON

ACKNOWLEDGMENTS

"The Battle of Cannae" by General Field Marshal Alfred von Schlieffen. From *Cannae* by Field Marshal Count Alfred von Schlieffen. Published in 1901 by E.G. Mittler and Son, Frankfurt, Germany. Permission granted by U.S. Army Command and General Staff College.

"Cannae" by Theodore Ayrault Dodge. From *Great Captains* by Theodore Ayrault Dodge. Original edition of 1889 reissued in 1968 by Kennikat Press, Port Washington, N.Y.

"The Defeat of the Spanish Armada, 1588" by Major General J.F.C. Fuller. Excerpt from *The Defeat of the Spanish Armada* by J.F.C. Fuller published by Eyre & Spottiswoode, London, 1955. (Agent) David Higham Associates, Ltd., 5–8 Lower John Street, Golden Square, London, W1R 4HA.

"The Battle of Blenheim, 1704" by Sir Edward Shepherd Creasy. From *Fifteen Decisive Battles of the World* by Sir Edward Creasy. Published in 1851 by Harper, New York.

"The Battle of Saratoga: October 17, 1777" by F.J. Hudleston. From *Gentleman Johnny Burgoyne* by F.J. Hudleston. Copyright © 1927 by The Bobbs-Merrill Company, Inc., 1955, reprinted by permission of the publisher.

"The Battle of Waterloo, A.D. 1815" by Sir Edward Shepherd Creasy. From *Fifteen Decisive Battles of the World* by Sir Edward Creasy. Published in 1851 by Harper, New York.

"The Battle for New Orleans, 1815" by John Spencer Bassett. From *The Life of Andrew Jackson* by John Spencer Bassett, reprinted 1967 by Archon Books, The Shoe String Press, Inc.

"The Battle of Gettysburg, 1863" by James Ford Rhodes. From *The History of the Civil War* by James Ford Rhodes. Published by Macmillan, 1917.

"The Generalship of Grant and Lee, 1864–65" by Major General J.F.C. Fuller. From *Grant and Lee* by J.F.C. Fuller. Published by Indiana University Press. Copyright © by J.F.C. Fuller. Reprinted by permission of Curtis Brown, Ltd.

"The Battle of the Marne" by Field Marshal Joffre. From *Personal Memoirs of Joffre, Field Marshal of the French Army*, translated by T. Bentley Mott. Copyright © 1932, 1960 by Harper & Row, Publishers, Inc. By permission of the publishers.

"Nach Paris!" by Georges Blond. From *The Marne* by Georges Blond. Published by Stackpole Books, Harrisburg, Pa.

"The Marne" by Joseph Delteil. Reprinted by permission of G.P. Putnam's Sons from *The Poilus* by Joseph Delteil.

"The Second Battle for Tobruk" by Field Marshal Erwin Rommel. Excerpted from *The Rommel Papers* edited by B.H. Liddell Hart. Copyright © 1953 by B.H. Liddell Hart. Reprinted by permission of Harcourt Brace Jovanovich, Inc.

"The Liberation of the South-West Pacific" by B.H. Liddell Hart. Reprinted by permission of G.P. Putnam's Sons from *History of the Second World War* by B.H. Liddell Hart. Copyright © 1970 by Lady Liddell Hart.

"I Turn North" by Fleet Admiral William F. Halsey. From *Admiral Halsey's Story* by Fleet Admiral William F. Halsey, USN and J. Bryan III. Published by Whittlesey House, McGraw-Hill Book Company, Inc. Copyright, 1947, by William F. Halsey. Copyright, 1947, by the Curtis Publishing Company. Reprinted by permission.

"Stalingrad—Point of No Return" by Hanson W. Baldwin. Abridged from "Stalingrad—The Point of No Return" in *Battles Won and Lost* by Hanson Baldwin. Copyright © 1966 by Hanson W. Baldwin. By permission of Harper & Row, Publishers.

"Postscript from the Battle for Stalingrad" by General Vasili I. Chuikov. From *The Battle for Stalingrad* by Marshal Vasili Chuikov. Translated by Harold Silver. Copyright © 1963 by MacGibbon and Kie, Ltd. Reprinted by permission of Holt, Rinehart and Winston, Inc.

"D Day, Normandy" by General of the Army Omar N. Bradley. From *A Soldier's Story* by Omar N. Bradley. Copyright © 1951 by Holt, Rinehart and Winston, Inc. Reprinted by permission of Holt, Rinehart and Winston, Inc.

"The Longest Day: June 6, 1944" by Cornelius Ryan. Excerpt from *The Longest Day* by Cornelius Ryan. Copyright © 1959 by Cornelius Ryan. Reprinted by permission of Simon and Schuster, Inc.

"Inchon—the Great Debate; the Great Victory, September 15, 1950" by Major General Courtney Whitney. Excerpt from *MacArthur: His Rendezvous With Destiny* by Courtney Whitney. Copyright © 1955 by Time, Inc. Reprinted by permission of Alfred A. Knopf, Inc.

GREAT BATTLES
AND THEIR
GREAT GENERALS

INTRODUCTION

Wars? Few men really want them, yet all of us fight in them. War is the traditional way of settling differences between nations, tribes and factions. In medieval times, the knights had rules of conduct in combat, but war has not always been an honorable affair on the various battlefields of history. In this anthology of great battles and their great generals, it was usually a grandiose, bloody slaughter. If the enemy was annihilated, he would not rise to fight again.

Wars and weapons have been with us since the beginning of man's dark history. The wooden war club of the earliest warrior became the many-spiked metal mace of the Middle Ages, able to pierce the armor of the foe, along with his head. The tools of war, refined by its artisans, the armorers, included catapults, fire, slings, lances, swords, bows, javelins—anything that assaulted, wounded and killed. When gunpowder and the rifle replaced the sword, the entire nature of war changed strategically and tactically. By the 17th Century the rifle had made armor useless, increasing the mobility of the soldier and changing the nature of the terrain on which battles were fought. When the cannon finally arrived and artillery and tanks became the major weapons of armies, everything in man's inhumanity to man became enlarged on the killing-grounds of history. When the planes came, the whole earth became the warring *Walpurgisnacht.*

The first wars were fought for tribal and city-state superiority. Later they were fought for colonies and national expansion, for new lands and the greater aggrandizement of nationalism and imperialism. Wars have been prompted by fear, by courage, by moral need, by honor—by everything that men live by. There have been wars of defense as well as wars of aggression in our time and through all of man's violent history. Today's wars have created massive military complexes and industries, taxing the taxpayers of the world about $220 billion a year. As Clausewitz, the great Prussian military strategist, once wrote in his famous book *On War,* "War is the continuation of politics by other means. . . ."

Wars, whether ancient or modern, cannot be fought without agile-moving armies, as the Egyptians first learned in 2600 B.C. The later Greeks organized the phalanx, the heavily armed infantry formed in deep files and in close array. Then came the Roman legions, made up of 6000 cavalry and foot soldiers—the basic organization of the successful Roman armies. But the nature of the army organization changed after the decline of the Roman Empire, giving way to private armies, to barbarian hordes, to vassals controlled by lords, barons, dukes—and finally by the 17th Century, to the mercenary army. With the unsettling times of revolutions, the citizen army finally arrived in the form that we know today, with Frederick the Great creating the first conscripted army.

In this anthology we will encounter many forms of challenging armies massing for great battles under élite genius-generals like Hannibal, Sir Francis Drake, the duke of Marlborough, General Horatio Gates, General Andrew Jackson, Marshal Napoleon and the duke of Wellington, General Robert E. Lee and General Ulysses S. Grant, Marshal Joffre and General Gallieni . . . and on to the great captains of World War II and the Korean War.

The Battle of Cannae, fought in 216 B.C., is the first battle of this selective anthology. The much smaller Carthaginian armies, under Hannibal, annihilated the much larger Roman legions. The Battle of Cannae, not oddly, has been called the classical battle of quick flanking movement, sudden surprise and superior strategy. It has also been called the most perfect battle of total annihilation. Taking place during the long, drawn-out Punic Wars, when Rome and Carthage clashed over the control of Northwest Africa, Italy, the Mediterranean, Cannae became Hannibal's greatest victory. But though he won one of the most merciless battles ever fought, Hannibal eventually lost the war because he did not march on Rome to seize all the fruits of his bloody victory.

In the second selection—the Spanish Armada—the noted English military historian, Major General Fuller, fills out the social, political and imperial conclusions inherent in the English defeat of the Spanish Armada. Says General Fuller about Queen Elizabeth: "She hated straight dealing for its simplicity, she hated conviction for its certainty, and above all she hated war for its expense." But with all her hatreds, her appointed captain, Sir Francis Drake, with the aid of storms at sea, destroyed 65 out of 130 ships carrying 30,000 Spanish soldiers ready to invade England . . . and as General Fuller concludes in his exciting account of the Spanish Armada, "The defeat of the Armada whispered the imperial secret into England's ear; that in a commercial age the winning of the sea is more profitable than the winning of the land, and though this may not have been clearly understood in 1588, during the following century the whisper grew louder and louder until it became the voice of every Englishman . . . it laid the cornerstone of the British Empire by endowing England with the prestige Spain lost."

But France replaced Spain as England's enemy by the time the causes of war brought about the Battle of Blenheim, in 1704. It was a test of many great generals under Louis XIV, the dominating genius of France. Europe again was the stakes. His generals in the field included Marshal Villeroy, Marshal Marsin, Marshal Tallard and the Elector of Bavaria. Opposing them at the Battle of Blenheim were England's duke of Marlborough, Lord Cutts, Prince Eugène of Austria and Louis of Baden. Blenheim, in the end, was another battle of annihilation, of the French and the Bavarians.

The fourth battle in this anthology moves on to colonial America, to the Battle of Saratoga, during the American War of Independence. The battle is part of America's early heritage and is considered one of the great victories of the former colony against its colonial master. The Continental armies were small, ill equipped and badly trained. The war, on occasion, was also a curiously gentlemanly affair, for the loser and the winner; it was often a lunch-party pageant, with the wives of generals looking on from nearby hills.

At the Battle of Saratoga the English general, John Burgoyne, faced a former Englishman, General Horatio Gates, who had joined the war of the colonials against his former mother country. There were Americans like Benedict Arnold as well as Aaron Burr, who took an active part in the overall tactics and strategy of the battle, though their contributions to the victory are still in dispute.

The fifth battle in this anthology took place during the War of 1812, rightfully called the Second War of Independence. The prime factors underlying this war were many, including political, social, commercial and maritime. The Battle for New Orleans, fought on January 8, 1815, took place three weeks after the war between England and the United States had actually ended in a peace treaty.

The British, under General Pakenham, were attempting to seize New Orleans, which was defended by General Andrew Jackson. At Chalmette, below New Orleans, the skilled British met their Waterloo by the unprepared, diverse, unskilled American frontier forces.

It was yet another battle of annihilation. When a temporary armistice was agreed upon, Gleig, the British officer who rode out to meet the Americans, later wrote about what he saw on the field of battle: "Of all the sights I ever witnessed, that which met me there was beyond comparison the most shocking and the most humiliating. Within a small compass of a few hundred yards were gathered together nearly a thousand bodies, all of them arrayed in British uniform; and they were thrown by the dozens into shallow holes, scarcely deep enough to furnish them with a slight covering of earth. Nor was this all. An American officer stood by smoking a segar, and apparently counting the slain with a look of savage exultation; and repeating over and over to each individual that approached him, that their losses came to only eight men killed, and fourteen wounded."

Of all the battles that France and England fought, the last of the Napoleonic battles—Waterloo, in 1815—has been called one of the most dramatic. It brought Napoleon, the former conqueror of Europe, to his final defeat and final exile. The French losses were 32,000 men; the English coalition, about 23,000 men. With hundreds of thousands of soldiers engaged, the final Hundred Days' War ended 15 years of constant rivalry between Great Britain, Russia, Austria, Prussia, Sweden, Denmark, Portugal—against France. Of it the poet Lord Byron wrote: "Thou first and last of fields, king-making victory!" And military historian Sir Edward Creasy wrote: "At such a fearful price was the deliverance of Europe purchased."

The American Civil War, which reintroduced an earlier form of trench warfare, was one of the most brutal wars between brothers and states, prior to the Spanish Civil War, 75 years later. The North and the South, politically dismembered in 1861 by the secession of the Southern Confederacy, plunged into four years of mutual military terror. Whatever the causes of the war, the wounds were eventually bound up, and an all-American literary phenomenon has sprung up about the Civil War in legend and in fact.

Great authors have written great stories and novels about the War Between the States. Place names and battlefields honoring the dead of both sides are now part of our national memory. The names of generals, northern and southern, are ever with us in our literature. The humor, the songs, the regalia are also ever present. One story comes to mind, alleged to come from President Lincoln regarding victorious General Grant's habit of drinking too much whiskey. Said Lincoln, "I'd like to know what sort of liquor General Grant drinks so that I can send barrels to all my other generals."

The American historian Burke Davis, who wrote the book *Our Incredible Civil War,* relates the following story regarding General Joseph (Joe) Hooker. When General Hooker took command of the Army of the Potomac, his realistic policy toward recreation for the troops changed Washington overnight. Red-light districts flourished. Tradition strongly insists that it was this benevolent commanding general who gave his name to the slang expression "hooker," signifying both an abandoned woman and a drink of whiskey, neat.

Bruce Catton, a historian equally sensitive to the folkways of Civil War literature, had the following story regarding General Joe Hooker. General Hooker's men were entrained, but the wandering general was not about. Hermann Haupt, chief of construction on U.S. military railways, queried P. H. Watson, assistant secretary of war, regarding Hooker's whereabouts. Back came the answer from Watson: "General Hooker was in Alexandria last night, but I will send to Willard's place [a brothel] to see if he is there. I do not know any other place that he frequents. Be as patient as possible with the generals; some of them will trouble you more than they do the enemy."

In the chapter on the American Civil War, I have used two authors who complement each other's keen analyses. One deals with the most important Battle of Gettysburg, as seen by the American military historian James Ford Rhodes; and the second is a study in depth of the two great opposing generals of the Civil War, Grant and Lee, by the celebrated English military historian, General Fuller. The end result of the Civil War was:

Casualties for the Union Forces—359,528 men out of 2,213,462 men serving.
Casualties for the Confederate Forces—133,821 men out of 1,500,000 men serving.

As Montesquieu wrote about Europe of a hundred years earlier: "If Europe should ever be ruined, it will be by its warriors."

The eighth battle in this anthology is the First Battle of the Marne, fought during World War I in 1914. This battle has captured the interest of many military and political historians. It was, at the end, a battle of innovation, of new forms of transporting men in a dash—specifically, the 2000 commandeered taxis of Paris that took, under General Gallieni's order, 50,000 soldiers in Paris to the front, 50 miles away.

The German armies, only one month at war, were heading for Paris. They could be seen from the Eiffel Tower. Count Ludwig von Moltke, leading the German armies advancing under the much-heralded Schlieffen Plan, met their first major disaster of the war at the Marne. If General Gallieni as a strategist had not come to the aid of Marshal Joffre, with his taxiing soldiery, Paris might have fallen and the war might have ended for France.

This chapter is a three-pronged view of the Battle of the Marne: first, as seen through the eyes of the commanding general in the field, Marshal Joffre; next, *"Nach Paris!"* by Georges Blond, gives the German views of those desperate days; and last, a short-tailing endpiece by Joseph Delteil, an appreciation of how the aged and sick General Gallieni acted when he saw, from the Eiffel Tower, the Germans marching on to Paris.

The American casualties, from less than two years in the war, were:

320,710 out of 4,743,826 men serving.

Of World War II, still with us in the wounded and the crippled, I have selected, in sequence of time, the following four battles: the Second Battle of Tobruk and El Alamein, as seen by the German panzer genius, Field Marshal Erwin Rommel, who led the Axis armies and his Afrika Korps to Pyrrhic victory—then to their final defeat on the sands of Africa in 1942; the Battle of Stalingrad, where the German General von Paulus surrendered with his hundreds of thousands of soldiers in 1943, and of which Prime Minister Winston Churchill then wrote, "The hinge of fate had turned." For the embattled Russians, it was total war under total winter brutality and siege conditions; for the Germans, it was their second harrowing defeat, en masse.

The third great battle selected from World War II is Operation OVERLORD—the invasion of Normandy. It was, without doubt, the largest and most overwhelming invasion of all wars in the world. Through the four years of their occupation of France and the coast, the Germans had built up their Atlantic Wall. They believed that, unlike the former French Maginot Line, it would really be an impregnable fortress. Thus, on the night of June 6, 1944, when the Americans, the British and the Canadians, under

General Bradley and General Montgomery, launched D day and the invasion of France, the Germans were taken by total surprise. So much so, in fact, that General Rommel, who then headed the German forces in France, was found asleep in his hometown in Germany, where he had gone for a short visit.

D day, Normandy, is exacting reading. I have used two sources to tell the Normandy story: General Bradley's rendering of those testing times, and an overall German view by Cornelius Ryan from his intensive study *The Longest Day.*

To fill out the naval battles of World War II, especially in the wide sweep of the Pacific, I have used the invasion of Leyte, also considered the greatest sea battle of all time. Actually there were at least four major sea battles before Leyte was secured and General MacArthur and the American forces finally returned to the Philippines. I have excerpted pertinent parts of Liddell Hart's acute analysis of those frantic maneuvers at sea by the navies of the United States and Japan; and from Admiral William Halsey, of the U.S. Third Fleet, I have used some of his colorful evaluations of those hit-and-find-and-run days as told by a great warrior-of-the-waters.

The errors are well told, for both sides. The new facts, from Japanese annals, make them part of the naval history of the war. What went wrong? What went right? How much of a role did the law of chance play in the defeat of the Japanese Navy at Leyte? An admiral and a historian tell us.

The American casualties in the Second World War: 1,078,162 out of 16,353,659 men serving.

The last great battle in this anthology, the Inchon Landing, took place during the Korean War in 1950. It was another surprise shock, planned and executed with enormous strategical logic and verve. Dennis Hart Mahan, a professor at West Point in its early days, once wrote: "Some operations if carried out to their logical end may change the entire aspect of war. . . . The entire movable army strikes at the enemy in the heart of his own country. Such resolutions by great generals are stamped with the mark of true genius."

The military genius of the Inchon Landing was the commander-in-chief of the U.N. Forces, Douglas MacArthur. The debates held prior to the massive landings at Inchon will make for challenging reading here, for MacArthur, from afar, literally took on most of the joint chiefs of staff in Washington who disapproved of the landing. But the entire "movable army [struck] at the enemy in the heart of his own country." And it was another battle of Cannae, soon enough, for the enemy.

The American casualties in the Korean War: 157,530 out of 5,764,143 men serving.

The 13 decisive battles in this anthology range through 2000 years of élite generals and their warriors for many causes. It is always life over death as a military finality; a fatal touch of chance and/or military genius at the moment of battle and victory; of great generals in their terrible defeats and in their glorious victories . . . and many millions of soldiers, of all nations and all times, in their agony of war's hell. It was always brutal, as all wars must be despite the final victories by the civilized Hannibals of history.

CHAPTER I

CANNAE, PUNIC WARS, 216 B.C.

The Battle of Cannae has been called the most perfect battle of total annihilation. Taking place during the Punic Wars, when Rome and Carthage clashed for many years over the control of Northwest Africa, Italy, the Mediterranean and its great naval uses, Cannae became Hannibal's greatest victory. But though he won one of the most merciless battles ever fought, he eventually lost the war because he did not march on Rome, to seize all the fruits of his bloody victory.

The two versions of the battle, hardly differing in substance, were written by military men of the 19th and the early 20th Centuries. General von Schlieffen was chief of the German general staff from 1892 to 1906. He is most famous for the creation of the Schlieffen Plan worked out between 1905 and 1913. It consisted of a bold flanking movement—using Belgium and Holland as the annihilating pivot—to roll, via a right-wing advance, the French Army into Alsace-Lorraine and Switzerland. The first selection is from his book *Cannae*. General von Schlieffen died in 1913, a year before Moltke tried out the plan during World War I but failed because of his weak use of the enveloping right wing of the German Army.

Theodore Ayrault Dodge, an American, born in 1842, studied at the University of Heidelberg and was a soldier in the New York Militia in 1861. He was wounded in the Virginia campaign and lost a leg at the Battle of Gettysburg. He became a noted military historian. The second version of Cannae is from his book *Great Captains*, first published in 1889. Dodge died in 1909.

The Battle of Cannae
by
General Field Marshal Alfred von Schlieffen

The army of Hannibal, facing west, was located on 2 August, 216 B.C., in the Apulian plain to the left of the Aufidus in the vicinity of Cannae village, near the mouth of that river. Opposite them were the troops of Consul Terentius Varro. The other consul, Aemilius Paulus, had transferred the daily alternating command to him.

The Roman forces numbered:

> 55,000 heavily armed men
> 8,000 lightly armed men
> <u>6,000</u> mounted men
> 69,000 men

In addition there were in the two fortified camps:

> 2,600 heavily armed men
> <u>7,400</u> lightly armed men
> 10,000 men

The total strength of the Roman Army thus amounted to 79,-000 men.

Hannibal had 50,000 men disposed as follows:

> 32,000 heavily armed men
> 8,000 lightly armed men
> <u>10,000</u> mounted men
> 50,000 men

His situation, with a superior enemy to his front and the sea to his rear, was by no means favorable. Consul Aemilius Paulus, in concurrence with Proconsul Servillius, wished to avoid a battle.

Both feared the superior Carthaginian cavalry to which Hannibal owed his victories on the Ticinus, on the Trebia, and at the Trasimene lake. Terentius Varro, on the other hand, desired battle and to avenge the defeats suffered. He counted on the superiority of his 55,000 heavily armed men as against the hostile 32,000, consisting of only 12,000 Carthaginians and 20,000 Iberians and Gauls who, in equipment and training, could not be considered as of full value. In order to give increased weight to the attack, Terentius gave his army a new battle formation. According to regulation, the heavy infantry (hoplites) was to be arranged in three closely formed echelons. The first two echelons (hastati and principes) were of equal strength, organized into 12 units, each of 4,000 men. The third echelon (triarii) was half strength and consisted of 160 units each of 60 men, arranged 10 men front, 6 files deep.

This formation, 18 files deep, appeared too shallow to the commander-in-chief, so he changed it to a formation of 36 files, with a front of only 1,600 men. Both these formations, the shallow as well as the deep, required 57,600 men for full strength. There was therefore a deficit of 2,600 men. The cavalry was placed on the flanks. The lightly armed troops, destined to begin the battle, to swarm around the enemy, and to support the cavalry, were not much considered by either side.

Hannibal opposed to the enemy's center his 20,000 Iberians and Gauls, which were probably 12 files deep. The greater part of his cavalry under Hasdrubal was placed on the left flank and the light Numidian on the right. On the flanks, in rear of this cavalry the 12,000 highly armed Carthaginian infantry was formed in two equal parts.

Both armies advanced against each other. Hasdrubal overpowered the weaker, hostile cavalry on the right flank. The Roman knights were killed, thrown into the Aufidus, or scattered. Hasdrubal advanced behind the hostile infantry against the Roman cavalry on the other flank which, until then, had merely skirmished with the Numidian light horse. Attacked on both sides, the Romans were completely routed here as well. After the destruction of the hostile cavalry, Hasdrubal turned against the rear of the Roman phalanx.

In the meanwhile, both infantry masses had advanced. The

Iberians and Gauls were driven back, not so much on account of the strength of the attack of the 36 Roman files as on account of their inferior armament and poorer training for close combat. The advance of the Romans was, however, checked as soon as the Carthaginian flanking echelons, held back so far, came up and enveloped the enemy on the right and left, and Hasdrubal's cavalry threatened the Roman rear. The triarii turned back, the maniples of both wings moved outward. A complete rectangle had been formed, forced to halt, and was now attacked on all sides by the infantry with short swords and by the cavalry, with javelins, arrows, and slingshots, never scoring a miss in the compact, hostile mass. The Romans were constantly being pushed back and crowded together. Disarmed and helpless, they expected death. Hannibal, his heart full of hatred, circled the bloody arena encouraging the zealous, lashing on the sluggish. His soldiers desisted only hours later. Weary of slaughter, they took the remaining 3,000 men prisoners. Forty-eight thousand Roman corpses lay in heaps. Both Aemilius Paulus and Servilius had fallen, Varro had escaped with a few cavalrymen, a few of the heavily armed, and the greater part of the lightly armed men. Thousands fell into the hands of the victors in the village of Cannae and in both camps. The conquerors lost about 6,000 men, mostly Iberians and Gauls.

A battle of complete extermination had been fought, remarkable because, in spite of all theories, it had been won by a numerical inferiority. Clausewitz said "Concentric action against the enemy behooves not the weaker," and Napoleon taught "the weaker must not envelop both flanks." The weaker Hannibal had, however, acted concentrically, contrary to all tradition, and not only enveloped both flanks, but even encircled the hostile rear.

Tactics and technique have undergone a complete change during these 2,000 years. No bodily attack is made any more with short swords. One side fires at the other at a range of thousands of yards; the bow has been replaced by the field gun, the slingshot by machine guns. Capitulations have taken the place of slaughter. But the principles of strategy have remained unchanged. The battle of extermination may be fought today according to the same plan as then executed by Hannibal. The hostile front is not the objective of the principal attack. It is not against that point that the troops should be massed and the reserves disposed; the essential thing is to crush the flanks. They ought not to be sought merely in front, but along the entire depth and extension of the hostile formation. The extermination is completed by an attack against the rear of the enemy. This is primarily the mission of the cavalry. It need not attack "intact infantry," but may wreak havoc among the hostile masses by its fire-power.

A prerequisite to success lies, it is true, in a deep formation of the hostile forces with a constricted front attended by a massing of reserves, thus deepening the flanks and increasing the number of combatants forced to remain inactive. It was Hannibal's good luck to have opposed to him Terentius Varro, who eliminated his numerical superiority by disposing his infantry 36 men deep. At all times there have been generals of Varro's school, but not during the period when Prussia wanted them most.

Cannae
by
Theodore Ayrault Dodge

It is impossible, even slightly, to touch on many of Hannibal's campaigns and battles. I prefer to give a short description of the battle of Cannae, which, in its conduct and results, is typical of Hannibal's methods. And first, a few words about the organization of either army.

The Carthaginian discipline was based on the Macedonian idea, and the formation of the troops was phalangial, that is, in close masses. But Hannibal's army contained troops of all kinds, from the Numidian horseman, whose only clothing was a tiger-skin, on his tough little runt of a pony, or the all but naked Gaul with his long, curved sword, to the Carthaginian heavy-armed hypaspist. All these diverse tribes had each its own manner of fighting, and it required a Hannibal to keep up discipline or tactical efficiency in such a motley force. The Roman Army, on the contrary, was wonderfully homogeneous, carefully disciplined, in all parts organized and drilled in the same manner, and the legion was a body which was the very opposite of the phalanx. It had much more mobility, the individual soldiers were more independent in action, and instead of relying on one shock or on defense, the several lines could relieve each other, and renew a failing battle three or even four times with fresh troops. After Trasymene, Hannibal not only armed his men with captured Roman weapons, but modified his organization somewhat to the legion pattern.

The legion was at this time formed in three lines of maniples (or companies) placed checkerwise. In front were the hastati, the least efficient; behind this the principes; and in the rear the triarii, or veterans. Each maniple was an excellent tactical unit. Each of these lines could relieve the other, and thus give a succession of hammerlike blows.

The phalanx we already know, and while it was wonderful for one shock, it had no reserve, and if demoralization set in, it was gone. The tendency of formation in ancient days, as now, was towards greater mobility, and later on the Roman legion in Greece, particularly at Pydna (168 B.C.), proved that it was superior, if properly handled, to the phalanx.

In B.C. 216, Æmilius Paulus and Varro were consuls. The former was a man of high character and attainments; Varro came of plebeian stock, was overbearing and self-sufficient. The Roman and Carthaginian armies lay facing each other near the Aufidus, Hannibal backing on Cannae. His position here had been the result of an admirable maneuver. The consuls commanded on alternate days. There had been a serious combat on the last day of Varro's command, in which the Carthaginians had been outnumbered two to one, and been defeated. This had greatly elated Varro, and whetted his appetite for battle. He left the troops at evening in such a manner that next day his associate was badly placed. Æmilius scarcely wished to withdraw, lest his men should be disheartened; he could not remain where he was, as he was exposed to Hannibal's better cavalry. He took a middle course, on the whole unwise. He sent a third of his force to the north of the

Aufidus, a trifle upstream, to sustain some foragers he had there, and make a secondary camp, from which to annoy Hannibal's parties in search of corn. This division of forces was very risky. Hannibal had long been trying to bring the consuls to battle, and now saw that the moment had come, for Varro was precipitate, and would probably draw Æmilius into active measures.

Each general made a stirring address to his army. Polybius gives both. Hannibal's has the true ring of the great captain. "Let us hasten into action. I promise you victory, and, the gods willing, I will make my promise good." Two days later Hannibal offered Æmilius battle. But Æmilius declined it, and Hannibal sent his Numidians to the other side to annoy the Roman foragers. The succeeding day, knowing Varro to be in command, Hannibal again offered battle, aware that the hot-tempered Roman would be burning to avenge the yesterday's taunt. He left eight thousand men to guard his camp.

There has been much discussion as to which bank of the Aufidus was the scene of the battle. It seems to me that the plan in the diagram comes nearest to fitting all the statements, however conflicting, of the several authorities. Near Hannibal's camp the Aufidus makes a bold, southerly sweep. Here Hannibal forded the stream in two columns, drew up his army, and leaned his flanks on the riverbanks so as to prevent the Romans, with their numerical superiority, from overlapping them. His front he covered with archers and slingers, so as to hide his formation from the Roman generals. Varro, as Hannibal anticipated, thought the Carthaginians were crossing to attack the lesser camp, and leaving eleven thousand men to guard the larger one, with orders to attack Hannibal's camp during the battle, he also crossed and drew up in the plain opposite the Carthaginians, he and every Roman in the ranks craving to come to blows with the hated invaders.

Varro also threw out his light troops in advance. He had sixty-five thousand foot and seven thousand horse, to Hannibal's thirty-two thousand foot and ten thousand horse. He could not overlap Hannibal's flanks, so he determined to make his line heavier, and seek to crush him at the first impact. He changed the formation of the maniples so as to make them sixteen men deep and ten men front, instead of sixteen men front by ten deep, as usual. This was a grievous error. His men were unapt to maneuver or fight well in this unwonted form. He should have employed his surplus, say twenty-five thousand men, as a reserve for emergencies. His army was in the usual three lines, fifteen legions in all, the Roman on the right, the allied on the left. The intervals between the maniples always equalled their front, and the distance between the lines the depth of the maniples. The Roman cavalry, twenty-four hundred strong, was on the right. The allied, forty-eight hundred strong, on the left. It would have been better massed in one body. But such was the only formation then known. Æmilius commanded the right, Varro the left wing.

Hannibal placed on his left, opposite the Roman cavalry, his heavy Spanish and Gallic horse, eight thousand strong, two-thirds in a first, and one-third in a second line. This body was strong enough to crush the Roman horse, and thus cut off the retreat of the legions to their camps and towards Rome. In other words, Hannibal's fighting was to be forced on the Romans' strategic flank. He had a perfectly lucid idea of the value of a blow from this direction. On his right, facing the allied cavalry, were his Numidians, two thousand strong. Of the infantry, the Spaniards and Gauls were in the center in alternate bodies. His best troops, the African foot, he placed on their either flank. He expected these veterans to leaven the whole lump. The foot was all in phalanxes of one thousand and twenty-four men each, the African foot in sixteen ranks, as usual, the Spaniards and Gauls in ten. Hannibal had been obliged thus to make his center thin, from lack of men, but he had seething in his brain a maneuver by which he proposed to make this very weakness a factor of success. He had been on the ground and had seen Varro strengthen the Roman center. This confirmed him in his plan.

Hannibal commanded the center in person, Hanno the right, Hasdrubal the left, Maharbal the cavalry of the left. Hannibal relied on Maharbal to beat the Roman cavalry, and then, riding by the rear of the Roman Army, to join the Numidians on the Carthaginian right, like Coenus at the Hydaspes. His cavalry was superior in numbers, and vastly outranked in effectiveness the Roman horse.

Hannibal was, no doubt, familiar with Marathon. He proposed

to better the tactics of that day. Remember that Miltiades had opposed to him Orientals; Hannibal faced Roman legions. His general plan was to withdraw his center before the heavy Roman line—to allow them to push it in—and then to enclose them in his wings and fall on their flanks. This was a highly dangerous maneuver, unless the withdrawal of the center could be checked at the proper time; but his men had the greatest confidence in him; the river in his rear would be an aid, if he could but keep his men steady; and in war no decisive result can be compassed without corresponding risk. Hannibal had fully prepared his army for this tactical evolution, and rehearsed its details with all his subordinates. He not only had the knack of making his lieutenants comprehend him, but proposed to see to the execution of the work himself.

The Carthaginians faced north, the Romans south. The rising sun was on the flank of either. The wind was southerly, and blew the dust into the faces of the Romans. The light troops on either side opened the action, and fiercely contested the ground for some time. During the preliminary fighting, Hannibal advanced his center, the Spanish and Gallic foot, in a salient or convex order from the main line, the phalanxes on the right and left of the central one being, it is presumed, in *echelon* to it. The wings, of African foot, kept their place.

While this was being done, Hannibal ordered the heavy horse on his left to charge down on the Roman horse in their front. This they did with their accustomed spirit, but met a gallant resistance. The Roman knights fought for every inch with the greatest obstinacy, when dismounted, continuing the contest on foot. The fighting was not by shocks, it was rather hand to hand. But the weight and superior training of the Carthaginian horse soon told. They rode down the Romans and crushed them out of existence. Æmilius was badly wounded, but escaped the ensuing massacre and made his way to the help of the Roman center, hoping there to retrieve the day. On the Carthaginian right the Numidians had received orders to skirmish with the allied horse and not come to a decisive combat till they should be joined by the heavy horse from the Carthaginian left. This they did in their own peculiar style, by riding around their opponents, squadron by squadron, and by making numberless feigned attacks. The battle in the center had not yet developed results, when Maharbal, having destroyed the Roman cavalry, and ridden around the Roman Army, appeared in the rear of the allied horse. The Numidians now attacked seriously, and between them, in a few minutes, there was not a Roman horseman left upon the field alive. The Numidians were then sent in pursuit, Maharbal remaining upon the field.

While this was going on, the light troops of both sides had been withdrawn through the intervals, and had formed in the rear and on the flanks of legion and phalanx, ready to fill gaps and supply the heavy foot with weapons. This had uncovered Hannibal's salient. Varro had committed still another blunder. In the effort to make his line so strong as to be irresistible, he had ordered his maniples of principes from the second line forward into the intervals of the maniples of hastati in first line, thus making one solid wall and robbing the legionaries of their accustomed mobility, as well as lending them a feeling of uncertainty in their novel formation. Still, with its wonted spirit, the heavy Roman line advanced on Hannibal's salient. The Carthaginian wings could not yet be reached, being so much refused. Striking the apex, the fighting became furious. Hannibal's salient, as proposed, began to withdraw, holding its own in good style. Varro, far too eager, and seeing, as he thought, speedy victory before him, was again guilty of the folly of ordering the third line, the triarii, and even the light troops, up to the support of the already overcrowded first and second lines. The Carthaginian center, supported by its skirmishers, held the ground with just enough tenacity to whet the determination of the Romans to crush it. Varro now insanely ordered still more forces in from his wings to reenforce his center, already a mass so crowded as to be unable to retain its organization, but pressing back the Carthaginians by mere weight of mass. He could not better have played into Hannibal's hands. The Romans—three men in the place of one—struggled onward, but became every moment a more and more jumbled body. Its maniple formation, and consequent ease of movement, was quite lost. Still, it pushed forward, as if to certain victory, and still the Carthaginian salient fell back, till from a salient it became a line, from a line a reentering angle or crescent. Hannibal, by great personal exertions, had in an extraordinary manner preserved the steadiness and formation of his center, though outnumbered four to one. The Carthaginian wings he now ordered slowly to advance, which all the more edged the Roman center into the *cul-de-sac* Hannibal had prepared. The Roman legionaries were already shouting their eager cry of victory; but so herded together had they got that there was no room to use their weapons. Hannibal had kept the Carthaginian center free from any feeling of demoralization, and ready at his command to turn and face the enemy. The wings, by their advance, had hustled the Roman legions into the form of a wedge without a vestige of maniple formation left. The decisive moment had come. Hannibal seized it with the eye of the born soldier. Arresting the backward movement of the center, which still had elbow-room to fight, as the Romans had not, he gave orders to the wings which they were impatiently awaiting. These veteran troops, in perfect order, wheeled inward to right and left, on the flanks of the struggling mass of legionaries. The Roman Army was lost beyond a ray of hope, for, at the same instant, Maharbal, having finished the destruction of the cavalry, rode down upon its rear. The cry of victory changed to a cry of terror. Defeat degenerated into mere slaughter. The Carthaginian cavalry divided into small troops and rode into the midst of the Roman soldiers, sabring right and left. Some squadrons galloped around to the flanks and lent a hand to the African phalanx in its butchery. No quarter was given, or indeed asked. The Romans died with their faces to the foe. The bloody work continued till but a handful was left. Livy and Polybius place the killed at from forty to seventy thousand men. Varro had already escaped with a mere squad of horse. Æmilius Paulus died, sword in hand, seeking to stem the tide of disaster. Three proconsuls, two quæstors, twenty-one military tribunes, a number of ex-consuls, prætors, and ædiles, and eighty senators perished with the army.

Hannibal's loss had been barely six thousand men, but he had annihilated the splendid army of eighty-seven thousand men—the flower of Rome. It had vanished as if swallowed up in an earthquake. The battle had been won by crisp tactical skill and the most effective use of cavalry—as fine as that at the Hydaspes. It was, indeed, the gorgeous handling of the cavalry which made the infantry maneuver possible.

Few battles in history are more marked by ability on the one side and crass blundering on the other than the battle of Cannae. The handling of the cavalry was quite beyond praise. The manner in which the far from reliable Spanish and Gallic foot was advanced in a wedge in *echelon,* and, under the mettlesome attack of the Roman legions, was first held there, and then withdrawn step by step, until it had reached the converse position of a reentering angle, and was then steadied in place by ordering up the light troops into its intervals—all this being done under the exultant Roman shouts of victory—is a simple *chef d'oeuvre* of battle-tactics, due solely to Hannibal's magnificent personality; and the advance at the decisive instant of the African infantry, and its wheel right and left upon the flanks of the disordered and over-crowded legionaries, caps the master-stroke. The whole battle, from the Carthaginian standpoint, is a consummate piece of art, having no superior, few equals in the history of war.

CHAPTER II

THE SPANISH ARMADA, 1588

Major General John Frederick Charles Fuller (1878–1966) is considered one of the world's greatest military historians who also developed some of the basic concepts of armored warfare. He was a colonel in the British Army during the World War I tank battles at the Somme and Cambrai.

From chief instructor at the Staff College in 1922, he rose to the general staff. He became a major general in 1930 and retired in 1933 to write his military studies. Among his more than 30 books is his classical study *The Decisive Battles of the Western World,* from which the selection on the Spanish Armada is extracted.

The Defeat of the Spanish Armada, 1588
by
Major General J. F. C. Fuller

Before Calais was lost in 1558 the security of England depended theoretically on defending her shores by fighting battles on the Continent, which was looked upon as the counterscarp of England's defenses. After the loss of Calais this dependence had to be replaced by the command of the English Channel; yet, when the crisis of 1586 occurred, although Queen Elizabeth possessed a private fleet of 34 warships, which in time of war could be augmented by many armed merchantmen, no national navy existed, and so things stood until the days of the Commonwealth. Added to this, there was no standing army—the feudal levies had long disappeared—and though, as in the days of the Saxon *fyrd,* her Majesty's lieutenants were still authorized to call out levies of armed men, except for those in London they were little more than undisciplined bodies of soldiers which, at their best, would have been unable to meet in the field the highly organized soldiers of Spain.

The trouble was that, as Fortescue says of Elizabeth, "she hated straight dealing for its simplicity, she hated conviction for its certainty, and above all she hated war for its expense." These three idiosyncrasies, particularly the last, persuaded her to rely on diplomacy, and because she lacked the force necessary to make it effective she was outwitted consistently by the Duke of Parma who, until the Armada sailed, covered his preparations in the Netherlands by constant proposals of peace, which Elizabeth largely accepted at face value.

Nevertheless, because of the Babington Plot it became apparent that a crisis had been reached, and on December 25, 1586, Elizabeth was persuaded to order the mobilization of her fleet at Portsmouth and to hold a squadron in the Channel during the winter of 1586–1587 to frustrate any possible attempt by the Guises to rescue Mary Queen of Scots. In March, 1587, Mary was dead, and while the main fleet was mobilized at Portsmouth, Sir Francis Drake was making ready at Plymouth to sail "to impeach the joining together of the King of Spain's fleets out of their several ports, to keep victuals from them, to follow them in case they should come forward towards England or Ireland and to cut off as many of them as he could and impeach their landing. . . ." As usual, as soon as these orders were issued Elizabeth feared that they might precipitate a war and greatly modified them; but Drake, who knew what to expect, put to sea on April 2, before he could receive her counterorder, and arrived at Cadiz on April 19. "We stayed there," he writes, "until the 21st, in which meantime we sank a Biscayan of 1,200 tons, burnt a ship of the Marquess of Santa Cruz of 1,500 tons, and 31 ships more of 1,000, 800, 600, 400 to 200 tons the piece; carried away four with us laden with provisions, and departed thence at our pleasure. . . ." Next, being "furnished with necessary provisions," he made for Lisbon, from where on April 27 he writes: "There was never heard of so great a preparation [as] the King of Spain hath and doth continually prepare for an invasion. . . ."

Lisbon was where the ships of the Armada were being assembled, and though Santa Cruz had established his headquarters there, as yet he had not mustered a man. It was a powerfully defended port. Outside the bar and to the north was an anchorage commanded by Cascaes Castle, and close to it lay the strong fortress of St. Julian. On May 10 Drake cast anchor in Cascaes Bay. The port was thrown into consternation, every vessel cut her cables and sped for the nearest refuge. Thousands of tons of shipping and a vast quantity of stores were then destroyed; the Spanish return puts the loss at 24 ships with cargoes valued at 172,000 ducats. Drake, who had no land forces with him, could not hold the port, so he made for Cape St. Vincent—the strategic point between Lisbon and the Mediterranean. "We hold this Cape," writes Thomas Fenner—Drake's Flag-Captain—"so greatly to our benefit and so much to their disadvantage as a great blessing [is] the attaining thereof. For the rendezvous is at Lisbon, where we understand of some 25 ships and 7 galleys. The rest, we lie between home and them, so as the body is without the members; and they cannot come together by reason that they are unfurnished of their provisions in every degree, in that they are not united together."

Near St. Vincent immense damage was done to the Portuguese Algarve fisheries and thousands of tons of hoops and pipe-staves for casks were destroyed. Could Drake have remained there he might well have prevented altogether the assembly of the Armada, but this was not possible unless he were reinforced. On May 17 he wrote to Sir Francis Walsingham: "If there were here 6 or more of her Majesty's good ships of the second sort, we should be the better able to keep the forces from joining and haply take or impeach his fleet from all places in the next month and so after, which is the chiefest times of their return home, which I judge, in my poor opinion, will bring this great monarchy to those conditions which are meet."

This was not to be and he set out for the Azores. Sixteen days out from St. Vincent, on June 8, he sighted a large vessel off St. Michael's and took her the next day. She was the *San Felipe,* the king of Spain's own East Indiaman, with a cargo valued at

£114,000 and papers which revealed the long-kept secrets of the East India trade. On June 26 Drake was back in Plymouth. He had wrecked all possibility of the Armada sailing that year. This was most fortunate for England, for had the Armada been able to put to sea before the end of September, as Philip intended, Parma might have crossed the Channel. As he writes in a letter to the king: "Had the Marquis come when I was first told to look for him, the landing could have been effected without difficulty. Neither the English nor the Dutch were then in a condition to resist your fleet."

Meanwhile Santa Cruz hastened to make good the damage done and to be ready by the end of February, 1588; but he died suddenly on January 30. Again the expedition was delayed. His death proved to be as great a calamity to the Spaniards as Drake's raid, for he was the ablest sailor in Spain. In his stead Philip appointed Don Alonzo Perez de Guzman, duke of Medina Sidonia, who, though a grandee of highest rank, had never seen service either with the fleet or with the army. He wrote to the king asking to be excused, but Philip appointed a competent seaman, Don Diego de Valdez, to be his naval adviser and nominated the duke of Parma commander-in-chief of the entire expedition once Medina Sidonia had sailed up the Channel and joined him.

While Medina Sidonia made ready, the main preparations of the duke of Parma were the cutting of a ship canal from Antwerp and Ghent to Bruges; the building of 70 landing-craft on Waten River, each to carry 30 horses and equipped with embarking and disembarking gangways; the building of 200 flat-bottomed boats at Nieuport; the assembly of 28 warships at Dunkirk; the recruiting of mariners in Hamburg, Bremen, Emden, and other ports; the construction of 20,000 casks at Gravelines; and near Nieuport and Dixmude the building of camps for 20,600 foot, and at Courtrai and Waten for 4,900 horse. . . .

The English, then, had three times as many long-range pieces as the Spaniards and the Spaniards had three times as many heavy-shotted medium-range pieces as the English. These differences in range and smashing-power dictated the respective tactical policies; the English concentrated on long-range fighting and the Spaniards on medium- and short-range action. Whereas the Span-

Fleet	No. of ships	Cannon	Periers	Culverins	Total
English	172	55	43	1,874	1,972
Spanish	124	163	326	635	1,124

ish tactical aim was to reduce a hostile ship to impotence and then to board her, the English was to sink the enemy or to force her to strike her flag. Although the English culverin had the greater range, it was not powerful enough decisively to batter a ship at long range. Equally important, the inaccuracy of its fire was such that at long range few shots hit their target. Inaccuracy of fire dogged naval warfare, as it also did that on land, until the introduction of the rifled gun and musket. Theoretically, therefore, the Spanish, who relied on close-range battering power, were in advance of their enemy as artillerists.

Philip realized clearly the type of tactics the English would adopt and, before Medina Sidonia sailed, he gave him this warning: "You are especially to take notice that the enemy's object will be to engage at a distance, on account of the advantage which they have from their artillery and the offensive fireworks with which they will be provided; and on the other hand, the object of our side should be to close and grapple and engage hand to hand." But apparently he did not realize so fully that the true advantage of the English lay not in their longer-range ordnance, but in their superior seamanship and in the fact that their ships were handier than the Spanish. The Spaniard was a fair-weather sailor, the Englishman was not; the Spanish ships were looked upon more as fortresses than vessels and were crowded with soldiers and undermanned with sailors, who were considered little better than galley slaves. In the English ships their crews not only manned but fought them, and though pressed into service received fourpence a day. The greatest difference and advantage of all was that the Spaniard continued to make use of the galley tactics of line abreast in groups, whereas Drake or Howard introduced a rough formation of line ahead in groups and so began to revolutionize naval fighting. . . .

During the autumn a small English squadron under Sir Henry

Palmer, in conjunction with a Dutch squadron, in all some 90 warships of small burden "meete to saile upon their rivers and shallow seas," blockaded the havens of Flanders; but it was not until November 27 that the queen assembled a council of war to discuss such problems as likely landing places; the employment of land forces; the weapons to be used; and internal security. On December 21 she appointed Lord Howard of Effingham "lieutenant-general, commander-in-chief, and governor of the whole fleet and army at sea." She selected him instead of Drake—her most able admiral—not only to enhance the prestige of her fleet, but because it was essential to have in command a man of so high a rank that he could command obedience. Drake was later appointed vice-admiral to reinforce Howard on the technical side. Of Howard, Thomas Fuller says: "True it is he was no deep seaman; but he had skill enough to know those who had more skill than himself and to follow their instructions, and would not starve the Queen's service by feeding his own sturdy wilfulness, but was ruled by the experienced in sea matters; the Queen having a navy of oak and an Admiral of osier." . . .

Philip wrote to Medina Sidonia: "When you have received my orders, you will put to sea with the whole Armada, and proceed direct for the English Channel, up which you will sail as far as the point of Margate, then open communication with the Duke of Parma, and ensure him a passage across." He warned him to avoid the English fleet, and said that should Drake appear in the Channel, except for rearguard actions he was to ignore him. He also gave Medina Sidonia a sealed letter for Parma in which he informed the duke what to do should the expedition fail.

Philip placed at Medina Sidonia's disposal 130 ships: 20 galleons; 44 armed merchantmen; 23 *urcas,* or hulks; 22 *pataches,* or dispatch-vessels; 13 *zabras,* or pinnaces; 4 galleasses; and 4 galleys. These ships aggregated 57,868 tons burden, were armed with 2,431 guns, were manned by 8,050 seamen, and carried 18,973 soldiers. With galley slaves and others the total number of men was 30,493.

The whole fleet was divided into 10 squadrons as follows:

(1)   The squadron of Portugal, Medina Sidonia, 10 galleons and two pinnaces.

(2)   The squadron of Castile, Diego Flores de Valdez, 10 galleons, 4 armed merchantmen, and 2 pinnaces.

(3)   The squadron of Andalusia, Pedro de Valdez, 10 armed merchantmen and 1 pinnace.

(4)   The squadron of Biscay, Juan Martinez de Recalde, 10 armed merchantmen and 4 pinnaces.

(5)   The squadron of Guipuzcoa, Miguel de Oquendo, 10 armed merchantmen and 2 pinnaces.

(6)   The squadron of Italy, Martin de Bertendora, 10 armed merchantmen and 2 pinnaces.

(7)   The squadron of *Urcas,* Juan Gomez de Medina, 23 ships.

(8)   The squadron of *Pataches,* Antonio Hurtado de Mendoza, 22 ships.

(9)   The squadron of 4 galleasses, Hugo de Moncada.

(10)   The squadron of 4 galleys, Diego de Medrado.[1]

On April 13, Drake wrote to the queen, and added: "The advantage of time and place in all martial actions is half a victory; which being lost is irrecoverable." And again on April 28 he wrote: "Most renowned Prince, I beseech you to pardon my boldness in the discharge of my conscience, being burdened to signify unto your Highness the imminent dangers that in my simple opinion do hang over us; that if a good peace for your Majesty be not forthwith concluded—which I as much as any man desireth—then these great preparations of the Spaniard may be speedily prevented as much as in your Majesty lieth, by sending your forces to encounter them somewhat far off, and more near their own coasts, which will be the better cheap [the more advantageous] for your Majesty and people, and much the dearer for the enemy."

The outcome was that Howard was ordered to carry the bulk of his fleet to Plymouth, after he had detached a squadron under Lord Henry Seymour to watch the Channel. He set out from the

---

[1]This squadron did not sail.

Downs on May 21 and joined Drake two days later. He then took over supreme command and appointed Drake his vice-admiral; as such he became president of the Council of War. After this, Howard wrote to Burghley: "I mean to stay these two days to water our fleet, and afterwards, God willing, to take the opportunity of the first wind serving for the coast of Spain, with the intention to lie on and off betwixt England and that coast, to watch the coming of the Spanish forces. . . ."

Meanwhile rumors and reports arrived from Spain and the high seas. In April it was rumored that the Armada would make for Scotland, and on May 16 it was reported that 300 sail had assembled at Lisbon, and "that they stand greatly upon their guard hearing but of the name of Drake to approach them." On May 28 it was reported that the Armada was ready to sail. Howard accordingly put to sea on May 30 and Drake's daring project seemed about to be attempted, but on June 6 the fleet was forced back into the Sound by contrary winds. A few days later a dispatch from Walsingham was received which showed that timidity had again crippled the Council; Howard was ordered not to take his fleet to Spain, but instead "to ply up and down in some indifferent place between the coast of Spain and this realm. . . ." Howard, on June 15, answered:

"Sir, for the meaning we had to go on the coast of Spain, it was deeply debated by those which I think [the] world doth judge to be men of greatest experience that this realm hath.

"And if her Majesty do think that she is able to detract time with the King of Spain, she is greatly deceived which may breed her great peril. For this abusing [of] the treaty of peace doth plainly show how the King of Spain will have all things perfect, [as] his plot is laid, before he will proceed to execute. . . .

"The seas are broad; but if we had been [on] their coast, they durst not have put off, to have left us [on] their backs . . ."

Even more disastrous than this faulty strategy of Elizabeth and her Council was their administration. Again and again we find complaints by Howard of lack of victuals, a lack due partly to contrary winds, partly to the inefficiency of the period, but mainly to the parsimony of the queen and her councilors. Already, on

May 28, Howard had written to Burghley: "My good Lord, there is here the gallantest company of captains, soldiers and mariners that I think ever was seen in England. It were pity they should lack meat when they are so desirous to spend their lives in her Majesty's service." Again he appealed, this time to Walsingham, on June 15, and from then on much of Howard's and Drake's correspondence falls under two headings: "let us attack," and "in heaven's name send us food." . . .

At length, on June 17, the Council gave way on the first point and authorized Howard to do what he "shall think fittest." On June 23 the victuals had arrived and Howard informed the queen that he was about to sail. He added: "For the love of Jesus Christ, Madam, awake thoroughly, and see the villainous treasons round about you, against your Majesty and your realm, and draw your forces round about you, like a mighty prince, to defend you. Truly, Madam, if you do so, there is no cause to fear. If you do not, there will be danger."

Directly the ships were provisioned—probably on June 24— Howard, Drake, and Hawkins put to sea. Howard kept the body of the fleet together in mid-Channel while Drake, with a squadron of 20 ships, stood out toward Ushant, and Hawkins, with an equal number, lay toward Scilly. Soon afterward the wind shifted into the south-west and the fleet had to return to Plymouth, from where, on July 16, Howard informed Walsingham: "We have at this time four pinnaces on the coast of Spain; but, Sir, you may see what [may come] of the sending me out with so little victuals, and the [evil of the same]"; which suggests that it was not the wind alone which forced him back. Lastly, on July 17, we find him writing to the same minister: "I never saw nobler minds than be here [in our] forces; but I cannot stir out but I have an [infinite number] hanging on my shoulders for money."

Such was the condition of the English fleet, which in four days was to face the Armada. It consisted of the Royal Navy, 34 ships with *The Ark Royal* (800 tons) as flagship; the London squadron, 30 ships; Drake's squadron, 34 ships; Lord Thomas Howard's squadron (merchant ships and coasters), 38 ships; 15 victuallers and 23 voluntary ships; and Lord Henry Seymour's squadron— off the Downs—which numbered 23 ships.

On May 20, while the English fleet gathered at Plymouth, the

Armada dropped down the Tagus and put to sea, but was so buffeted in the Atlantic that, on June 9, Medina Sidonia sought refuge in Coruña, where to his consternation he found that much of the provisions was putrid and much water had leaked out of the newly made casks. He also found that so many ships needed repair and so many men were sick, that on the advice of a council of war he sent a message to the king recommending a postponement of the expedition until the following year. This Philip refused to consider, so after fresh supplies had been requisitioned, on July 12, in spite of the stormy weather, the Armada sailed again. On July 19, the *Lizard* was sighted, and there Medina Sidonia rested for a few hours until all his ships had come up. The following day he sailed eastward and shortly before midnight learnt from a captured English fishing boat that the admiral of England and Drake had put to sea that afternoon. This was untrue.

As soon as the Armada sighted the *Lizard,* Captain Thomas Fleming—who commanded one of the four pinnaces Howard had left in the Channel—reported its approach. The surprise was complete and Howard and Drake found themselves in the very position they had intended for their enemy—namely, "to meet the Spanish fleet upon their own coast, or in any harbour of their own, and there to defeat them." Nevertheless, on this Saturday, July 20, "his Lordship, accompanied with 54 sail of his fleet . . . plied out of the Sound; and being gotten out scarce so far as Eddystone, the Spanish army was discovered, and were apparently seen of the whole fleet to the westwards as far as Fowey." Howard then struck sail and lay under bare poles.

Because no fighting instructions are known to have been issued during the reign of Elizabeth it is impossible to say what order of battle Howard adopted. There was probably no order, other than "follow my leader," since, as yet, his fleet was not even organized into squadrons. And although the formation the Spanish fleet was found in was described as that of a crescent, no records support this. All that is known for certain is that it was divided into the usual main battle, vanguard (right wing) and rear guard (left wing). . . . The diagram illustrates his suggested distribution, which if viewed from the rear might well appear to look like a crescent.

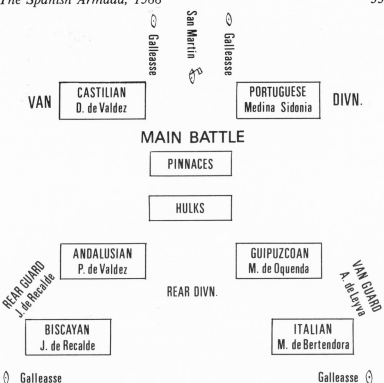

As Drake had not been met with in the Channel, Medina Sidonia concluded that he had been caught napping and was still at Plymouth. The opportunity to destroy him was so apparent that Don Alonzo de Leyva, captain-general of the Armada, and others urged Medina Sidonia to attack him before he could get out of the Sound. This was common sense, because in order to carry out their broadside tactics the English required sea-room to maneuver in and the Spaniards, dependent on boarding, required a fight in narrow waters. Had de Leyva's suggestion immediately been adopted, it is possible that the English fleet might have suffered as disastrous a defeat as the Turkish fleet did at Lepanto. But the king's orders stood in the way, and Medina Sidonia refused to listen to de Leyva.

Strangely enough, so it would appear, during the whole of July 20 the English fleet was unseen by the Spaniards, and it was not until one o'clock the following morning that they discovered from some prisoners that both Drake and Howard were out of Plymouth. Medina Sidonia at once anchored and ordered his squadron leaders to form order of battle.

While they did this, the moon rose and revealed their position to the English. Next, when the attention of the Spaniards was riveted on a small squadron of eight English ships bearing out from Plymouth to windward between the shore and the port side of the Armada, which was erroneously assumed to be the van of the English main fleet, Howard and his 50-odd ships "recovered the wind of the Spaniards two leagues to the westward of Eddystone . . ." and at daybreak Medina Sidonia was dumbfounded to discover a large enemy fleet to windward of him, bearing down to the attack. He realized that he could not avoid battle and ran up the royal standard—the signal for a general engagement.

The English got the weather gauge and drew up in a single long line—*en ala* as the Spaniards called it. Then, writes Corbett, they passed the Spanish vanguard "which formed the starboard and leeward wing of the rear division, firing upon it at long range as they went, and fell on the rearguard, a maneuver they can only have executed close-hauled in line-ahead. . . . The effect was immediate . . . a number of rearguard captains began crowding in a disgraceful panic upon Sidonia's division." To check the rout, Recalde came up with the *Gran Grin,* and was at once surrounded by Drake, Hawkins, and Frobisher, who poured into his ship a murderous fire "such as never before had been seen at sea." Next, Pedro de Valdez, in the *Nuestra Señora del Rosario,* was also engaged, and a little later Medina Sidonia in the *San Martin* came into action. But it was not until Recalde's vessel was completely disabled that Medina Sidonia could collect sufficient ships to relieve him. Howard then broke off the engagement, and soon after this the *San Salvador,* carrying the paymaster-general of the Armada and his chests, blew up and dropped out of the fleet in flames. Howard signalled to his ships to make sail for the burning wreck, which resulted in a fresh fight, after which he again signalled the retreat.

This engagement, the first between the two fleets, was of outstanding moral importance. It showed that the English ships and gunners were vastly superior to the Spanish. The latter were greatly depressed by their failure to board, and also by the abandonment of the *San Salvador*. As Medina Sidonia says: "The enemy's ships were so fast and handy that there was nothing which could be done with them."

That night, "his Lordship appointed Sir Francis Drake to set the Watch . . ." and then assembled a council of war in the *Ark Royal*, at which the general opinion held was that the Spaniards would make for the Isle of Wight—obviously the correct thing to do—in order to establish a base on English soil and to gain an anchorage for the fleet. This was the course the Spanish captains persuaded Medina Sidonia to adopt; for the English tactics had led to so excessive an expenditure of Spanish ammunition that they considered it essential for Medina Sidonia to occupy a port or roadstead on the south coast of England—actually the Isle of Wight—whence the Armada could cover the necessary flow of munitions from Spain and stand fast until action had been concerted with Parma. To prevent such a contingency, the English war council decided to give chase to the enemy: Drake lit the great poop lantern of the *Revenge* and set out to lead the fleet through the night.

As the night wore on, suddenly his light disappeared, and immediately many of the ships astern of him hove to, while others held on their course. The result was confusion, and when the sun rose on July 22 the *Revenge* was nowhere to be seen.

What had happened was that when he heard that Don Pedro de Valdez's ship lay helpless, Drake extinguished his lantern and put about, for he had been told that she contained much treasure. In the morning he captured her, sent her into Torbay, and rejoined the lord admiral. Apparently his privateering spirit had got the upper hand, which so incensed Frobisher that he exclaimed: "He thinketh to cozen us of our shares of fifteen thousand ducats; but we will have our shares, or I will make him spend the best blood in his belly. . . ."

The respite granted to Medina Sidonia by the confusion in his enemy's fleet enabled him to reorganize his rear division. He now placed it under the command of de Leyva, but continued to maintain the van division as it was, because Seymour's squadron was still unaccounted for; then he set sail again. But the English fleet could not be got together until the evening of July 22, when the wind died away and both fleets were becalmed within cannon shot of each other between Portland and St. Alban's Head.

At dawn the following day the wind rose from the north-east, and as this gave the weather gauge to the Spaniards, Medina Sidonia signalled a general engagement, and fighting was resumed. Soon Frobisher's ship, the *Triumph* (1,100 tons and the largest English ship), and five others got into trouble, and when he saw this ". . . the Duke of Medina Sidonia . . . came out with 16 of his best galleons to impeach his Lordship [Howard] and to stop him from assisting the *Triumph*. At which assault, after wonderful sharp conflict, the Spaniards were forced to give way and to flock together like sheep." Howard's account continues: "This fight was very nobly continued from morning until evening, the Lord Admiral being always in the hottest of the encounter, and it may well be said that for the time there was never seen a more terrible value of great shot, nor more hot fight than this was; for although the musketeers and harquebusiers of crock [a rest or swivel] were then infinite, yet could they not be discerned nor heard for the great ordnance came so thick that a man would have judged it to have been a hot skirmish of small shot, being all the fight long within half musket shot of the enemy."

The next day, Howard informs us, "there was little done," as much ammunition had been spent; therefore he sent "divers barks and pinnaces unto the shore for a new supply of such provisions," and divided his fleet into four squadrons, respectively commanded by himself, Drake, Hawkins, and Frobisher. Here for the first time we find a clear attempt to bring order out of disorder. Hitherto, with the possible exception of their first engagement, the English had fought their ships in swarms, in which the ships of their most noted captains had done the bulk of the fighting. Now these captains were to lead their own squadrons, and although this did not mean that Howard and Drake had decided henceforth to fight in line ahead, because each squadron had its own leader it was a definite step in that direction. Further, to facilitate his attack, Howard arranged that during the night six armed merchantmen from each squadron should keep the Spaniards in constant alarm.

Unfortunately, the wind fell and these distracting attacks had to be abandoned. Meanwhile Medina Sidonia told off 40 ships as a rearguard to protect his rear and then continued on his way, but soon after he was becalmed a few miles to the south of the Isle of Wight.

The following morning—Thursday, July 25—Howard noticed that Recalde's flagship, the *Santa Ana,* was "short of her company to the southwards" and ordered Sir John Hawkins to lower some boats and attack her. Immediately three galleasses rowed toward the boats, and were "fought a long time and much damaged" by "the Lord Admiral in the Ark, and the Lord Thomas Howard in the Golden Lion." The wind then rose, the fleets clinched, and for several hours the fighting was intense. This is noted by Sir George Carey, who writes: ". . . with so great expense of powder and bullet, that during the said time the shot continued so thick together that it might rather have been judged a skirmish with small shot on land than a fight with great shot on sea. In which conflict, thanks be to God, there hath not been two of our men hurt"— somewhat of an anticlimax to so desperate a struggle.

Medina Sidonia had hoped much of this day—St. Dominic's, his patron-saint—but when he found his ships again outclassed he abandoned all idea of seizing the Isle of Wight, sent ahead a dispatch boat to warn Parma of his arrival, and stood out for Calais. Howard then made for Dover to link up with Lord Henry Seymour and Sir William Wynter.

This day's fighting really decided the fate of the whole enterprise. The Spaniards had not yet been beaten, for so far their losses were insignificant, but the English tactics of refusal to close—that is, refusal to be pounded by the Spanish heavy cannon—had exhausted the ammunition of both sides, and whereas Howard could replenish his from coastal ports near by, Medina Sidonia could not do so until he had reached Flanders.

When Friday, July 26, dawned, "The Spaniards," says Howard, "went away before the English army like sheep," not out of fear, but for want of round shot. On Saturday evening, when he was near Calais, Medina Sidonia cast anchor between the town and Cape Gris-Nez and the English fleet anchored "within culverin shot of the enemy." Howard had been joined by Seymour's and Wynter's squadrons and had in all under his command 136 ships,

46 of which were "great ships," whereas the ships of the Armada had been reduced to 124.

The tactical situation was changed completely, for Howard, who had been able, in part at least, to replenish his powder and shot, whereas Sidonia had been unable to do so, could, whenever he wished, close in to small arms range and use his culverins as true ship-battering pieces. The crisis had been reached—the Armada was cornered. But to board the Spanish ships would clearly be both a desperate and a costly operation, for their soldiers were trained and armed to meet this type of attack.

This situation had been foreseen, and some days before the Armada put into Calais Roads Walsingham had sent orders to Dover to collect some fishing craft, pitch, and faggots, to make fire-ships. This suggestion must have come from Howard and Drake, who could not have failed to see that if their enemy could not hold the Channel he would be compelled to put into some roadstead or port.

Early on Sunday, July 28, a council of war was assembled in the main cabin of the *Ark Royal,* at which it was decided that so urgent was it to attack there would not be sufficient time to bring the fire-craft from Dover. Instead eight ships of 200 tons or under were selected from the fleet and prepared so hastily that not even their guns were removed.

Immediately after he reached Calais, Medina Sidonia sent his secretary to Parma to urge haste; but no sooner had he gone than another messenger, who had been sent by boat sometime before, returned to say that Parma was at Bruges and that so far no men had been embarked. Then the secretary returned to say that it was impossible for Parma to get his army on board in under a fortnight.

The truth would appear to be not that Parma's embarkation was delayed, but that, because of the Dutch fleet under Justinian of Nassau, Parma could not get out of port. It was useless to embark his men before Justinian's ships were driven away. Had it not been for the Dutch blockading fleet, which played a vitally important part in the campaign, in spite of Lord Henry Seymour's squadron, Parma might have chanced a crossing to Margate when the Armada was off the Isle of Wight. Emanuel van Meteren is definite on the effectiveness of the Dutch blockading fleet. "The shippes of Holland and Zeeland," he says, "stood continually in their sight [in the sight of Parma's ships] threatening shot and powder, and many inconveniences unto them: for feare of which shippes, the Mariners and Sea-men secretly withdrew themselves both day and night, lest that the duke of Parma his souldiers should compell them by maine force to goe on board, and to breake through the Hollanders Fleete, which all of them judged to bee impossible by reason of the straightnesse of the Haven." . . .

Midnight struck and passed, when early on Monday, as all lay still, the Spanish sentries saw several shadowy ships approach them and then burst into flames. The memory of the "hell-burners" of Antwerp, which three years before had destroyed a thousand of Parma's men, flashed across the minds of the terrified Spaniards. Medina Sidonia gave the fatal order for cables to be cut. He meant to reoccupy the anchorage once the fire-ships had passed by, but a panic followed and in confusion many of his ships crashed into each other in the dark and were borne out to sea. "Fortune," wrote a Spanish officer, "so favoured them [the English] that there grew from this piece of industry just what they counted on, for they dislodged us with eight vessels, an exploit which with one hundred and thirty they had not been able to do nor dared to attempt."

As soon as the fire-ships had drifted clear—they did no damage —Medina Sidonia ordered a signal gun to be fired for the fleet to regroup at Calais. The *San Marcos* (a Portuguese galleon) and one or two others obeyed the signal, but most of the ships, with two anchors lost and unable to get at their spare ones, drifted northeastward along the coast. When at last he realized that because the wind blew from the south-southwest it would be impossible for these ships to close in on the *San Martin,* Medina Sidonia weighed anchor and stood out to sea to follow the rest.

When morning broke, a triumphant sight greeted the eyes of Howard's men: right along the coast toward Dunkirk the Armada lay scattered, with no possibility of regaining Calais Road, where, stranded on the sand, close under the guns of the town, lay the *Capitana* galleasse with Don Hugo de Moncada and 800 men on board. Now was Howard's chance to attack and overwhelm his enemy, and he set out to seize it, but when he saw the great galleasse, she proved too tempting a bait. Instead of following the fleeing enemy, he made for the galleasse and took her after a stiff fight, in which Moncada was killed.

Drake, Hawkins, and Frobisher crowded on all sail and set out after the Armada. As they were short of powder and shot they closed in on their enemy so that every shot should tell. This they could do at little risk because the Spanish cannon shot had been exhausted. In this running fight their aim was to cut off the weathermost of the Spanish ships and to drive the rest to leeward on to the banks of Zeeland. . . .

The battle was continued along the coast toward Dunkirk, and at about nine o'clock the two fleets were engaged off Gravelines. The fight lasted until six in the evening. On the Spanish side Estrade's account is interesting, because it describes the severity of the English fire:

"So we bare out of the north and north-east," he writes, "with great disorder investing one with another and separated; and the English in the wind of us discharging their cannons marvellously well, and discharged not one piece but it was well employed by reason we were on so nigh another and they a good space asunder one from the other. The Vice-Admiral St. Martin went before, shooting her artillery. This day was slain Don Philip de Cordova, with a bullet that struck off his head and struck with his brains the greatest friend that he had there, and 24 men that were with us trimming our foresail. And whereas I and other four where, there came a bullet and from one struck away his shoe without doing any other harm, for they came and plied so very well with shot." . . .

As the crisis of the battle approached—it was six o'clock in the evening—it seemed that the Armada was doomed to inevitable destruction, when, to the relief of its sorely tried men, a squall of wind swept down upon the contending fleets. Then Howard and Drake broke off the fight, and the *Maria Juan* of 665 tons—one of Recalde's ships—foundered. With the squall the battle ended, and as Medina Sidonia had been forced out of the Channel and to leeward of Dunkirk the possibility of joining hands with Parma grew more and more remote.

As night closed in the wind freshened to a half-gale and the *San Mateo,* the *San Felipe,* and a third ship were driven on to the Zeeland coast. When Tuesday, July 30, dawned, Medina Sidonia looked from his flagship to see 109 English sail little more than half a league astern of his scattered fleet. . . .

Throughout the entire week's fighting, and in spite of "upwards of 100,000 rounds of great shot" expended by the Spaniards, no English ship was seriously damaged and only one captain and a score or two of seamen were killed. On the other hand, in the battle of Gravelines alone the Spaniards lost 600 killed and 800 wounded.

On the evening of July 29 Medina Sidonia had summoned a council of war, which decided that if the wind changed the Armada would regain the Channel, in spite of the fact that his ships were short of provisions and out of great shot. But, should it not regain the Channel, the sole course open was to return to Spain by way of the North Sea. As the wind did not change the latter course was adopted.

It was a desperate venture, for not only were many of the ships now unseaworthy, but they were not provisioned for so long a voyage. Nevertheless, though driven northward by an evil wind and pursued by Drake, to whom had been allotted the post of honor in the chase, it was still possible for Medina Sidonia in part to redeem the disaster. This he could have done if he had landed in the Forth and raised Scotland against the queen. But his one thought was to get back to Spain; he sailed past the mouth of the Forth on August 2, and in a single body the Armada stood out for the Orkneys. The next day Howard abandoned the chase, and, on August 7, his ships recovered the Downs, Harwich, and Yarmouth.

From Margate Road, on August 8, he wrote to Walsingham: "I pray to God we may hear of victuals, for we are generally in great want." To guard against an enemy return, he urged Walsingham to look to the country's defenses, and then added: "Some made little account of the Spanish force by sea; but I do warrant you, all the world never saw such a force as theirs was; and some Spaniards that we have taken, that were in the fight at Lepanto, do say that the worst of our four fights that we have had with them did exceed far the fight they had there; and they say that at some

of our fights we had 20 times as much great shot as they had there.
. . . Sir, in your next letters to my brother Stafford [ambassador
at Paris] I pray write to him that he will let Mendoza [Spanish
ambassador in Paris] know that her Majesty's rotten ships dare
meet with his master's sound ships; and in buffeting with them,
though they were three great ships to one of us, yet we have
shortened them 16 or 17: whereof there is three of them a-fishing
in the bottom of the seas." To this letter he added the postscript
—"Sir, if I hear nothing of my victuals and munition this night
here, I will gallop to Dover to see what may be got there, or else
we shall starve."

The rest of the story, a dramatic one, is soon told, for during
the Armada's dreadful voyage home, the galleasse *Girona* went to
pieces near Giant's Causeway, and carried to their deaths her crew
and Don Alonso de Leyva; the *El Gran Grifon* sank off Fair
Island; the *Rata Coronada* was wrecked on the coast of Erris; the
Duquesa Santa Ana was lost in Glennagiveny Bay; and the *Nuestra Señora de la Rosa* was beaten to pieces on the Blaskets. The
San Marcos, San Juan, Triniada, Valencera, and *Falcon Blanco
Mediano* were lost off the coast of Ireland, and the *San Pedro
Mayor,* blown off course, was wrecked in Bigbury Bay, near Ply-
mouth.

Of the 130 sail which stood out from Lisbon in May, 63 are
believed to have been lost. Two were abandoned to the enemy;
three were lost off the French coast; two were lost off Holland; two
were sunk off Gravelines; 19 were wrecked off Scotland or Ireland;
and the fate of 35 is unknown. The English did not lose a ship.

Even more horrible than the fate of the castaways on the Irish
coast, most of whom were butchered, was that of the crews who
were not shipwrecked; thousands of men died of untended
wounds, of fever, of hunger, and of thirst—some ships were without water for 14 days. At length, in the middle of September, a
messenger arrived posthaste at the Escorial from Santander with
the news that Medina Sidonia had returned to that port on September 12. When the messenger gave the king this fatal news,
Philip was sitting at his desk. Without change of countenance he
observed: "Great thanks do I render Almighty God, by whose
generous hand I am gifted with such power, that I could easily,

if I chose, place another fleet upon the sea. Nor is it of very great importance that a running stream should be sometimes intercepted, so long as the fountain from which it flows remains inexhaustible."

It was God's will, and so he accepted his defeat. Yet he was not unconscious of the sufferings of the brave men who had risked and undergone so much in this disastrous crusade. He did all in his power to alleviate their ills, and instead of blaming Medina Sidonia, he ordered him to return to Cadiz, there to resume his former governorship.

Very different was the behavior of Queen Elizabeth, whose first consideration was to cut expense. Unlike Philip, there was nothing either chivalrous or generous in her character, and though Professor Laughton goes out of his way to exonerate her meanness, there is no shadow of doubt that, had she been a woman of heart as well as of head, it would have been impossible for her to have left her gallant seamen to die by scores of want and disease immediately after the victory was won.

The correspondence of Howard proves this conclusively. On August 10—that is, three days after his return from the pursuit —he wrote to Burghley: "Sickness and mortality begins wonderfully to grow amongst us; and it is a most pitiful sight to see, here at Margate, how the men, having no place to receive them into here, die in the streets." Again, on August 29, he wrote to him: "It were too pitiful to have men starve after such a service. . . . Therefore I had rather open the Queen Majesty's purse something to relieve them, than they should be in that extremity for we are to look to have more of their services; and if men should not be cared for better than to let them starve and die miserably, we should very hardly get men to serve."

Although little realized at the time, the influences of this campaign on naval strategy and tactics were profound, and out of them gradually emerged many of the principles which were to govern warfare at sea until the advent of the steamship.

First, the campaign showed the vital importance of bases in relation to command of the sea. Drake's 1587 attack on Cadiz and Lisbon was in idea a more certain method of protecting England against invasion than to meet and beat the Armada in the Channel, and had it been repeated in 1588, as it readily could have been, the high probability is that the Armada would never have sailed. Conversely, the lack of a Spanish naval base near England was the fundamental reason why the Armada was unable to carry out its task. Hence onward, because it is seldom possible to compel an enemy to accept battle at sea, to bottle up his fleet in its home ports and simultaneously to deny him naval bases near her shores became the foundations of England's naval policy.

Secondly, the campaign had shown clearly the futility of reliance on armed merchantmen in battle. They took next to no part in the Channel fighting, and the best that can be said of them is that they added grandeur and with it, possibly, terror, to the respective fleets. As raiders, they were of use, but as ships of the line, an impediment rather than a support. Had the English done without them much money could have been saved without in any way jeopardizing the issue.

Thirdly, as artillerists both sides had failed to achieve their respective ends. The English culverins were neither powerful enough nor sufficiently accurate to hit and smash a ship except at close range, and though the Spanish cannon could do so, their ships were not nimble enough nor their seamen sufficiently skillful to bring their superior armament within close range of their enemy. Hence the indecisive nature of the fighting and the tendency for cannon increasingly to become the primary naval weapon in battle.

Historically, the importance of the defeat of the Armada was, as Merriman says, that it constituted "the supreme disaster of Philip's reign." Nevertheless the war meandered on until 1604, to end in a peace of exhaustion which was neither creditable nor profitable to England, nor of any great consequence to Spain. It did not add an acre to Spanish territory, nor subtract an acre from English. It did not change the dynasties of England or Spain, nor did it modify the policies of the contending parties or influence their respective religions. Wherein, then, lay the decisiveness of the battle?

To answer that it spared England from invasion is true, but only conditionally so, for the part played by Justinian of Nassau was as important in gaining the victory as that played by Howard and

Drake. Even had these two never put to sea, it is improbable that the Armada could have dislodged the Sea Beggars of Brill, because their nimble, light draught ships could still sail the shallow coastal waters of Flanders and Zeeland and the cumbersome and larger Spanish ships could not. Yet, even should this hypothesis be set aside, the defeat of the Armada is to be reckoned the most decisive English battle fought since Hastings—it saved England and it mortally wounded Spanish prestige. It showed to the world at large that the colossus had feet of clay; that the edifice of Spanish power was built upon sand, and that the security of her empire was largely a mirage. It was this illusion which for nearly a century had imposed itself upon the credulity of the world to an extent unwarranted either by the resources, the wealth, or the population of Spain. . . .

The defeat of the Armada whispered the imperial secret into England's ear; that in a commercial age the winning of the sea is more profitable than the winning of the land, and though this may not have been clearly understood in 1588, during the following century the whisper grew louder and louder until it became the voice of every Englishman. . . .

The historical importance of the defeat of the Armada is this: it laid the cornerstone of the British Empire by endowing England with the prestige Spain lost. And it was this prestige, this faith in her destiny, that urged the English along their imperial way, until their flag floated over the greatest empire the world has so far seen: the empire of the oceans and the seas, which from rise to fall was to endure for over 300 years.

CHAPTER III

CARNAGE AT THE
BATTLE OF BLENHEIM

The British historian Sir Edward Creasy (1812–1878) was a professor at the University of London, as well as a lawyer. He was, later, the chief justice of Ceylon and he was knighted in 1860. He has written the most notable military and political evaluations of the world's greatest battles—specifically Cannae, Marathon, Hastings, The Spanish Armada—and here sets the historical stage for the Battle of Blenheim.

It was a test of many great generals and causes. Louis XIV was the gracious, cultured but dominating genius of France. The stakes were Europe. His generals in the field included Marshal Tallard, Marshal Marsin, Marshal Villeroy and the Elector of Bavaria. Opposing them were England's duke of Marlborough, Prince Eugène of Austria, Louis of Baden and Lord Cutts, the English general.

The French-Bavarian armies outnumbered the armies of Marlborough and his Grand Alliance. When the battle was over, 40,000 French and Bavarians were killed, wounded, captured or missing—as against 12,000 soldiers of Marlborough and his allies. It was another annihilating Cannae almost 2000 years later.

The Battle of Blenheim, 1704
by
Sir Edward Shepherd Creasy

The decisive blow struck at Blenheim resounded through every part of Europe. It at once destroyed the vast fabric of power which it had taken Louis XIV, aided by the talents of Turenne and the genius of Vauban, so long to construct.

—Alison

Though more slowly molded and less imposingly vast than the Empire of Napoleon, the power Louis XIV had acquired and was acquiring at the commencement of the eighteenth century was almost equally menacing to the general liberties of Europe. If tested by the amount of territory that each procured *permanently* for France, the ambition of the royal Bourbon was more successful than were the enterprises of the imperial Corsican. At the end of all the devastating wars of the Consulate and the Empire, France was left with virtually the same boundaries as at the beginning of the French Revolution. . . .

When Louis took the reins of his government into his own hands, there was a union of ability with opportunity such as France had not seen since the days of Charlemagne. Moreover Louis's career was no brief one. For over forty years, for a period equal to the duration of Charlemagne's rein, Louis steadily followed an aggressive and a generally successful policy. He passed a long youth and manhood of triumph before the military genius of Marlborough made him acquainted with humiliation and defeat. The great Bourbon lived too long. Had he died when his great antagonist William III died in 1702, just before the opening of the

War of the Spanish Succession, his reign would be cited as unequaled in French annals. But he lived on to see his armies beaten, his cities captured, and his kingdom wasted by disastrous war.

Still, Louis XIV had forty years of success, and from the permanence of their fruits we may judge what the results would have been if the last fifteen years of his reign had been equally fortunate. Had it not been for Blenheim, the greater part of Europe might have come under French domination, with England perhaps standing alone, protected by her navy, somewhat as in the later days of Napoleon, but with different allies. It would be hazardous to attempt to predict the ultimate result of such a situation; it is enough to classify this battle as of tremendous importance, and decisive in its effects upon the course of history.

When Louis XIV began to exercise personal control over the affairs of his kingdom, he found all the materials for a strong central government at hand. Richelieu had completely tamed the turbulent spirit of the French nobility and destroyed the political power of the Huguenots. The assemblies of the States-General were obsolete. The royal authority alone remained. When he said, "L'Etat c'est moi," it was a simple statement of fact. He was the state; he knew it and fearlessly played the part.

Not only was his government a strong one, but the country which he governed was strong—strong in its geographical position, in the compactness of its territory, in the number and martial spirit of its inhabitants, and in their complete and undivided nationality. Furthermore, there were an extraordinary number of talented men in France eager to serve their king. One of the surest proofs of Louis's own genius was his skill in discovering genius in others and his promptness in calling it into action. Under him, Minister of War Louvois organized, and Turenne, Condé, Villars, and Berwick led, the armies of France; and Vauban, the greatest fortification engineer of all time, designed her defenses. Throughout his reign French diplomacy was marked by skillfulness and activity. Great strides were made in the internal administration of the government, the building of roads, and in the provision of public services.

François Guizot, in his lectures on *The History of Civilization in Europe,* admiringly says that "the government of Louis XIV was the first that presented itself to the eyes of Europe as a power acting upon sure grounds, which had not to dispute its existence with inward enemies, but was at ease as to its territory and its people, and solely occupied with the task of administering government, properly so called. All the European governments had been previously thrown into incessant wars, which deprived them of all security as well as of all leisure, or so pestered by internal parties or antagonists that their time was passed in fighting for existence. The government of Louis XIV was the first to appear as a busy, thriving administration of affairs, as a power at once definitive and progressive, which was not afraid to innovate, because it could reckon securely on the future. There have been in fact very few governments equally innovating. Compare it with a government of the same nature, the unmixed monarchy of Philip II of Spain; it was more absolute than that of Louis XIV and yet it was far less regular and tranquil. How did Philip II succeed in establishing absolute power in Spain? By stifling all activity in the country, opposing himself to every species of amelioration, and rendering the state of Spain completely stagnant. The government of Louis XIV on the contrary exhibited alacrity for all sorts of innovations, and showed itself favorable to the progress of letters, arts, wealth —in short, of civilization. This was the veritable cause of its preponderance in Europe, which arose to such a pitch that it became the type of a government, not only to sovereigns, but also to nations, during the seventeenth century."

While France was thus strong and united, and ruled by a martial, an ambitious, and (with all his faults) an enlightened and high-spirited sovereign, what European power was there fit to cope with her or keep her in check?

Both Spain and Austria had been humbled during the Thirty Years' War. Cardinal Richelieu had made sure that his country would be more powerful than they. Also, on several occasions the French king was able to acquire allies among the numerous princes of the Empire.

As for the northern countries at the beginning of the eighteenth century, when the last of Louis's wars began, Russia, Poland, and Denmark were fully occupied in the Great Northern War, trying to curb the power of Sweden.

If we turn to the two remaining European powers of importance in this era, to England and to Holland, we find the position of England, from 1660 to 1688, most painful to contemplate. Bolingbroke rightly says that during these twenty-eight years prior to the Glorious Revolution of 1688 which brought William of Orange to the throne of England, the very period in which Louis XIV was acquiring such great power, the Stuarts' conduct of foreign policy was unworthy. England was either an idle spectator of what happened on the Continent, or a faint and uncertain ally against France, or a warm and sure ally on her side, or a partial mediator between her and the powers attempting to defend themselves against her. But the crime was not national; the people of England objected strongly to the policies of their Stuart kings.

The Dutch Netherlands, alone of all the European powers, opposed from the very beginning a steady and uniform resistance to the ambition and strength of the French king. It was against Holland that the fiercest attacks of France were made and, though often apparently on the eve of complete success, they were always ultimately baffled by the stubborn bravery of the Dutch and the heroism of their great leader, William of Orange. When he became king of England, the contest became less equal, although France retained her general superiority.

This is not the place for any narrative of the first three wars of Louis XIV which resulted in his adding to his kingdom territory to the north, and along the Rhine. He thus conquered and annexed valuable lands and people who would increase his strength. However, throughout this period from 1667 to 1697, he had always in mind the possibility of a far greater expansion of his kingdom to the south, that is, to acquire for the House of Bourbon the empire of Spain.

As time passed and the prospect of Charles II of Spain dying without lineal heirs became more and more certain, the claims of the House of Bourbon to the Spanish crown after his death became matters of urgent international concern. At length when Charles died in 1700 he named Philip of Anjou, Louis XIV's grandson, to succeed him. Louis well knew that a general European war would follow if he accepted for his house the crown thus bequeathed, but he had been preparing for this crisis throughout his reign. When he announced that his grandson would go to Spain as King Philip V, the Spanish ambassador coined the memorable words, "There are no longer any Pyrenees."

The Empire, which now received the grandson of Louis XIV, comprised, besides Spain itself, part of the Netherlands, Sardinia, Sicily, the Kingdom of Naples, the Duchy of Milan; the Philippine Islands in Asia; and in the New World, lower California, Mexico, Florida, Central America, and a large part of South America.

Loud was the wrath of Austria whose prince, the Archduke Charles, was the rival claimant for the empire of Spain. The wrath is understandable, but of far greater importance were the alarm and fear that swept through Europe. It was evident that Louis aimed at consolidating France and the Spanish dominions into one huge empire. The peril that menaced England, Holland, Austria, and the other powers is well summed up by Alison: "Spain had threatened the liberties of Europe in the end of the sixteenth century. France had all but overthrown them in the close of the seventeenth. What hope was there of their being able to make head against them both, united under such a monarch as Louis XIV?"

William III began to form a Grand Alliance against the House of Bourbon. It included England, Holland, Austria, and some of the Germanic princes. At this point Louis, who professed to desire peace, took a step forward that made war inevitable. The treaty concluding the last war had stipulated that the principal Spanish fortresses along the northern frontier of France would be garrisoned by Dutch troops as a barrier against French invasion. Under pretense of securing these barrier fortresses for the young king of Spain, Louis sent his troops to occupy them. The result was that all the famous strongpoints in what is now southern Belgium became Louis's property without a struggle. It seemed as if everything the allies had striven for in the last war was gone and that Louis was stronger than ever.

Then William, the guiding light of the allied league, died on March 8, 1702; but England's new queen took prompt action. Queen Anne immediately declared her intention to adhere to the Grand Alliance and to support the measures planned by her predecessor. The man primarily responsible for the rapidity of this decision and for the conduct of the war that followed was John

Churchill, soon to become famous in history as the duke of Marlborough. Many have attempted to cast a blot upon his reputation. It has been claimed that his advancement was due *primarily* to court intrigue, and it has been pointed out that he was once accused of treason. However it must be remembered that the latter charge, during those perplexing times of shifting allegiances, could be applied with equal ease to many prominent figures of the day. Furthermore, if his advancement was due *partially* to court intrigue it was indeed fortunate for England that this occurred. The fact is that without some influence at court it was almost impossible in that day and age to reach a high position.

It is, however, only in his military career that we must now consider him. There are few generals of ancient or modern times, possibly only one other English general, the duke of Wellington, whose campaigns will bear comparison with those of Marlborough. He had served in his earlier years under Turenne and had obtained the praise of that great tactician. It would be difficult to name a single quality a general ought to have, with which Marlborough was not eminently gifted. What principally attracted the attention of contemporaries was the imperturbable evenness of his spirit. Voltaire says of him: "He had, to a degree above all other generals of his time, that calm courage in the midst of tumult, that serenity of soul in danger, which the English call *a cool head* (que les Anglais appellent *cold head, tête froide*), and it was perhaps this quality, the greatest gift of nature for command, which formerly gave the English so many advantages over the French in the plains of Crécy, Poitiers and Agincourt."

In his last illness King William recommended Marlborough, whom he had appointed commander in chief of the English forces in Holland, to his successor Queen Anne as the fittest person to command her armies. Since William knew how highly Marlborough already stood in her favor, because of his ability and because his wife was the queen's favorite companion and confidante, this recommendation was not at all necessary. It simply shows how thoroughly the two men, previously estranged by that unproved charge of treason, had become reconciled, and how anxious William was that no one but Marlborough be given the task of leading the armies in the coming crisis.

He was not only made captain-general of the English forces at home and abroad but also, upon his arrival on the Continent, he made such a good impression that the Dutch made him commanding general of their armies, and so did many of the Germanic princes. Unfortunately, however, in addition to commanding the armies, he had to deal with the civilian governments and try to reconcile their conflicting interests, jealousies, and disagreements. He was never permitted to carry out his plans without obtaining approval from the various states whose troops he supposedly commanded. This required all the tact and persuasiveness for which he became justly famous. At one point at the beginning of the Blenheim campaign, as we shall see, he found it necessary actually to conceal his true plans from all but a few selected persons in authority. Had it not been for his enduring patience, his intuitive ability to judge which persons could be thoroughly trusted, his resourcefulness, and his unrivaled diplomatic skill as a courtier and statesman, he would never have led the allied armies to victory on the Danube. His great political adversary, Bolingbroke, does him ample justice here. After referring to the loss that King William's death seemed to inflict on the allied cause, Bolingbroke observes that: "By his death the Duke of Marlborough was raised to the head of the army and, indeed, of the confederacy; where he, a new, a private man, a subject, acquired by merit and by management a more deciding influence than high birth, confirmed authority, and even the crown of Great Britain had given to King William. Not only all the parts of that vast machine, the Grand Alliance, were kept more compact and entire, but a more rapid and vigorous motion was given to the whole. Instead of languishing and disastrous campaigns, we saw every scene of the war full of action. All those wherein he appeared, and many of those wherein he was not then an actor, but abettor, however, of their action, were crowned with the most triumphant success.

"I take with pleasure this opportunity of doing justice to that great man, whose faults I knew, whose virtues I admired; and whose memory, as the greatest general and the greatest minister that our country, or perhaps any other, has produced, I honor."

War was formally declared by the allies against France in May, 1702. In that year the principal scenes of operation were along the

Dutch border and in north Italy. Marlborough headed the allied troops in Holland and succeeded in conquering several fortresses along the Meuse; for these victories he was created a duke by the queen. In Italy Prince Eugène, although outnumbered by the French, was able to hold his own. But in September the Elector of Bavaria decided to join the French. Louis XIV was quick to seize the opportunity thus presented of aiming a blow at Austria through the territory of his new ally. By the end of the year 1703 the French and Bavarian armies had seized a number of vital points on the line of communications through the allied territory of Baden, joined forces, and were threatening Vienna. Because of political pressure Marlborough had been forced to confine his activities to northern France, the Meuse and the area around Cologne on the Rhine.

Louis XIV's plan for the 1704 campaign would have done credit to Napoleon himself. On the extreme left of his line, in the west, the French armies in the Netherlands were to act on the defensive. The fortresses still in French hands were so many and so strong that it seemed unlikely that the allies could make any serious impression upon them in one campaign. The French king was thus making proper use of fortifications, to hold a line with fewer men while he massed his strength for decisive blows against the enemy in another region. Austria was his target; he could eliminate her from the war while remaining on the defensive opposite the Netherlands.

Large detachments were therefore to be made from troops holding the line on the left. They were to be led by Marshal Villeroy to the Rhine. The French Army already in that region, commanded by Marshal Tallard, was to march through the Black Forest to join the Elector of Bavaria and the French troops of Marshal Marsin near Ulm. The French Grand Army of the Danube was then to march upon Vienna. High military genius was shown in the formation of this plan, but it was met and baffled by a genius higher still.

Marlborough had watched with the deepest anxiety the progress of French arms on the Rhine and in Bavaria. He saw the futility of carrying on a war of posts and sieges in the Netherlands while death-blows were being dealt on the Danube. Unlike most of the generals of his day, he believed not in the strength of the defensive but in the power of the attack with the bayonet. He taught his cavalry to rely on shock action, to charge with drawn weapons at a full trot. His belief in offensive tactics naturally led to the offensive in strategy. He resolved, therefore, to let the war in the west languish for a year, while he moved with all the forces he could collect to the central scene of decisive operations. Thus, unknown to each other, Louis XIV and Marlborough were both planning decisive victories in the same region.

In one important respect the French king had a tremendous advantage over the English general. Louis's word was law; when he ordered his armies to march there was no one to question his decision or obstruct his plans. Marlborough, on the other hand, had to overcome the objections of his own countrymen and of the Dutch, whose frontier he proposed to weaken. Fortunately he had a staunch ally, Anton Heinsius, the Chief Minister of Holland, who had been the cordial supporter of King William, and who now supported Marlborough in the council of the allies. To him, and a few others, the duke communicated his plan; but to the general councils of his allies he disclosed only part of his scheme. His proposal to them was that he should march to the Moselle with the English troops and part of the foreign auxiliaries, and commence vigorous operations in that region, while a defensive war was maintained in the Netherlands. Having with difficulty obtained the consent of the Dutch to his portion of his project, he exercised the same diplomatic zeal with the same success, in urging the other princes of the empire to increase the number of troops they supplied, and to post them in places convenient for his own intended movements.

Crossing the Meuse, Marlborough marched toward Koblenz on the Rhine. On May 23 he reached Bonn and learned that Marshal Villeroy was moving east. Louis XIV was also putting his plan of movement toward the Danube into effect, but Marlborough had moved first. When he reached Koblenz everyone, friend and foe, expected him to turn south and follow the Moselle. We have noted the advantage the French king had over Marlborough, of being able to dictate his orders without having to consult anyone else. Here we find Marlborough with the tremendous advantage of surprise on his side. The French could not believe that he had obtained permission from the Dutch to move any farther east than the Moselle. Therefore when he continued toward Mainz they were greatly puzzled until they learned that bridges were being built across the Rhine at Philippsburg. Believing that he had now divined his enemy's true purpose, Marshal Tallard made preparations to resist an advance from that direction.

Therefore when Marlborough reached Weisloch and turned southeast toward the Danube, revealing unmistakably his destination, he had already accomplished a great deal. He was between Marshal Tallard's army and his target, the armies of Marshal Marsin and the Elector of Bavaria. Marshal Tallard could do nothing but follow and hope he would arrive in time. Marshal Villeroy was left far behind.

Crossing the Neckar River, Marlborough met for the first time Prince Eugène, the famous general of Austria's forces, who had been called back from Italy to defend Vienna. There began a lasting friendship that grew into a feeling of mutual trust and confidence; the partnership of these two brilliant leaders would bring victory on many a famous battlefield.

Continuing toward Ulm, Marlborough was joined by the army of Louis of Baden and other reinforcements. Then while Prince Eugène undertook to delay, with a small force, the approach of Marshal Tallard from the Rhine, Marlborough marched down the Danube. On July 2 he stormed the heights of the Schellenberg at Donauwörth and, after a stout resistance, captured the fortress. This was a prize well worth securing. With this stronghold in his possession, he marched south, across the Danube, into Bavaria. But the elector's army, although part of it had been defeated at Donauwörth, was still numerous and strong; also Marshal Tallard was at last coming to join forces. When these two united they moved north across the Danube and fortified a position on the north bank at Blenheim. Marlborough also recrossed the Danube and joined Prince Eugène; together they occupied a position downriver a few miles to the east, facing their enemy. Prince Louis of Baden had been sent farther eastward to besiege Ingolstadt.

At this point the French-Bavarian Army consisted of about 60,000 men, outnumbering the combined forces of Marlborough and Prince Eugène who had fewer guns and could count no more than 56,000 men, although they did have a preponderance of cavalry. According to all the rules of warfare as practiced in that age, the allies should therefore retreat; certainly they should not attack. For the first time since the beginning of the campaign, the French felt confident of ultimate victory. Eventually Marshal Villeroy would arrive with his army, which would give them sufficient strength to overwhelm the force under Marlborough and Eugène; then they could carry out King Louis's original plan and push forward to Vienna.

This was exactly what Marlborough had come all the way to the Danube to prevent. He had inflicted heavy losses upon his enemy at Donauwörth and had maneuvered Marshal Villeroy out of position. He was an exponent of offensive warfare and had no intention whatsoever of either retreating or waiting for Marshal Villeroy.

On August 12, 1704, he rode out to reconnoiter the enemy lines. He found that they occupied a very strong position facing to the east. The French-Bavarian right (south) flank rested on the Danube; their left was protected from assault by wooded high ground. They could be attacked only from the front, but here also he found himself confronted with serious obstacles. The enemy was posted behind a little stream called the Nebel, which runs into the Danube immediately in front of the little village of Blenheim. The Nebel flowed through a marshy little valley which he would have to cross before reaching their position on the rising ground to the west. Blenheim, which they were now engaged in fortifying, formed a strongpoint on their right flank. The village of Lutzingen formed another strongpoint on their left flank, while near the center of the line a third strongpoint was being constructed around the hamlet of Oberglau.

The average general would have decided that an attack upon such a position could have little chance of success, but Marlborough needed a victory. The fatal consequences if he were to retreat were obvious. His prestige would be lowered; the morale of the allied forces would decrease as the enemy increased in strength; and ultimately he might be defeated in battle far from his homeland, with little chance of returning safely. The allied confederacy, the Grand Alliance, would fall apart and Louis XIV's fondest hopes would be realized.

Marlborough and Eugène were well aware of the consequences of defeat, but they made their plans with victory in mind, and they counted heavily on two factors—surprise and maintaining the initiative by offensive action. The first element, surprise, they attained by beginning their march at 2:00 A.M., August 13. As they approached the enemy Marlborough's troops formed the left and center, while Eugène's forces were on the right. A thick haze covered the ground that morning, and it was not until the allied left and center had advanced nearly within cannon-shot that Tallard on the French right was aware of their approach. He made his preparations with haste, and about eight o'clock opened a heavy fire of artillery on Marlborough's advancing left wing.

With so little time to form, Tallard had done the best he could under the circumstances, but the result was that he formed as a separate army would form, with his main infantry force near the strongpoint of Blenheim and his cavalry on each side of his infantry. The army of Marsin and the Elector of Bavaria did the same thing, with their infantry near Oberglau, and their cavalry on each side. The result, for all practical purposes, was a formation of two separate armies in line beside each other. The gap between the strongpoint of Blenheim (held by Tallard's infantry) and Oberglau (held by Marsin's infantry, with the elector's infantry alongside them) was therefore held by cavalry. Later both Tallard and Marsin made an effort to strengthen the center of their combined line, but essentially it remained Tallard's left-wing cavalry and Marsin's right-wing cavalry.

The ground Eugène's column had to traverse was peculiarly difficult, especially for the artillery. It was noon before he could get his troops into line. Marlborough waited therefore until all was ready before launching his attack at 12:30. First he sent Lord Cutts with a strong brigade of infantry to assault the village of Blenheim. The attack was gallantly made and as valiantly repulsed. A second assault met the same result; the losses on both sides were severe. Marlborough made no further efforts to carry the village but turned his energies to effecting a crossing of the Nebel in the center of the allied line.

Meanwhile, farther to the north, a crisis was developing opposite Oberglau. The attack of the prince of Holstein-Beck on that little hamlet had been driven back by the Irish brigade which held that village. The Irish were pressing forward in pursuit when Marlborough came up in person to restore order. With help from some of Prince Eugène's men, this was accomplished. Thus the fighting had centered around two strongpoints in the French line, neither of which had been captured. But both had been continuously exerting that power of attraction which is so common on any battlefield. The defending forces, including a large portion of the French reserves, had been gradually drawn to these two points.

Marlborough's next move, to keep the initiative in his own hands, was to press forward between Blenheim and Oberglau. Temporary bridges had already been prepared, and planks and fascines collected. With the aid of these he had already succeeded in getting troops across the Nebel. The French artillery had not been idle, nor had the French cavalry, but by degrees the allies had struggled forward across the bloodstained marshy streams and were now lined up on the enemy side of the river. Though the French saw the attack coming, there was little they could do to alter their situation. Very few reserves were available; they had been permitted to be drawn into the struggles at Blenheim and Oberglau. Nor were any available from their left flank. Prince Eugène's attacks had made little progress in that area, but here also the defenders had permitted their reserves to be drawn into the battle. The only commander on the field able to make an attack at this point was Marlborough.

The allied cavalry, strengthened and supported by foot and guns, advanced up the slope to where the French cavalry awaited them. On riding up the summit, the allies were received with so hot a fire from artillery and small arms that at first the cavalry recoiled, but without abandoning the high ground. The guns and the infantry they had brought with them maintained the contest with spirit and effect. The French fire seemed to slacken. The duke instantly ordered a charge all along the line. The allied cavalry, with the duke himself leading the charge, went forward in long, sweeping lines. It was of course impossible for the defending cavalry to wait halted, and meet the shock of a mounted charge. They wheeled and spurred from the field. The few infantry left alone were ridden down by the torrent of allied horsemen. By never losing the initiative, by pinning down the enemy's reserves near their strongpoints, and then charging through between them the battle had been won.

Tallard and Marsin, severed from each other, thought only of retreat. Tallard drew up his remaining squadrons in a line extended toward Blenheim, and sent orders to the infantry in that village to join him without delay. But long before his orders could be obeyed, the conquering squadrons of Marlborough had wheeled to their left and thundered down on the array of the French marshal. Part of Tallard's force was driven into the Danube. Part fled with their general to the village of Sonderheim where they were soon surrounded and compelled to surrender. Meanwhile, Eugène had renewed his attack and was enveloping the Bavarian left; Marsin, finding his colleague routed and his own right flank uncovered, beat a retreat. Though he and the elector succeeded in withdrawing a portion of their troops, the large body of French remaining in Blenheim were left to certain destruction. Marlborough speedily occupied all the outlets of the village; then, collecting his artillery around it, he methodically began a cannonade that would have destroyed Blenheim and all who were in it. After several gallant but unsuccessful attempts to cut their way through, the French in Blenheim were compelled to surrender. Twenty-four battalions and twelve squadrons laid down their arms.

In the Battle of Blenheim the allies lost 4,500 killed and 7,500 wounded out of a total of 56,000 engaged. The French and Bavarian losses have never been accurately computed. Their army totaled 60,000 men; of these no more than 20,000 were ever reassembled. This means a loss of about 40,000 killed, wounded, captured, or missing. Almost all the artillery and almost all the supplies were captured. The army had not just suffered a defeat; it had been practically destroyed.

Before the year ended, Ulm, Landau, Trarbach, and Trier had surrendered. Bavaria submitted to the emperor. Germany was completely delivered from France. The military ascendancy of allied arms was established; throughout the rest of the war Louis XIV fought only in defense. Blenheim had dissipated forever his once-proud visions of universal conquest.

CHAPTER IV

SARATOGA, 1777

General John Burgoyne, British (1722–92), was a hero of the Seven Years' War (1756–63) that England fought against France and Austria. Prior to retiring from the army to continue his parliamentary activities and eventually become a famous playwright, he was sent to Boston in 1775 to assist General Gage in putting down the American rebellion. His major military actions were the reoccupation of Crown Point, the capture of Ticonderoga, as well as his victory at Bemis Heights, though his losses there were overwhelming. The greatest victory of the American colonials was the Battle of Saratoga, where General Burgoyne was forced to surrender his force of less than 5000 men to General Gates's 16,000 colonial soldiers—the turning point in the American Revolution.

General Horatio Gates (1729–1806), born in England, served in the British Army during the French and Indian Wars in America. He returned to England, but George Washington encouraged him to become a planter in West Virginia. Later, favoring the cause of the American colonies, he became a brigadier general when the Revolutionary War began. He was considered an excellent training officer and tactician. There is, however, a permanent dispute as to whether it was his role or Benedict Arnold's action in the Battle of Saratoga that helped to bring about the surrender of General Burgoyne.

General Gates was always controversial and was involved in a plot to make him commander-in-chief. He was stationed in the South after the loss of Charleston and he commanded the colonial troops when Camden was lost to the British. After the war, Gates retired to his plantation in West Virginia, freed his slaves in 1790 and retired to Newburgh, New York.

General James Wilkinson (1757–1825), born in Maryland, has been everything to every historian of early American history. He was on General Gates's staff and was a born plotter among plotters. His friendship with Benedict Arnold and Aaron Burr, and the various conspiracies that he was part of during and after the war, have given Wilkinson a bizarre reputation. He served in the War of 1812 and did so poorly as a general in the North that he was the subject of a court of inquiry. He wrote his memoirs in 1816 and retired to Mexico.

The Battle of Saratoga: October 17, 1777
by
F. J. Hudleston

"The army must not retreat." So Burgoyne had said, and it is very evident, if you look at any portrait of him in profile in the books of his day, why he would not retreat. He has the jowl of a prizefighter, he is a regular Gentleman Jackson. The painter Ramsay was right to take a front view of him; in that charming portrait there is little hint of the set and dogged jaw that you see in the old prints.

So on September fourteenth Burgoyne and his army crossed the Hudson by a bridge of boats and encamped "on the heights and in the plains of Saratoga." In short, as the old saying is, he burned his boats, and definitely committed himself to an advance at all costs. It was just before this date that Mrs. General Riedesel observed with surprise that the wives of the officers were beforehand informed of all the military plans. Like Corporal Brewster she adds: "This would not have done for the Dook," her duke being Ferdinand of Brunswick, under whom her husband had served in the Seven Years' War.

The Americans were at Stillwater. Let us now briefly consider General Gates. He was, in two words, an intriguer and a humbug.

Also, he wore spectacles. A godson of Horace Walpole—hence his name, Horatio—he had served under Prince Ferdinand, and with Braddock (who carried military pride to such heights that he thought it cowardly to take cover) and, having married an English lady of fortune, bought an estate in Berkeley County, Virginia, which he called (it sounds rather like a road-house) "Traveller's Rest." But Mrs. Gates did little to make it so. Charles Lee describes her, with some acerbity, as "a tragedy in private life, a farce to all the world." He also pleasantly alludes to her as a Medusa. Gates got great credit, which should have been Schuyler's and Arnold's, for the operations which led to the Convention of Saratoga, but in later life he lost his military reputation. At Camden, when the militia broke and fled, he exclaimed, with burning indignation, "I will bring the rascals back with me into line." He pursued the rascals, and such was his zeal that he is said not to have drawn rein until he was over sixty miles from the battlefield. The best that can be said for him as a soldier is that he had some considerable insight into Burgoyne's character. Writing of him on October fourth to the American General Clinton, he said: "Perhaps Burgoyne's despair may dictate to him to risque all upon one throw; he is an old gamester, and in his time has seen all chances. I will endeavour to be ready to prevent his good fortune, and, if possible, secure my own." . . .

Gates owed his appointment to succeed Schuyler to intrigue and to the fact that New England did not like New York, which was too aristocratic; Vons and Vans always are. He arrived on August nineteenth with a commission in his pocket making him commander-in-chief of the Northern Department and he seems to have treated Schuyler with a certain hauteur; Schuyler, a true patriot and a thorough gentleman, took no notice of it. At the same time there arrived Benedict Arnold, a far better fighting general then Gates (although indeed a "Damaged Soul," to quote Mr. Gamaliel Bradford), and Morgan's Riflemen, the most famous corps of the Continental Army, all of them crack shots.

Burgoyne's troops were beginning to feel the pinch. Food for the men and forage for the horses were running short, and the soldiers were lightly clad, their winter clothing having been sent back to Ticonderoga in anticipation of a walk-over to Albany. It was at this time that Major Acland and his wife, Lady Harriet, were nearly burned to death, owing to a "restless" Newfoundland dog—the British camp, quite apart from Mrs. Commissary, was full of pets—upsetting a candle in their tent.

The first of the Saratoga battles took place on September nineteenth. It is known as Freeman's Farm, Bemis's Heights or Bemus's Heights. Other variants are "Behmus" and "Braemus." The baroness goes bravely for "Bimese's." The American position, chosen by Arnold, had been fortified by Kosciusko. Wilkinson, Gates's aide-de-camp, says that the battle was an accident, and that neither general contemplated an attack. This is wrong. Burgoyne knew where Gates's camp was—four miles away—and deliberately advanced upon it in three columns, leading the center himself, the right wing being commanded by Fraser, the left and the artillery by Riedesel and Phillips. Gates wanted to stay in his earthworks, in the rear of which he had the baggage-wagons all packed ready for the retreat which he evidently anticipated. It was the Damaged Soul, Arnold, who was all for action.

There was heavy fighting from two in the afternoon to sunset. On the British side the 20th, 21st, and 62nd regiments, immediately under the command of Burgoyne, particularly distinguished themselves. Each side went at it, hammer and tongs. "Such an explosion of fire," writes Digby, "I never had any idea of before, and the heavy artillery joining in concert like great peals of thunder, assisted by the echoes of the woods, almost deafened us with the noise." And in addition to the usual battle din could be heard Morgan's "turkey-call," the instrument normally used to decoy turkeys, but employed by him to collect his riflemen, who, perched up in trees, did deadly work as snipers, picking out the British officers by their uniforms. Burgoyne ended his despatch to Germain: "Just as the light closed, the enemy gave ground on all sides, and left us completely masters of the field of battle, with the loss of about 500 men on their side, and, as supposed, thrice that number wounded." He wrote to Brigadier-General Powell at Ticonderoga: "We have had a smart and very honourable action and are encamped on the front of the field, which must demonstrate our victory beyond the power of even an American newspaper to explain away."

As a matter of fact, gallantry apart, it was, as a victory, nothing to write home or to Ticonderoga about. The youthful Digby puts it better when he calls it "a dear-bought victory, if I can give it that name as we have lost many brave men." Wilkinson uses a picturesque phrase; writing on the twentieth, he says: "The enemy have quietly licked their sores this day." He adds the very interesting statement, which he says he got later from General Phillips: "Burgoyne had intended to renew the attack on the 20th, but Fraser, saying that the grenadiers and light infantry wanted a rest, persuaded him to put it off." It is enormously to Burgoyne's credit that, Fraser being dead, he never said a word of this when he was defending himself against those who attacked him, with more than Indian craft, at home. Meanwhile Clinton's letter that he intended to move against the highlands arrived, and Burgoyne decided to wait. Wilkinson was of the opinion that, had he attacked at once, he would probably have obtained a decisive victory. . . .

Clinton's letter was dated September twelfth. In it he said that in ten days he intended to attack Fort Montgomery. Burgoyne received it on September twenty-first. In his despatch he says: "I continued fortifying my camp and watching the enemy whose numbers increased every day. I thought it advisable on the 3rd of October to diminish the soldiers' ration in order to lengthen out the provisions, to which measure the army submitted with the utmost cheerfulness. The difficulties of a retreat to Canada were clearly foreseen, as was the dilemma, should the retreat be effected, of leaving at liberty such an army as General Gates's to operate against Sir William Howe." . . .

Some historians have argued that it was Burgoyne's vanity which now operated to dissuade him from giving the order for a retreat to Canada. This is not altogether fair. Obstinacy, a regular John Bullish obstinacy, perhaps. But we must remember that, as he so often said himself, there was no "latitude" in his instructions. Had he retreated to Canada—probably the best course he could have taken—Germain, that authority on not advancing, would have pounced upon it. Burgoyne's orders were to get to Albany and he thought it his duty, at all hazards, to try to do so. He knew by now that St. Leger had failed, and he must have realized that there was no likelihood of Howe advancing to Albany to meet him. . . .

On the twenty-seventh of September Burgoyne had sent Captain Scott, and on the following day Captain Campbell, with letters in duplicate to Clinton, urging him to cooperate with him. Campbell arrived on the fifth of October, Scott on the ninth. Clinton sent home to Whitehall an account of his "Conversation with Captain Campbell sent by General Burgoyne to me."

"He said he was desired by General Burgoyne to tell me that the General's whole army did not exceed 5,000 men; that the consequences of the battle on the 19th were the loss of between five and six hundred men; that the enemy were within a mile and a half of him; that he knew not their number for certain, but believed them to be twelve or fourteen thousand men; that there was besides that a considerable body in his rear. That he wished to receive my orders whether he should attack, or retreat to the lakes; that he had but provisions to the 20th of this month; and that he would not have given up his communications with Ticonderoga, had he not expected a co-operating army at Albany. That he wished to know my positive answer, as soon as possible, whether I could open a communication with Albany, when I should be there, and [whether] when there keep my communication with New York; that if he did not hear from me by the 12th instant he should retire.

"To which I returned the following answer by Capt. Campbell, viz. That not having received any instructions from the commander-in-chief [Howe] relative to the Northern Army, and [being] unacquainted even of his intentions concerning the operations of that army, excepting his wishes that they should get to Albany, Sir H. Clinton cannot presume to give any orders to General Burgoyne. General Burgoyne could not suppose that Sir H. Clinton had an idea of penetrating to Albany with the small force he mentioned in his last letter. What he offered in that letter he has now undertaken: cannot by any means promise himself success, but hopes it will be at any rate serviceable to General Burgoyne, as General Burgoyne says in his letter answering the offer, 'that even the menace of an attack would be of use.' ". . .

The two armies were now engaged in fortifying their respective positions, but Burgoyne's army was growing smaller and smaller as the Indians responded to the "call of the wild"—farther back —and the Canadians found themselves unable to resist the temptation to go home. Gates's army was getting larger every day. The discomfort in the British camp was intense. "Many bodies not buried deep enough in the ground appeared (from the great rain) as the soil was a light sand and caused a most dreadful smell." About eight hundred sick and wounded were in tents and roughly constructed huts, dignified with the name of hospital; it was necessary to be on the alert night and day, and supplies were running out like the sand in an hour-glass. . . .

On the fourth of October Burgoyne held a small council of war, Riedesel, Phillips, and Fraser being present. Burgoyne proposed that two hundred men should be left in the camp to defend it and that the rest should march out and attack the enemy in the rear. Riedesel suggested a retreat to Fort Edward, which Fraser approved. Phillips would not give an opinion. As so often happens in councils of war, there was plenty of talk, but no decision.

Meanwhile, what of Sir Harry Clinton? He had come up the Hudson with three thousand men and captured Forts Montgomery and Clinton. Here he rested on his oars and wrote Burgoyne a letter, which the latter never received. The bearer of it had it in a hollow silver bullet: blundering into the American General Clinton's camp, and perceiving his mistake, he promptly and loyally swallowed it. A "severe dose of tartar emetic" recovered it, but perhaps it was as well that it never reached Burgoyne, for it would not have brought much comfort to that distracted general. . . .

Clinton returned with his whole force to New York. . . . He feared that when his force was "removed out of the power of co-operating with you," Burgoyne might be overwhelmed, but he had hoped that Howe would get possession of Philadelphia and be able to send him reinforcements so that he might "try something in your favour." He goes on: "Could you with reason my dear friend expect that I should form the most distant idea of penetrating to Albany? Had I thought that with the small number I could spare from hence I should have been equal to forcing the highlands, I should not have conceived myself justified in detaching part of my garrison further, without extraordinary motives. . . . I feel for you as a friend and will not look amiss upon anything that passed when you had so much to perplex and distress you." It is really rather difficult not to agree with the opinion expressed at home that Clinton was jealous of Burgoyne.

On the sixth a rum ration was served out to the British troops and on the seventh Burgoyne led out some fifteen hundred men, with ten guns, "to discover whether there were any possible means of forcing a passage should it be necessary to advance," that is to say it was a reconnaissance in force. The movement was perceived and reported to Gates, who said, "Order out Morgan to begin the game." The game began, and a bloody one it proved. "There was a very sudden and rapid attack of the enemy on our left." Arnold, who was in the American camp with no position and no authority, was here, there, and everywhere. He and Gates had quarreled over the question of the command of Morgan's corps. Arnold complained bitterly that he was "huffed in such a manner as must mortify a person with less pride than I." But he forgot all his grievances in the thick of this fight. Wilkinson, not an unbiased witness where Arnold is concerned, says that he "had been drinking freely" and "behaved like a madman"; possibly, but a very heroic and courageous madman. When talebearers reported that Grant drank, did not Abraham Lincoln want to know, for the benefit of his other generals, what brand of whisky it was?

On the British side Fraser and Sir Francis Clark were mortally wounded; Acland was shot through both legs and taken prisoner; Burgoyne got one shot through his hat while another tore his waistcoat. The British were driven back into their camp, against which Arnold led a desperate attack, in the course of which he was wounded. [Lamb writes] "The intrenchments of the German reserve, commanded by Lieut.-Col. Breymann, who was killed, were carried and, although ordered to be recovered, they never were so, and the enemy by that misfortune gained an opening on our right and rear. The night put an end to the action." As a matter of fact, the Germans did not behave well, or rather they behaved very badly. After Breymann's death, writes Lamb, "The Germans retreated, firing until they had gained their tents in the rear of the entrenchments, but, supposing that the assault was general, they gave one discharge, after which some retreated to the British camp, but others surrendered prisoners."

In short it was a British defeat, the credit of which was entirely due to Arnold, for Gates spent the greater part of the action having what began as an academic, but ended in being a very hot, discussion on the merits of the Revolution with Sir Francis Clark, who, taken prisoner after his wound, was lying upon the American commander's bed. . . .

On the eighth, leaving the so-called hospitals, full of wounded, with a letter recommending them to Gates's sympathy, Burgoyne fell back to Schuylerville, where it was found necessary to burn General Schuyler's house, storehouses, and mills. It was on the evening of the ninth that, according to the Baroness Riedesel, Burgoyne entertained his lady friend at supper. Gates and his troops had come hot in pursuit and by the eleventh the British Army was completely surrounded; "their cannon and ours began to play on each other: it was impossible to sleep from the cold and rain and our only entertainment was the report of some popping shots heard now and then from the other side [of] the great river." The British horses and livestock were living on the leaves of trees: as for the army itself, let us again quote from the baroness: "The greatest misery and confusion prevailed; the Commissaries had forgotten to distribute provisions; there were plenty of cattle but none had been killed. More than thirty officers, driven by hunger, came to me. I had tea and coffee made for them and shared my food with them." She then proceeds to represent herself as a *deus ex machina;* she sent for (!) Burgoyne, talked to him like a Dutch uncle, or rather aunt, and, according to her account, he thanked her with emotion for having shown him what was his duty. The baroness had, as her countrymen would say, too much ego in her cosmos. She remarks on another occasion that Phillips said to her he wished she was in command of the expedition instead of Burgoyne. She wrote her book some time after the war and here and there probably her memory may have misled her. On this particular occasion Burgoyne was probably excessively courteous and excessively sorry, and no doubt that was all. On the whole the Riedesels had no great cause to grumble, for the general saved quite a lot of money when in North America. The baroness was so fond of the continent that of two daughters born there one was christened "Canada" and the other "Amerika." How lucky that she was not more definite: just suppose one of them had been born at Oshkosh! . . .

On the twelfth of October a council of war was held on the Heights of Saratoga, "Burgoyne, Baron Riedesel, Phillips and Brig.-Gen. Hamilton being present." Burgoyne put the case very clearly to his council. They were practically surrounded; the provisions might hold out to the twentieth, but "there is neither rum nor spruce beer." There were four possible courses of action, or inaction. 1. To wait the chance of favorable events. 2. To attack. 3. To retreat, repairing the bridges for the artillery. 4. To retreat by night, leaving the artillery and the baggage. The fourth was chosen, but, scouts being sent out, it was reported that it would be impossible to move without the march being immediately discovered.

And so on the thirteenth another council of war was held, all the general officers and field officers and captains commanding corps being present. Burgoyne behaved like a gentleman—and a scholar. He began by stating that he himself, and he alone, was responsible for the situation in which they found themselves, as he had asked no officer for advice, but had given instructions which were to be followed. He then, the scholar part of him coming to the surface, asked whether in military history any army in a similar case had capitulated. (Here, I feel sure, some of the younger officers must heartily have wished, probably for the first time in the expedition, that they were somewhere else.) The next questions were, whether they were in such a situation that there was nothing left but to capitulate, and whether such a capitulation would be dishonorable. The answer of the council to the first was yes, and to the second no. While this council was sitting a cannon-ball whizzed over the table in the tent where they were collected. Burgoyne must have been reminded of La Lippe's practical exposition of gunnery in Portugal.

There is a detailed account of the negotiations in a War Office manuscript volume, *Capitulations.* On the thirteenth Burgoyne wrote to Gates that he was desirous of sending a field officer to him "upon a matter of high moment to both Armies." Gates agreed that the field officer should be received "at the advanced post of the Army of the United States" at ten o'clock the following morning, from whence he would be conducted to Headquarters. On the fourteenth Major Kingston was entrusted with the following message to General Gates; one cannot but admire the bravado of its beginning:

"After having fought you twice, Lieut.-Gen. Burgoyne has waited some days, in his present position, determined to try a third conflict against any force you could bring to attack him.

"He is apprised of the superiority of your numbers, and the disposition of your troops to impede his supplies, and render his retreat a scene of carnage on both sides. In this situation he is impelled by humanity, and thinks himself justifiable by established principles and precedents of state, and of war, to spare the lives of brave men upon honourable terms. Should Maj.-Gen Gates be inclined to treat upon that idea, General Burgoyne would propose a cessation of arms during the time necessary to communicate the preliminary terms by which, in any extremity, he and his army mean to abide." . . .

We now come to Gate's preliminary "Propositions." These were:

1. General Burgoyne's army being exceedingly reduced by repeated defeats, by desertion, sickness, etc., their provisions exhausted, their military stores, tents and baggage taken or destroyed, their retreat cut off and their camps invested, they can only be allowed to surrender as prisoners of war. . . .
2. The officers and soldiers may keep their baggage belonging to them, the generals of the United States never permit private individuals to be pillaged.
3. The troops under his excellency, General Burgoyne, will be conducted by the most convenient route to New England, marching by easy marches and sufficiently provided for by the way.

4. The officers will be admitted on parole, may wear their side arms, and will be treated with the liberality customary in Europe, so long as they, by proper behavior, continue to deserve it; but those who are apprehended having broken their parole (as some British officers have done) must expect to be close confined.

To this Burgoyne replied—can you not hear his quill pen sputtering with indignation?—"There being no officers in this army under, or capable of being under, the description of breaking parole, this article needs no answer."

5. All public stores, artillery, arms, ammunition, carriages, horses, etc., must be delivered to commissaries appointed to receive them.

Answer: "All public stores may be delivered, arms excepted."

6. These terms being agreed to and signed, the troops under his excellency's, General Burgoyne's, command may be drawn up in their encampment, when they will be ordered to ground their arms and may thereupon be marched to the river side to be passed over on their way toward Bennington.

The cold and severe answer to this was: "This article inadmissible in any extremity. Sooner than this army will consent to ground their arms in their encampment, they will rush on the enemy determined to take no quarter."

7. A cessation of arms to continue till sunset to receive General Burgoyne's answer.

It was the sixth article which was the crux. Kingston was instructed to give Wilkinson a verbal answer: "If General Gates does not mean to recede from the 6th Article the treaty ends at once. The Army will to a man proceed to any act of desperation rather than submit to that article." According to Wilkinson, at one moment Burgoyne said the truce must end in an hour and he says that he and the British General "set watches." Turning to Colonel Sutherland, Wilkinson said: "You will not only lose your fusee but your whole baggage," and goes on to explain "this fusee Col. Sutherland had owned for thirty-five years and had desired me to except it from the surrendered arms and save for him as *she* was a favourite piece." Another difficulty was that Burgoyne had received intelligence that "a considerable force has been detached from the Army under the command of General Gates during the course of the negotiations": this he argued was "not only a violation of the Cessation of Arms but subversive of the principles on which the treaty originated, *viz.,* a great superiority of numbers in General Gates's Army." He even "required" that two of his officers should have ocular proof of this, to which Gates briefly replied that no violation of the treaty had taken place on his part. In addition rumors that Clinton was at hand had reached both Burgoyne and Gates.

Another British council of war was held and it was decided that "should General Clinton be where reported, yet the distance is such as to render any relief from him improbable during the time our provisions could be made to last." Gates, on his side, gave better terms than he would otherwise have done, and "after many flags passing and repassing the terms were at last mutually agreed to," though Burgoyne insisted that it was to be a convention and not a capitulation. The convention contained thirteen articles. They were as follows:

ARTICLES OF CONVENTION
between
Lieut.-General Burgoyne and Major-General Gates.

1.

The Troops under Lieut.-Genl. Burgoyne, to march out of their Camp with the honors of War, & the Artillery of the Intrenchment to the Verge of the River where the Old Fort stood, where the arms & Artillery are to be left. The arms to be piled by word of command from their own officers.

2.

A Free Passage to be granted to the Army under Lieut.-

Genl. Burgoyne to Great Britain, upon condition of not serving again in North America, during the present Contest; and the Port of Boston is Assigned for the Entry of Transports to Receive the Troops whenever General Howe shall so Order.

3.

Should any Cartel take place by which the Army under Lieut.-General Burgoyne, or any part of it, may be exchang'd, the foregoing Article to be void as far as such exchange shall be made.

4.

The Army under Lieut.-Genl. Burgoyne to March to Massachusetts Bay by the Easiest, Most Expeditious, & Convenient Route, and to be quartered in, near, or as convenient as possible to Boston, that the march of the Troops may not be delay'd when Transports arrive to receive them.

5.

The Troops to be Supplied on the March & during their being in Quarters with Provisions by Genl. Gates's Orders, at the same rates of Rations as the Troops of his own Army, & if possible the Officers Horses, & Cattle are to be Supplied with Forage at the usual Rates.

6.

All officers to Retain their Carriages, Bat Horses, & other Cattle, and no Baggage to be molested or searched; Lieut.-Genl. Burgoyne giving his honor there are no public Stores contained therein. Major-General Gates will, of course, take the necessary measures for the due performance of this Article. Should any Carriages be wanting during the March for the Transportation of officers' Baggage, they are, if possible, to be supplied by the Country at the usual Rates.

7.

Upon the March and during the time the Army shall remain in Quarters in the Massachusetts Bay the officers are not, as far as Circumstances will Admit, to be separated from their Men. The officers are to be Quartered according to Rank, and are not to be hindered from assembling their Men for Roll-calling & other purposes of Regularity.

8.

All Corps whatever of General Burgoyne's Army, whether compos'd of Sailors, Batteau-men, Artificers, Drivers, Independant Companies, & followers of the Army who come under no particular Description, are to be permitted to return there; they are to be conducted immediately, by the Shortest Route to the first British Post on Lake George, are to be supplied with Provisions in the same manner as the other Troops, and to be bound by the same condition of not serving during the present Contest in North America.

10.

Passports to be immediately granted for three officers not exceeding the Rank of Captains, who shall be appointed by Lieut.-Genl. Burgoyne to carry Dispatches to Sir William Howe, Sir Guy Carleton, & to Great Britain by the way of New York; and Maj.-Gen'l Gates engages the Publick Faith that these Dispatches shall not be opened. These officers are to set out immediately after receiving their Dispatches and are to Travel by the Shortest Route & in the most expeditious manner.

11.

During the stay of the Troops in the Massachusetts Bay the officers are to be admitted on Parole, and are to be permitted to wear side Arms.

12.

Should the Army under Lieut.-General Burgoyne find it necessary to send for their Cloathing & other Baggage from Canada, they are to be permitted to do it in the most convenient manner and the necessary Passports granted for that purpose.

13.

These Articles are to be mutually Signed & Exchanged tomorrow at 9 o'clock; and the Troops under Lieut.-Genl. Burgoyne are to march out of their Intrenchments at three o'clock in the afternoon.
Camp at Saratoga, October 16, 1777.

On the seventeenth, early in the morning, Burgoyne called all his officers together and "entered into a detail of his manner of acting since he had the honour of commanding the army; but he was too full to speak." Digby goes on in a simple and very moving strain: "About 10 o'clock we marched out, according to treaty, with drums beating and the honours of war, but the drums seemed to have lost their former inspiriting sounds, and though we beat the Grenadiers' march, which not long before was so animating, yet then it seemed by its last feeble effort as if almost ashamed to be heard on such an occasion." He adds, and he echoed the feeling of every officer in the expedition: "Thus was Burgoyne's Army sacrificed to either the absurd opinions of a blundering ministerial power, the stupid inaction of a general who, from his lethargic disposition, neglected every step he might have taken to assist their operations, or lastly, perhaps, his own misconduct in penetrating so far as to be unable to return."

Burgoyne "in a rich royal uniform" and Gates in a plain blue frock met at the head of Gates's camp: "When," writes Wilkinson, "they had approached nearly within swords' length they reined up and halted: I then named the gentlemen and General Burgoyne raising his hat said, 'The fortune of war, General Gates, has made me your prisoner,' to which the conqueror, returning a courtly salute, replied, 'I shall always be ready to bear testimony that it has not been through any fault of your excellency.' "

CHAPTER V

WATERLOO

The French Revolution, in part, unleashed the Napoleonic Wars.
At various times between 1799 and 1815, Russia, Great Britain,
Austria, Prussia, Sweden, Denmark, Portugal—as allies—fought
against Napoleon's armies then conquering much of Europe. But
allies deserted allies, and the Russians went over briefly to Napoleon for economic reasons. In 1812 Napoleon turned against the
Russians, and Moscow was burned. But eventually defeated by the
Russian winter, short supplies and the intense suffering of his men,
Napoleon returned to France with his bedraggled armies. Defeated at the Battle of Nations at Leipzig, in 1813, Napoleon was
captured when Paris fell and exiled to the island of Elba, from
where he escaped in 1815.

This chapter concerns Napoleon's final battle—the Hundred
Days' War, ending almost 15 years of the Napoleonic Wars.

We met the author, Sir Edward Shepherd Creasy, in an earlier
chapter on Blenheim. The following excerpt is from his noted
historical work *Fifteen Decisive Battles of the World.*

The Battle of Waterloo, A.D. 1815
by
Sir Edward Shepherd Creasy

Thou first and last of fields, king-making victory!
—Byron

England has now been blessed with thirty-six years of peace. At no other period of her history can a similarly long cessation from a state of warfare be found. It is true that our troops have had battles to fight during this interval for the protection and extension of our Indian possessions and our colonies, but these have been with distant and unimportant enemies. The danger has never been brought near our own shores, and no matter of vital importance to our empire has ever been at stake. We have not had hostilities with either France, America, or Russia; and when not at war with any of our peers, we feel ourselves to be substantially at peace. There has, indeed, throughout this long period, been no great war, like those with which the previous history of modern Europe abounds. There have been formidable collisions between particular states, and there have been still more formidable collisions between the armed champions of the conflicting principles of absolutism and democracy; but there has been no general war, like those of the French Revolution, like the American, or the Seven Years' War, or like the War of the Spanish Succession. It would be far too much to augur from this that no similar wars will again convulse the world; but the value of the period of peace which Europe has gained is incalculable, even if we look on it as only a long truce, and expect again to see the nations of the earth recur to what some philosophers have termed man's natural state of warfare.

No equal number of years can be found during which science, commerce, and civilization have advanced so rapidly and so extensively as has been the case since 1815. When we trace their progress, especially in this country, it is impossible not to feel that their wondrous development has been mainly due to the land having been at peace. Their good effects can not be obliterated even if a series of wars were to recommence. When we reflect on this, and contrast these thirty-six years with the period that preceded them—a period of violence, of tumult, of unrestingly destructive energy—a period throughout which the wealth of nations was scattered like sand, and the blood of nations lavished like water, it is impossible not to look with deep interest on the final crisis of that dark and dreadful epoch—the crisis out of which our own happier cycle of years has been evolved. The great battle which ended the twenty-three years' war of the first French Revolution, and which quelled the man whose genius and ambition had so long disturbed and desolated the world, deserves to be regarded by us not only with peculiar pride as one of our greatest national victories, but with peculiar gratitude for the repose which it secured for us and for the greater part of the human race.

One good test for determining the importance of Waterloo is to ascertain what was felt by wise and prudent statesmen before that battle respecting the return of Napoleon from Elba to the imperial throne of France, and the probable effects of his success. For this purpose, I will quote the words, not of any of our vehement anti-Gallican politicians of the school of Pitt, but of a leader of our Liberal party, of a man whose reputation as a jurist, a historian, and afar-sighted and candid statesman was, and is, deservedly high, not only in this country, but throughout Europe. Sir James Mackintosh said of the return from Elba.

"Was it in the power of language to describe the evil? Wars which had raged for more than twenty years throughout Europe; which had spread blood and desolation from Cadiz to Moscow, and from Naples to Copenhagen; which had wasted the means of human enjoyment, and destroyed the instruments of social improvement; which threatened to diffuse among the European nations the dissolute and ferocious habits of a predatory soldiery— at length, by one of those vicissitudes which bid defiance to the foresight of man, had been brought to a close, upon the whole, happy, beyond all reasonable expectation, with no violent shock to national independence, with some tolerable compromise between the opinions of the age and the reverence due to ancient institutions; with no too signal or mortifying triumph over the legitimate interests or avowable feelings of any numerous body of men, and, above all, without those retaliations against nations or parties which beget new convulsions, often as horrible as those which they close, and perpetuate revenge, and hatred, and blood from age to age. Europe seemed to breathe after her sufferings. In the midst of this fair prospect and of these consolatory hopes, Napoleon Bonaparte escaped from Elba; three small vessels reached the coast of Provence; their hopes are instantly dispelled; the work of our toil and fortitude is undone; the blood of Europe is spilled in vain—

'Ibi omnis effusus labor!' "

The exertions which the allied powers made at this crisis to grapple promptly with the French emperor have truly been termed gigantic, and never were Napoleon's genius and activity more signally displayed than in the celerity and skill by which he brought forward all the military resources of France, which the reverses of the three preceding years, and the pacific policy of the Bourbons during the months of their first restoration, had greatly diminished and disorganized. He reentered Paris on the 20th of March, and by the end of May, besides sending a force into La Vendée to put down the armed risings of the Royalists in that province, and besides providing troops under Massena and Suchet for the defense of the southern frontiers of France, Napoleon had an army assembled in the northeast for active operations under his own command, which amounted to between 120 and 130,000 men, with a superb park of artillery, and in the highest possible state of equipment, discipline, and efficiency.

The approach of the many Russians, Austrians, Bavarians, and other foes of the French emperor to the Rhine was necessarily slow; but the two most active of the allied powers had occupied Belgium with their troops while Napoleon was organizing his forces. Marshal Blucher was there with 116,000 Prussians, and the duke of Wellington was there also with about 106,000 troops, either British or in British pay. Napoleon determined to attack these enemies in Belgium. The disparity of numbers was indeed great, but delay was sure to increase the number of his enemies much faster than reenforcements could join his own ranks. He considered also that "the enemy's troops were cantoned under the command of two generals, and composed of nations differing both in interest and in feelings." His own army was under his own sole command. It was composed exclusively of French soldiers, mostly of veterans, well acquainted with their officers and with each other, and full of enthusiastic confidence in their commander. If he could separate the Prussians from the British, so as to attack each in detail, he felt sanguine of success, not only against these, the most resolute of his many adversaries, but also against the other masses that were slowly laboring up against his southeastern frontiers.

The triple chain of strong fortresses which the French possessed on the Belgian frontier formed a curtain, behind which Napoleon was able to concentrate his army, and to conceal till the very last moment the precise line of attack which he intended to take. On the other hand, Blucher and Wellington were obliged to canton their troops along a line of open country of considerable length, so as to watch for the outbreak of Napoleon from whichever point of his chain of strongholds he should please to make it. Blucher, with his army, occupied the banks of the Sambre and the Meuse, from Liege on his left, to Charleroi on his right; and the duke of Wellington covered Brussels, his cantonments being partly in front of that city, and between it and the French frontier, and partly on its west; their extreme right being at Courtray and Tournay, while their left approached Charleroi and communicated with the Prussian right. It was upon Charleroi that Napoleon resolved to level his attack, in hopes of severing the two allied armies from each other, and then pursuing his favorite tactic of assailing each separately with a superior force on the battlefield, though the aggregate of their numbers considerably exceeded his own.

On the 15th of June the French Army was suddenly in motion, and crossed the frontier in three columns, which were pointed upon Charleroi and its vicinity. The French line of advance upon Brussels, which city Napoleon resolved to occupy, thus lay right through the center of the line of the cantonments of the allies. The Prussian general rapidly concentrated his forces, calling them in from the left, and the English general concentrated his, calling them in from the right toward the menaced center of the combined position. On the morning of the 16th, Blucher was in position at Ligny, to the northeast of Charleroi, with 80,000 men. Wellington's troops were concentrating at Quatre Bras, which lies due north of Charleroi, and is about nine miles from Ligny. On the 16th, Napoleon in person attacked Blucher, and, after a long and obstinate battle, defeated him, and compelled the Prussian Army to retire northward toward Wavre. On the same day, Marshal Ney, with a large part of the French Army, attacked the English troops at Quatre Bras, and a very severe engagement took place, in which Ney failed in defeating the British, but succeeded in preventing their sending any help to Blucher, who was being beaten by the emperor at Ligny. On the news of Blucher's defeat at Ligny reaching Wellington, he foresaw that the emperor's army would now be directed upon him, and he accordingly retreated in order to restore his communications with his ally, which would have been dislocated by the Prussians falling back from Ligny to Wavre if the English had remained in advance at Quatre Bras. During the 17th, therefore, Wellington retreated, being pursued, but little molested by the main French Army, over about half the space between Quatre Bras and Brussels. This brought him again parallel, on a line running from west to east, with Blucher, who was at Wavre. Having ascertained that the Prussian Army, though beaten on the 16th, was not broken, and having received a promise from its general to march to his assistance, Wellington determined to halt, and to give battle to the French emperor in the position, which, from a village in its neighborhood, has received the ever-memorable name of the field of WATERLOO.

Sir Walter Scott, in his "Life of Napoleon," remarks of Waterloo that "the scene of this celebrated action must be familiar to most readers either from description or recollection." The narratives of Sir Walter himself, of Alison, Gleig, Siborne, and others, must have made the events of the battle almost equally well known. . . . In particular, the description by Captain Siborne of the Waterloo campaign is so full and so minute, so scrupulously accurate, and, at the same time, so spirited and graphic, that it will long defy the competition of far abler pens than mine. I shall only aim at giving a general idea of the main features of this great event, of this discrowning and crowning victory.

When, after a very hard-fought and a long-doubtful day, Napoleon had succeeded in driving back the Prussian Army from Ligny, and had resolved on marching himself to assail the English, he sent, on the 17th, Marshal Grouchy with 30,000 men to pursue the defeated Prussians, and to prevent their marching to aid the duke of Wellington. Great recriminations passed afterward between the marshal and the emperor as to how this duty was attempted to be performed, and the reasons why Grouchy failed on the 18th to arrest the lateral movement of the Prussian troops from Wavre toward Waterloo. It may be sufficient to remark here that Grouchy was not sent in pursuit of Blucher till late on the 17th, and that the force given to him was insufficient to make head against the whole Prussian Army; for Blucher's men, though they were beaten back, and suffered severe loss at Ligny, were neither routed or disheartened; and they were joined at Wavre by a large division of their comrades under General Bulow, who had taken no part in the battle of the 16th, and who were fresh for the march to Waterloo against the French on the 18th. But the failure of Grouchy was in truth mainly owing to the indomitable heroism of Blucher himself, who, though severely injured in the battle at Ligny, was as energetic and active as ever in bringing his men into action again, and who had the resolution to expose a part of his army, under Thielman, to be overwhelmed by Grouchy at Wavre on the 18th, while he urged the march of the mass of his troops upon Waterloo. "It is not at Wavre, but at Waterloo," said the old field-marshal, "that the campaign is to be decided"; and he risked a detachment, and won the campaign accordingly. Wellington and Blucher trusted each other as cordially, and cooperated as zealously, as formerly had been the case with Marlborough and Eugène. It was in full reliance on Blucher's promise to join him that the duke stood his ground and fought at Waterloo; and those who have ventured to impugn the duke's capacity as a general ought to have had common sense enough to perceive that to charge the duke with having won the battle of Waterloo by the help of the Prussians is really to say that he won it by the very means on which he relied, and without the expectation of which the battle would not have been fought.

Napoleon himself has found fault with Wellington for not having retreated beyond Waterloo. The short answer may be, that the duke had reason to expect that his army could singly resist the French at Waterloo until the Prussians came up, and that, on the Prussians joining, there would be a sufficient force, united under himself and Blucher, for completely overwhelming the enemy. And while Napoleon thus censures his great adversary, he involuntarily bears the highest possible testimony to the military character of the English, and proves decisively of what paramount importance was the battle to which he challenged his fearless opponent. Napoleon asks, *"If the English army had been beaten at Waterloo, what would have been the use of those numerous bodies of troops, of Prussians, Austrians, Germans, and Spaniards, which were advancing by forced marches to the Rhine, the Alps, and the Pyrenees?"*

The strength of the army under the duke of Wellington at Waterloo was 49,608 infantry, 12,402 cavalry, and 5645 artillerymen, with 156 guns. But of this total of 67,655 men, scarcely 24,000 were British, a circumstance of very serious importance, if Napoleon's own estimate of the relative value of troops of different nations is to be taken. In the emperor's own words, speaking of this campaign, "A French soldier would not be equal to more than one English soldier, but he would not be afraid to meet two Dutchmen, Prussians, or soldiers of the Confederation." There were about 6000 men of the old German Legion with the duke: these were veteran troops, and of excellent quality. But the rest of the army was made up of Hanoverians, Brunswickers, Nassauers, Dutch, and Belgians, many of whom were tried soldiers, and fought well, but many had been lately levied, and not a few were justly suspected of a strong wish to fight under the French eagles rather than against them.

Napoleon's army at Waterloo consisted of 48,950 infantry, 15,-765 cavalry, 7232 artillery-men, being a total of 71,947 men, and

246 guns. They were the élite of the national forces of France; and of all the numerous gallant armies which that martial land has poured forth, never was there one braver, or better disciplined, or better led, than the host that took up its position at Waterloo on the morning of the 18th of June, 1815.

Perhaps those who have not seen the field of battle at Waterloo, or the admirable model of the ground and of the conflicting armies which was executed by Captain Siborne, may gain a generally accurate idea of the localities by picturing to themselves a valley between two and three miles long, of various breadths at different points, but generally not exceeding half a mile. On each side of the valley there is a winding chain of low hills, running somewhat parallel with each other. The declivity from each of these ranges of hills to the intervening valley is gentle but not uniform, the undulations of the ground being frequent and considerable. The English Army was posted on the northern, and the French Army occupied the southern ridge. The artillery of each side thundered at the other from their respective heights throughout the day, and the charges of horse and foot were made across the valley that has been described. The village of Mont St. Jean is situated a little behind the center of the northern chain of hills, and the village of La Belle Alliance is close behind the center of the southern ridge. The high road from Charleroi to Brussels runs through both these villages, and bisects, therefore, both the English and the French positions. The line of this road was the line of Napoleon's intended advance on Brussels.

There are some other local particulars connected with the situation of each army which are necessary to bear in mind. The strength of the British position did not consist merely in the occupation of a ridge of high ground. A village and ravine, called Merk Braine, on the duke of Wellington's extreme right, secured him from his flank being turned on that side; and on his extreme left, two little hamlets, called La Haye and Papillote, gave a similar though a slighter protection. It was, however, less necessary to provide for this extremity of the position, as it was on this (the eastern) side that the Prussians were coming up. Behind the whole British position is the great and extensive forest of Soignies. As no attempt was made by the French to turn either of the

English flanks, and the battle was a day of straightforward fighting, it is chiefly important to see what posts there were in front of the British line of hills of which advantage could be taken either to repel or facilitate an attack; and it will be seen that there were two, and that each was of very great importance in the action. In front of the British right, that is to say, on the northern slope of the valley toward its western end, there stood an old-fashioned Flemish farmhouse called Goumont or Hougoumont, with out-buildings and a garden, and with a copse of beech-trees of about two acres in extent round it. This was strongly garrisoned by the allied troops; and while it was in their possession, it was difficult for the enemy to press on and force the British right wing. On the other hand, if the enemy could occupy it, it would be difficult for that wing to keep its ground on the heights, with a strong post held adversely in its immediate front, being one that would give much shelter to the enemy's marksmen, and great facilities for the sudden concentration of attacking columns. Almost immediately in front of the British center, and not so far down the slope as Hougoumont, there was another farmhouse, of a smaller size, called La Haye Sainte,[1] which was also held by the British troops, and the occupation of which was found to be of very serious consequence.

With respect to the French position, the principal feature to be noticed is the village of Planchenoit, which lay a little in the rear of their right (i.e., on the eastern side), and which proved to be of great importance in aiding them to check the advance of the Prussians.

As has been already mentioned, the Prussians, on the morning of the 18th, were at Wavre, about twelve miles to the east of the field of battle at Waterloo. The junction of Bulow's division had more than made up for the loss sustained at Ligny; and leaving Thielman, with about 17,000 men, to hold his ground as he best could against the attack which Grouchy was about to make on Wavre, Bulow and Blucher moved with the rest of the Prussians upon Waterloo. It was calculated that they would be there by three o'clock; but the extremely difficult nature of the ground

---

[1]Not to be confounded with the hamlet of La Haye, at the extreme left of the British line.

which they had to traverse, rendered worse by the torrents of rain that had just fallen, delayed them long on their twelve miles' march.

The night of the 17th was wet and stormy; and when the dawn of the memorable 18th of June broke, the rain was still descending heavily. The French and British armies rose from their dreary bivouacs and began to form, each on the high ground which it occupied. Toward nine the weather grew clearer, and each army was able to watch the position and arrangements of the other on the opposite side of the valley.

The duke of Wellington drew up his infantry in two lines, the second line being composed principally of Dutch and Belgian troops, whose fidelity was doubtful, and of those regiments of other nations which had suffered most severely at Quatre Bras on the 16th. This second line was posted on the northern declivity of the hills, so as to be sheltered from the French cannonade. The cavalry was stationed at intervals along the line in the rear, the largest force of horse being collected on the left of the center, to the east of the Charleroi road. On the opposite heights the French Army was drawn up in two general lines, with the entire force of the Imperial Guards, cavalry as well as infantry, in rear of the center, as a reserve. English military critics have highly eulogized the admirable arrangement which Napoleon made of his forces of each arm, so as to give him the most ample means of sustaining, by an immediate and sufficient support, any attack, from whatever point he might direct it, and of drawing promptly together a strong force, to resist any attack that might be made on himself in any part of the field.[2] When his troops were all arrayed, he rode along the lines, receiving everywhere the most enthusiastic cheers from his men, of whose entire devotion to him his assurance was now doubly sure. On the southern side of the valley the duke's army was also arrayed, and ready to meet the menaced attack.

"The two armies were now fairly in presence of each other, and their mutual observation was governed by the most intense interest and the most scrutinizing anxiety. In a still greater degree did these feelings actuate their commanders, while watching each

---

[2]Siborne, vol. i., p. 376.

other's preparatory movements, and minutely scanning the surface of the arena on which tactical skill, habitual prowess, physical
strength, and moral courage were to decide, not alone their own,
but, in all probability, the fate of Europe. Apart from national
interests and considerations, and viewed solely in connection with
the opposite characters of the two illustrious chiefs, the approaching contest was contemplated with anxious solicitude by the whole
military world. Need this create surprise when we reflect that the
struggle was one for mastery between the far-famed conqueror of
Italy and the victorious liberator of the Peninsula; between the
triumphant vanquisher of Eastern Europe, and the bold and successful invader of the south of France! Never was the issue of a
single battle looked forward to as involving consequences of such
vast importance—of such universal influence."[3]

It was approaching noon before the action commenced. Napoleon, in his memoirs, gives as the reason for this delay the miry
state of the ground through the heavy rain of the preceding night
and day, which rendered it impossible for cavalry or artillery to
maneuver on it till a few hours of dry weather had given it its
natural consistency. It has been supposed, also, that he trusted to
the effect which the sight of the imposing array of his own forces
was likely to produce on the part of the allied army. The Belgian
regiments had been tampered with; and Napoleon had well-
founded hopes of seeing them quit the duke of Wellington in a
body, and range themselves under his own eagles. The duke,
however, who knew and did not trust them, had guarded against
the risk of this by breaking up the corps of Belgians, and distributing them in separate regiments among troops on whom he could
rely.[4]

At last, at about half past eleven o'clock, Napoleon began the
battle by directing a powerful force from his left wing under his
brother, Prince Jerome, to attack Hougoumont. Column after
column of the French now descended from the west of the southern heights, and assailed that post with fiery valor, which was
encountered with the most determined bravery. The French won

[3]Siborne, vol. i., p. 377.
[4]Ibid., p. 373.

the copse round the house, but a party of the British Guards held the house itself throughout the day. Amid shell and shot, and the blazing fragments of part of the buildings, this obstinate contest was continued. But still the English held Hougoumont, though the French occasionally moved forward in such numbers as enabled them to surround and mask this post with part of their troops from their left wing, while others pressed onward up the slope, and assailed the British right.

The cannonade, which commenced at first between the British right and the French left, in consequence of the attack on Hougoumont, soon became general along both lines; and about one o'-clock, Napoleon directed a grand attack to be made under Marshal Ney upon the center and left wing of the allied army. For this purpose four columns of infantry, amounting to about 18,000 men, were collected, supported by a strong division of cavalry under the celebrated Kellerman, and seventy-four guns were brought forward ready to be posted on the ridge of a little undulation of the ground in the interval between the two main ranges of heights, so as to bring their fire to bear on the duke's line at a range of about seven hundred yards. By the combined assault of these formidable forces, led on by Ney, "the bravest of the brave," Napoleon hoped to force the left center of the British position, to take La Haye Sainte, and then, pressing forward, to occupy also the farm of Mont St. Jean. He then could cut the mass of Wellington's troops off from their line of retreat upon Brussels, and from their own left, and also completely sever them from any Prussian troops that might be approaching.

The columns destined for this great and decisive operation descended majestically from the French range of hills, and gained the ridge of the intervening eminence, on which the batteries that supported them were now ranged. As the columns descended again from this eminence, the seventy-four guns opened over their heads with terrible effect upon the troops of the allies that were stationed on the heights to the left of the Charleroi road. One of the French columns kept to the east, and attacked the extreme left of the allies; the other three continued to move rapidly forward upon the left center of the allied position. The front line of the allies here was composed of Bylant's brigade of Dutch and Belgians. As the French columns moved up the southward slope of the height on which the Dutch and Belgians stood, and the skirmishers in advance began to open their fire, Bylant's entire brigade turned and fled in disgraceful and disorderly panic; but there were men more worthy of the name behind.

The second line of the allies here consisted of two brigades of English infantry, which had suffered severely at Quatre Bras. But they were under Picton, and not even Ney himself surpassed in resolute bravery that stern and fiery spirit. Picton brought his two brigades forward, side by side, in a thin two-deep line. Thus joined together, they were not 3000 strong. With these Picton had to make head against the three victorious French columns, upward of four times that strength, and who, encouraged by the easy rout of the Dutch and Belgians, now came confidently over the ridge of the hill. The British infantry stood firm; and as the French halted and began to deploy into line, Picton seized the critical moment: a close and deadly volley was thrown in upon them, and then with a fierce hurrah the British dashed in with the bayonet. The French reeled back in confusion; and as they staggered down the hill, a brigade of the English cavalry rode in on them, cutting them down by whole battalions, and taking 2000 prisoners. The British cavalry galloped forward and sabred the artillery-men of Ney's seventy-four advanced guns; and then cutting the traces and the throats of the horses, rendered these guns totally useless to the French throughout the remainder of the day. In the excitement of success, the English cavalry continued to press on, but were charged in their turn, and driven back with severe loss by Milhaud's cuirassiers.

This great attack (in repelling which the brave Picton had fallen) had now completely failed; and, at the same time, a powerful body of French cuirassiers, who were advancing along the right of the Charleroi road, had been fairly beaten after a close hand-to-hand fight by the heavy cavalry of the English household brigade. Hougoumont was still being assailed, and was successfully resisting. Troops were now beginning to appear at the edge of the horizon on Napoleon's right, which he too well knew to be Prussian, though he endeavored to persuade his followers that they were Grouchy's men coming to aid them. It was now about half past three o'clock; and though Wellington's army had suffered severely by the unremitting cannonade and in the late desperate encounter, no part of the British position had been forced.

Napoleon next determined to try what effect he could produce on the British center and right by charges of his splendid cavalry, brought on in such force that the duke's cavalry could not check them. Fresh troops were at the same time sent to assail La Haye Sainte and Hougoumont, the possession of these posts being the emperor's unceasing object. Squadron after squadron of the French cuirassiers accordingly ascended the slopes on the duke's right, and rode forward with dauntless courage against the batteries of the British artillery in that part of the field. The artillery-men were driven from their guns, and the cuirassiers cheered loudly at their supposed triumph. But the duke had formed his infantry in squares, and the cuirassiers charged in vain against the impenetrable hedges of bayonets, while the fire from the inner ranks of the squares told with terrible effect on their own squadrons. Time after time they rode forward with invariably the same result; and as they receded from each attack, the British artillery-men rushed forward from the centers of the squares, where they had taken refuge, and plied their guns on the retiring horsemen. Nearly the whole of Napoleon's magnificent body of heavy cavalry was destroyed in these fruitless attempts upon the British right. But in another part of the field fortune favored him for a time. Donzelot's infantry took La Haye Sainte between six and seven o'clock, and the means were now given for organizing another formidable attack on the center of the allies.

There was no time to be lost: Blucher and Bulow were beginning to press upon the French right; as early as five o'clock, Napoleon had been obliged to detach Lobau's infantry and Domont's horse to check these new enemies. This was done for a time; but, as large numbers of the Prussians came on the field, they turned Lobau's left, and sent a strong force to seize the village of Planchenoit, which, it will be remembered, lay in the rear of the French right. Napoleon was now obliged to send his Young Guard to occupy that village, which was accordingly held by them with great gallantry against the reiterated assaults of the Prussian left under Bulow. But the force remaining under Napoleon was now numerically inferior to that under the duke of Wellington, which he had been assailing throughout the day, without gaining any other advantage than the capture of La Haye Sainte. It is true that, owing to the gross misconduct of the greater part of the Dutch and Belgian troops, the duke was obliged to rely exclusively on his English and German soldiers, and the ranks of these had been fearfully thinned; but the survivors stood their ground heroically, and still opposed a resolute front to every forward movement of their enemies.

Napoleon had then the means of effecting a retreat. His Old Guard had yet taken no part in the action. Under cover of it, he might have withdrawn his shattered forces and retired upon the French frontier. But this would only have given the English and Prussians the opportunity of completing their junction; and he knew that other armies were fast coming up to aid them in a march upon Paris, if he should succeed in avoiding an encounter with them, and retreating upon the capital. A victory at Waterloo was his only alternative from utter ruin, and he determined to employ his Guard in one bold stroke more to make that victory his own.

Between seven and eight o'clock the infantry of the Old Guard was formed into two columns, on the declivity near La Belle Alliance. Ney was placed at their head. Napoleon himself rode forward to a spot by which his veterans were to pass; and as they approached he raised his arm, and pointed to the position of the allies, as if to tell them that their path lay there. They answered with loud cries of "Vive l'Empereur!" and descended the hill from their own side into that "valley of the shadow of death," while their batteries thundered with redoubled vigor over their heads upon the British line. The line of march of the columns of the Guard was directed between Hougoumont and La Haye Sainte, against the British right center; and at the same time, Donzelot and the French, who had possession of La Haye Sainte, commenced a fierce attack upon the British center, a little more to its left. This part of the battle has drawn less attention than the celebrated attack of the Old Guard; but it formed the most perilous crisis for the allied army; and if the Young Guard had been there to support Donzelot, instead of being engaged with the

Prussians at Planchenoit, the consequences to the allies in that part of the field must have been most serious. The French tirailleurs, who were posted in clouds in La Haye Sainte, and the sheltered spots near it, completely disabled the artillery-men of the English batteries near them; and, taking advantage of the crippled state of the English guns, the French brought some field-pieces up to La Haye Sainte, and commenced firing grape from them on the infantry of the allies, at a distance of not more than a hundred paces.

The allied infantry here consisted of some German brigades, who were formed in squares, as it was believed that Donzelot had cavalry ready behind La Haye Sainte to charge them with, if they left that order of formation. In this state the Germans remained for some time with heroic fortitude, though the grape-shot was tearing gaps in their ranks, and the side of one square was literally blown away by one tremendous volley which the French gunners poured into it. The Prince of Orange in vain endeavored to lead some Nassau troops to their aid. The Nassauers would not or could not face the French; and some battalions of Brunswickers, whom the duke of Wellington had ordered up as a reenforcement, at first fell back, until the duke in person rallied them and led them on. The duke then galloped off to the right to head his men who were exposed to the attack of the Imperial Guard. He had saved one part of his center from being routed; but the French had gained ground here, and the pressure on the allied line was severe, until it was relieved by the decisive success which the British in the right center achieved over the columns of the Guard.

The British troops on the crest of that part of the position, which the first column of Napoleon's Guards assailed, were Maitland's brigade of British Guards, having Adam's brigade on their right. Maitland's men were lying down, in order to avoid, as far as possible, the destructive effect of the French artillery, which kept up an unremitting fire from the opposite heights, until the first column of the Imperial Guard had advanced so far up the slope toward the British position that any farther firing of the French artillery-men would endanger their own comrades. Meanwhile, the British guns were not idle; but shot and shell plowed fast through the ranks of the stately array of veterans that still moved imposingly on. Several of the French superior officers were at its head. Ney's horse was shot under him, but he still led the way on foot, sword in hand. The front of the massy column now was on the ridge of the hill. To their surprise, they saw no troops before them. All they could discern through the smoke was a small band of mounted officers. One of them was the duke himself.

The French advanced to about fifty yards from where the British Guards were lying down, when the voice of one of the band of British officers was heard calling, as if to the ground before him, "Up, Guards, and at them!" It was the duke who gave the order; and at the words, as if by magic, up started before them a line of the British Guards four deep, and in the most compact and perfect order. They poured an instantaneous volley upon the head of the French column, by which no less than three hundred of those chosen veterans are said to have fallen. The French officers rushed forward, and, conspicuous in front of their men, attempted to deploy them into a more extended line, so as to enable them to reply with effect to the British fire. But Maitland's brigade kept showering in volley after volley with deadly rapidity. The decimated column grew disordered in its vain efforts to expand itself into a more efficient formation. The right word was given at the right moment to the British for the bayonet-charge, and the brigade sprang forward with a loud cheer against their dismayed antagonists. In an instant the compact mass of the French spread out into a rabble, and they fled back down the hill pursued by Maitland's men, who, however, returned to their position in time to take part in the repulse of the second column of the Imperial Guard.

This column also advanced with great spirit and firmness under the cannonade which was opened on it, and, passing by the eastern wall of Hougoumont, diverged slightly to the right as it moved up the slope toward the British position, so as to approach the same spot where the first column had surmounted the height and been defeated. This enabled the British regiments of Adam's brigade to form a line parallel to the left flank of the French column, so that while the front of this column of French Guards had to encounter the cannonade of the British batteries, and the musketry of Maitland's Guards, its left flank was assailed with a destructive fire by a four-deep body of British infantry, extending all along it. In such a position, all the bravery and skill of the French veterans were in vain. The second column, like its predecessor, broke and fled, taking at first a lateral direction along the front of the British line toward the rear of La Haye Sainte, and so becoming blended with the divisions of French infantry, which, under Donzelot, had been pressing the allies so severely in that quarter. The sight of the Old Guard broken and in flight checked the ardor which Donzelot's troops had hitherto displayed. They, too, began to waver. Adam's victorious brigade was pressing after the flying Guard, and now cleared away the assailants of the allied center. But the battle was not yet won.

Napoleon had still some battalions in reserve near La Belle Alliance. He was rapidly rallying the remains of the first column of his Guards, and he had collected into one body the remnants of the various corps of cavalry, which had suffered so severely in the earlier part of the day. The duke instantly formed the bold resolution of now himself becoming the assailant, and leading his successful though enfeebled army forward, while the disheartening effect of the repulse of the Imperial Guard on the French Army was still strong, and before Napoleon and Ney could rally the beaten veterans themselves for another and a fiercer charge. As the close approach of the Prussians now completely protected the duke's left, he had drawn some reserves of horse from that quarter, and he had a brigade of Hussars under Vivian fresh and ready at hand. Without a moment's hesitation, he launched these against the cavalry near La Belle Alliance.

The charge was as successful as it was daring; and as there was no hostile cavalry to check the British infantry in a forward movement, the duke gave the long-wished-for command for a general advance of the army along the whole line upon the foe. It was now past eight o'clock, and for nine deadly hours had the British and German regiments stood unflinching under the fire of artillery, the charge of cavalry, and every variety of assault that the compact columns or the scattered tirailleurs of the enemy's infantry could inflict. As they joyously sprang forward against the discomfited masses of the French, the setting sun broke through the clouds which had obscured the sky during the greater part of the day, and glittered on the bayonets of the allies while they in turn poured down into the valley and toward the heights that were held by the foe. Almost the whole of the French host was now in irretrievable confusion. The Prussian Army was coming more and more rapidly forward on their right, and the Young Guard, which had held Planchenoit so bravely, was at last compelled to give way. Some regiments of the Old Guard in vain endeavored to form in squares. They were swept away to the rear; and then Napoleon himself fled from the last of his many fields, to become in a few weeks a captive and an exile. The battle was lost by France past all recovery. The victorious armies of England and Prussia, meeting on the scene of their triumph, continued to press forward and overwhelm every attempt that was made to stem the tide of ruin. The British Army, exhausted by its toils and suffering during that dreadful day, did not urge the pursuit beyond the heights which the enemy had occupied. But the Prussians drove the fugitives before them throughout the night. And of the magnificent host which had that morning cheered their emperor in confident expectation of victory, very few were ever assembled again in arms. Their loss, both in the field and in the pursuit, was immense; and the greater number of those who escaped, dispersed as soon as they crossed the frontier.

The army under the duke of Wellington lost nearly 15,000 men in killed and wounded on this terrible day of battle. The loss of the Prussian army was nearly 7000 more. At such a fearful price was the deliverance of Europe purchased.

CHAPTER VI

BATTLE FOR
NEW ORLEANS, 1815

The War of 1812, called the Second War of Independence, resulted from many factors that were as economic as they were political and maritime. Great Britain, then in the midst of the Napoleonic Wars, objected to American ships trading with France's possessions in the West Indies, and with France itself. American merchant seamen were forced to serve on British ships. When the United States declared war on Great Britain, it found Americans divided and hardly prepared for war. America, too, wanted to expand into Canada and into the West—and the last battle fought, for New Orleans, was fought after the United States and Great Britain signed the Treaty of Ghent, ending the war, on December 24, 1814. It was an irony of timing and history. Having been beaten in most battles, the United States, in winning the battle of New Orleans, helped to strengthen American nationalism and expand forcibly toward the western frontiers.

John Spencer Bassett, American (1867–1928), the author of the following selection on the Battle for New Orleans, was a professor of history at Duke University and Trinity College. He edited the *South Atlantic Quarterly* and wrote extensively about the federalist system and President Andrew Jackson. This chapter is from his book *The Life of Andrew Jackson.*

January the Eighth, 1815
by
John Spencer Bassett

When Jackson was fighting the battle of December 23rd, he was still uncertain about the plans of the enemy. He feared that Keane was attempting a ruse in order to draw the Americans to Villeré's, while the main body of the British landed at Chef Menteur and seized the city. Not daring, under these circumstances, to take all his troops with him, he ordered Carroll's 2,000 with three regiments of city militia to hold the road to Chef Menteur, at the eastern extremity of which Lacoste was stationed with his battalion of city Negroes. In fact, Jackson suspected that Lacoste was already taken; but soon after the battle he had definite news from that officer, who reported that the main body of the enemy were passing his position and entering Bayou Bienvenue. Convinced that no ruse was intended, Jackson at once ordered half of Carroll's force to his aid. His first impulse was to renew the fight at dawn, but on reflection he "determined not to play so deep a game of hazard as to attack them in their strong position,"[1] but to select a protected situation and await battle. There was a midnight conference with the engineers and it was decided to establish defenses at McCartey's old mill race, otherwise called Rodriguez's canal, two miles north of the scene of the night battle. It was no more than a dry ditch ten feet wide, running three-quarters of a mile from river to swamp, but it was the best natural protection in the neighborhood, and it was thought that with batteries placed at intervals it could be held against the enemy.

---

[1]From a fragmentary *Journal* of the battle of New Orleans in Jackson's "own hand," covering the period from December 23, 1814, to January 19, 1815. It seems to have been prepared some time after the battle but it was certainly before the death of Major Reid, in the winter of 1815–16. The sheets are missing which deal with events between December 28 and January 25 and from January 7 and to the battle on the west bank on January 8. It is among the Jackson Mss. in the Library of Congress.

The withdrawal of the troops began at four o'clock in the morning of the twenty-fourth. They broke away from the left, Coffee first, then Carroll, who was already on hand, and last the regulars. At sunrise they held the mill race, the regulars next the river and Coffee next the swamp, in the same order as they were formed before the British a few hours earlier. Hinds's dragoons and a small company of horse from Feliciana Parish were left to observe the enemy.

The British knew nothing of this movement but remained huddled on the field during the night and offered battle early in the morning. When no attack was made on them they withdrew, at eight o'clock, to their camp. All day reinforcements were hurried forward from the fleet, and by the morning of the twenty-fifth all the army which had arrived at the anchorage was landed. An old levee paralleled the new one at a distance of 300 yards and between the two the soldiers found some protection from the fire of the *Carolina* and *Louisiana* on the river and from the threatened attacks of Coffee's horsemen whom Jackson sent to annoy them by land. Here Pakenham found them when he arrived on the morning of the twenty-fifth. The first thing he did after taking command was to move them to the plain, placing a large body near the cypress swamp and extending his outposts across the intervening space to the river. By this time the two armies faced each other at an interval of two miles, one preparing to march straight on the city, the other utilizing every hour given it in erecting the works which would defeat such an advance.

Pakenham was an able general but a methodical one. With 5,500 troops in his camp he might have seized the American line, now barely more than a skeleton. But the *Carolina* and *Louisiana* annoyed his right flank, and he determined to silence or drive them away before he moved. By great exertion he got batteries in place during the night of the twenty-sixth and opened on them on the following morning with shell and hot shot. The second discharge of the latter fired the *Carolina,* which could not be taken away on account of contrary winds and a strong current. The batteries played on her for an hour, when she blew up. Meantime, the *Louisiana* with difficulty was towed out of range and saved. These operations delayed the British advance four days and gave the Americans a valuable opportunity to construct works of defense.

When Jackson fell back on the twenty-fourth his first care was to order heavy guns and entrenching tools from New Orleans. At 1:00 P.M., fifty spades and mattocks arrived and ground was immediately broken for the first battery. The general watched it with feverish anxiety, expecting at any moment to receive the advance of the British. At four o'clock he learned that they were being heavily reinforced and that they kept in close line formation. He concluded that they would not come at once and redoubled his efforts on the works, sending to the neighboring plantations for all available implements. Three times each day he rode down the lines and kept a part of his staff on them constantly. Although suffering from serious illness he did not sleep for three days and nights while the entrenchments were going through their first stages. He was "determined there to halt the enemy," as he himself said, "or bury himself on the ruins of that defense."[2]

Among Jackson's manuscripts is a fragmentary journal in which he gives us a view of the events of these trying days. In it we have a glimpse of the anxious haste with which were utilized the four days of grace which Pakenham fortunately allowed. During the night of the twenty-fourth the two six-pounders which served in the night battle were put in position six hundred yards from the river, being battery five on Latour's plan.[3] The next morning, the twenty-fifth, Hinds reported the British still in camp and fortifying on their flank. This seemed a good omen, and every effort was made to complete the three batteries then being constructed. The twenty-sixth, Hinds reported that the enemy during the night were busy bringing up heavy artillery, which indicated that they were not yet prepared to move forward. During the day three American batteries were completed, being numbers two, three, and four, commanded respectively by Lieutenant Norris, Captain Dominique, and Lieutenant Crawley. The morning of the twenty-seventh, Hinds reported that the British were still in camp but showed signs of activity. Early on the twenty-eighth he gave

---

[2]Jackson's fragmentary *Journal,* Jackson Mss.
[3]Latour, *Historical Memoir,* map number 7.

notice that they were forming in columns as if to advance. His messenger was hardly gone when the dragoons were attacked in force and compelled to withdraw behind the American lines. Following closely on their heels came the whole British Army in two compact columns, one near the river and the other marching parallel to it near the swamp. The sight of the American works surprised them, but they approached within cannon shot. The river column was immediately exposed to a heavy fire from the batteries on the line and from the *Louisiana* and floating batteries on the river: it was glad to seek any cover which offered and remained till evening in an uncomfortable position next to the levee from which it was brought with some loss and the appearance of a retreat. The other column deployed through the swamp where it encountered Coffee's riflemen and fell back when he prepared to outflank it. Pakenham was unwilling to try to carry the works and encamping at nightfall out of range of Jackson's cannon, sent for his great guns and prepared to erect batteries with which he could beat down his opponent's defenses. At that time the American earthworks, if we may believe a British eyewitness, were no more than "a few abattis with a low mound of earth thrown up in the rear."[4] Near the swamp they were weakly protected by the batteries, and it seems probable that a strong column massed here under the protection of the woods could have brushed away any defense Coffee and Carroll could have offered. It was the last opportunity the British had to break through: when their batteries were established, Jackson had strengthened his own works until they were impregnable.

For three days after the demonstration of the twenty-eighth, the cautious and methodical Pakenham gave himself to the task of erecting batteries in front of Jackson's lines. They began at the river, 700 yards from the Americans, and the first battery, containing seven light, long-ranged guns, was brought to bear on the river and the opposite shore where Commander Patterson had erected a battery. The Americans learned from deserters that hot shot was continually ready in these batteries for the *Louisiana,* if she should come within range. Facing Jackson's lines were four batteries with

---

[4] *Subaltern in America* (edition 1833), 235.

seventeen guns, eight eighteens, four twenty-fours, and five howitzers and field-pieces probably of twelve- and nine-pound capacity. It is estimated from the best sources that they threw a broadside of as much as 350 pounds of metal.

The British delay gave Jackson an opportunity to increase his artillery strength. On the twenty-eighth he had five guns in position, on the first of January fifteen. Three of these, one twenty-four and two long twelves, were on the west bank of the river, opposite the British batteries at a distance of three quarters of a mile. They were taken from the *Louisiana* and under Patterson's command did important service on January 1st. On the east bank the twelve guns were placed in eight batteries, thirty-twos, twenty-fours and smaller pieces. Together they threw a broadside of 226 pounds.[5]

At eight o'clock on New Year's morning these two lines of cannon began the best sustained artillery engagement of the war. The British were the attacking party, their object being to dismount the batteries so that the waiting infantry might go through the line. They had the opportunity to dismount, if they could, the opposite batteries one at a time by concentrating their fire. If they did not do so within a reasonable time their attack was a failure. The task of the Americans was to sustain the fire of their opponents, and in this respect they had the advantage of better earthworks, because they had longer time to construct them. They sought also to disable the opposing batteries and drive them from the attack. The infantry of the two sides remained, for the most part, inactive during the battle.

The British had great confidence in their artillerists, who now opened vigorously and incautiously, sending their shot for a time too high and thus wasting much of the ammunition which was brought from the fleet with great difficulty. The Americans began slowly, observing the effect of their fire and seeking the proper range. As they found it their fire grew stronger till in the course of an hour it became so accurate and penetrating that the British were surprised and forced to admit its superiority. Some of their cannon were dismounted, and five were reported as abandoned on

---

[5]This statement of artillery strength is taken from map five in Latour, *Historical Memoir;* his statement in the text (page 147), is slightly different, where he omits the two four-pounders and includes a howitzer in battery number one, making a total weight of metal of 224 pounds.

the field. By noon most of their batteries were silent, but their guns nearest the river were able to keep up a response at intervals till three in the afternoon. The British used hogsheads of sugar in their works, which proved to have slight power of resistance. To this they attributed the failure. In the night they withdrew their artillery, having lost something less than seventy-five men. "Such a failure in this boasted arm," said Admiral Codrington with a tinge of professional jealousy, "was not to be expected, and I think it a blot in the artillery escutcheon."[6] But we must not demand the impossible. The failure was due to the resistance of Jackson's earthworks and the excellence of his gunnery.

The Americans suffered little. In the cheeks of the embrasures of their batteries bales of cotton were placed, which were knocked out of position by the enemy's shot to the confusion of the gunners.[7] Three guns were somewhat damaged, two caissons were exploded, and thirty men were killed or wounded—a small price to pay for the knowledge that American gunners could meet their English brethren on equal terms. Jackson was satisfied with his success. Till nightfall the British guns lay in the empty batteries, but he made no attempt to bring them off. He realized that it behooved him to be cautious. His trenches and his army were the only defenses against conquest. It was for his antagonist to decide what the next move should be.

Pakenham's decision was duly made. He planned to throw to the west of the river a body of troops large enough to seize Patterson's guns which he would turn on Jackson's army on the east side, while with his main force he stormed the formidable works which sheltered the Americans. The movement was well designed, and if carried into effect with precision would be a dangerous one for Jackson. But the event showed that it was not easy to make the attack on the west bank at the right moment for cooperation with the assault on the east.

The experiences of the past fortnight had given the British

---

[6] *Life of Codrington,* I, 334.
[7] Much has been said by later writers of this incident, which contemporaries barely mention. Reid and Eaton seem to say that Jackson continued to use cotton bales in his earthworks till after January 8, *Life of Jackson,* 357. Jackson, on the other hand, said in his old age, when his memory was entirely reliable, that no cotton bales were in his works. See Parton, *Jackson,* III, 633.

greater respect for the resistance of the Americans, and their general was disposed to move cautiously. Major-General Lambert was daily expected with the 7th and 43rd regiments numbering together 1,570 men, and it was decided to await their arrival. Colonel Thornton, who led brilliantly the advance at Bladensburg, was appointed to command the movement on the west bank. To put him across the river, orders were given to dig Villeré's canal deep enough to carry the ships' barges, and on the night of the sixth the whole army by shifts labored silently to accomplish this vast undertaking. The boats might have been transported on rollers with less labor; for they were lighter than the artillery which the men had dragged up, but Pakenham preferred the canal since it would make it easier to conceal the movement of the boats, and, in order to make the deception surer, he commanded troops to maneuver in front of the canal while the boats were being moved. All this precaution was unnecessary; for, on the seventh, Patterson from the opposite side observed all that was done and understood its significance. It was not until January 6th that Lambert arrived in camp and gave the occasion for the final advance. On the seventh, fifty boats were ordered to be placed on the Mississippi for the embarkation of Thornton's command at nightfall.

These activities gave Jackson an opportunity to make further preparations for meeting his foe. The cannonade on the first showed that his works were not thick enough and they were ordered strengthened. To his men it seemed a hardship, this eternal digging, which might as well be left to the Negro slaves: the men came to fight, not to build fortifications. One of the battalions refused point-blank. Jackson, alarmed at this symptom of mutiny, sent for the officers of the discontented organization and told them plainly that he was prepared to take the most energetic measures if the men persisted in disobedience. The officers were impressed by his manner and assured him there would be no more trouble, and the promise was kept.[8]

On January 5th, Major Peire suggested that a bastion be placed on the levee at the right and in front of the line to rake the flank

---

[8] Jackson's fragmentary *Journal*, Jackson Mss.

of a charging column. Jackson objected on the ground that it would obstruct his fire, but yielded when Colonel Hayne, whose opinion he valued highly, seconded Peire's opinion. It was against his judgment that he gave in and it was, as he says, "for the first time in my life."[9] The event tended to justify his opinion. The bastion was easily seized by the British on the eighth; for its two six-pounders and small company of defenders were not able to resist the force concentrated against it; and retaking it was expensive.

January 2nd, General John Adair rode into Jackson's camp with the cheering news that the expected Kentuckians were near at hand. Two days later they arrived, 2,268 in all, commanded by Maj.-Gen. John Thomas. They were badly armed, two-thirds having no guns of any kind. Seven hundred and fifty, only 500 of whom had muskets, were stationed in the rear of Carroll's men as a support. They were under the command of Brig.-Gen. John Adair. The rest of the Kentuckians were placed on Jackson's second line at Dupree's plantation. Although strenuous efforts were made to get arms they were only slightly successful, and these good troops were nearly useless in the battle which was about to begin. But on January 7th, Adair armed 400 more of his men with guns he got in New Orleans and sent them to the advanced line. On the eighth, therefore, 1,100 Kentuckians fought by the side of Carroll's Tennesseeans.

Jackson's lines of defense were three and consisted of three parapets, each extending from the river to the swamp. The first was five miles from the city along Rodriguez's canal, the second two miles north of this at Dupree's plantation, and the third at Montreuil's, a mile and a quarter nearer New Orleans. The second and third lines were designed for rallying points in case it should be necessary to abandon the first. As no such necessity arose, this description is concerned with the details of the first line only.

When Jackson took possession of Rodriguez's canal it was a dry ditch, twenty-five feet wide and four or five feet deep. By cutting the levee a quantity of water was let into it, but the quick subsidence of the river left it very shallow. Thirty yards behind the

[9]From Jackson's fragmentary *Journal,* Jackson Mss.

canal a palisade of fence pales and other boards was made and the soil was banked against it in the rear. The supervision of the engineers was not strict, and the citizen soldiers of the various corps followed their own ideas, with the result that the parapet when completed was very irregular in height and width. In some parts it was twenty feet wide at the top, and in others it was hardly strong enough to stop a cannon-ball. Everywhere it was as much as five feet high and in some places higher. The batteries were placed in three groups, one bearing on the approach along the river road, one covering the center of the plain, and the other covering the approach along the edge of the swamp. Number one was seventy feet from the river with the bastion a short distance in front and to the right, number two was ninety yards farther east, number three was fifty yards beyond that, and number four twenty yards farther. These made the first group. Number five was 190 yards beyond number four, and number six about thirty-six yards farther, and these made the second group. Number seven was 190 yards beyond number six, and number eight—the crippled brass howitzer—was sixty yards still farther, and these made the third group. Fifty yards beyond number eight the line plunged into the woods, here not impassable, for 750 yards and then bent backward at right angles to its former direction until at the distance of 200 yards it ended in an impracticable swamp. The part within the woods had no batteries and was only thick enough to withstand rifle shots. Whenever necessary, the parapet was provided with a banquette.[10]

Besides the artillerymen, the troops behind the line consisted of the 7th regiment next the river and from that point in order Plauché's battalion, Lacoste's and Daquin's battalions of Negroes, the 44th regiment, General Carroll's command supported by Adair 400 yards in the rear, and Coffee's command which guarded the lines from the point at which it entered the woods, to the end. The total strength of these various bodies was 3,989 men.[11] Behind the line were 230 cavalry, in four small groups; and along the edge

---

[10]Latour, *Historical Memoir*, 145.

[11]This estimate is based on Latour, *Historical Memoir*, 150, and is not far from the estimate made by Jackson two years after the battle, when he was in his controversy with Adair.

of the woods were posted 250 Louisiana militia to prevent surprise in that quarter. Four hundred yards behind the line was placed a strong row of sentinels to prevent any soldier leaving the line without permission. In front of the line at a distance of 500 yards were the outposts. In this excellent position Jackson awaited the attack which various signs and bits of information led him to expect on the eighth of January.

The point at which Pakenham proposed to break this defense was at battery number seven, which could be approached within two hundred yards with some protection from the woods. In front of this position he formed a column of 2,150 men under the command of Major-General Gibbs, supporting it on the right by a regiment of West Indian Negroes, 520 strong, with direction to advance through the woods and occupy Coffee's attention, breaking his lines if possible. While Gibbs led this column in the charge on the right, a second column consisting of 1,200 men under Major-General Keane was formed to advance along the road by the edge of the river, making a demonstration in force against Jackson's right and drawing his fire, while Gibbs did the real work of carrying the line. A third column of 1,400 men under Major-General Lambert was held in reserve near the center of the field. During the night of the seventh, six eighteen-pounders were thrown forward to one of the redoubts erected for the artillery battle of the first and played on the American line during the attempted assault. Gibbs's and Keane's columns were ordered to form two hours before dawn on the eighth, and it was planned to hurl them against the Americans while it was still dark enough to conceal their movements. Pakenham hoped that the attack might take his opponent by surprise, but in that he was to be disappointed. Had no external agency informed Jackson of what was coming, his sleepless activity would have prevented a surprise.

In accurate cooperation with this assault were to be Thornton's operations on the west bank. With 1,400 men, 200 of whom were seamen and 520 of whom were blacks from the West Indies, he was directed to embark by nightfall on the seventh, cross the river to a point three miles below the American defenses, thence march in the night up the river, seize Patterson's batteries, and await the signal for the attack on the east bank. On getting it he was to turn

Patterson's captured guns on Jackson's flank with all possible energy. It was a well-arranged plan; for if at the moment of crisis in his front Jackson should find himself galled by his own guns from the west, the effect could be little less than demoralizing.[12]

Thornton's success, however, depended on accurate cooperation and this proved to be impossible. The capricious Mississippi suddenly fell leaving only two feet of water in the precious canal and the boats had to be dragged along slowly by the men. The caving of the banks stopped some of the largest ones and that created further delay. It was three o'clock before Thornton pushed off with a third of his force, and when he landed unopposed on the opposite side he heard the reports of the British batteries which opened the battle. It was nearly three hours before he could come within striking distance of Patterson's guns.

But not all of the delay was with Thornton. Pakenham had the misfortune to appoint the 44th regiment to lead Gibbs's column. The selection is unaccountable; for it was notorious in the army that Lieutenant-Colonel Mullins, then in command, was incapable, and if Pakenham did not know it, the fault was his own. Fascines made of bundles of sugar cane with ladders were collected behind the place designated for the formation of the charging column, and the 44th was ordered to take them up as they proceeded to the head of the division. When they arrived they had neither fascines nor ladders, and it was time for the assault to be made. Three hundred men were hurried back to get them, leaving the 44th at the head of the column with 127 men. As the moments elapsed, the dawn began to appear and all the advantage of a concealed attack was lost. Through this the troops became impatient and uneasy under the American cannonade which then began and the signal was given for the attack before the formation of the 44th could be restored. With this element of confusion at the head of the column Gibbs's advance lost the precision which was necessary in the severe ordeal to which Jackson's deadly fire subjected it. The men forgetting their duty to rush the works with the bayonets began to fire, the detail of the luckless 44th, rushing up with fascines and ladders, threw down their burdens and began

---

[12] *Subaltern* (edition 1833), page 257, James, *Military Occurrences*, II, 374–380.

to fire likewise, and the advance became a wavering, confused mass.

Gibbs was now in despair. All his commands were wasted, his column recoiled, and he rushed up to Pakenham a short distance in the rear exclaiming, "The troops will not obey me; they will not follow me!" Gibbs turned and dashed to the head of the column and Pakenham, his hat in his hand and shouting encouragement to his men, followed on horseback. Two hundred yards from the parapet the latter's horse was killed and the rider was wounded. He hardly mounted another when a grapeshot brought him to the ground and he was borne to the rear in a dying condition. Gibbs reached the head of the column which was now rallying and carried it forward up to the very lines of his opponents, but in the deadly fire from their rampart he fell mortally wounded within twenty yards of the canal. At the same moment Keane was severely injured and when the soldiers saw their three leaders carried off the field, they lost courage and fell back. Lambert coming up with reserves had not the hardihood to repeat the costly attempt.

Meantime, Keane on the left flank had been in action. With the signal for battle his brigade advanced along the river road, driving the sentinels so rapidly that his advanced companies rushed the bastion before its defenders could fire more than two rounds at them. Had the whole column now followed with vigor, the result might have been disastrous for the Americans; but mindful that his duty was merely to make a demonstration, Keane held his men back, while the Americans rallied and drove out the captors of the bastion. His main column was halting at a respectful distance from the American fire. It accomplished nothing: Keane himself was severely wounded at the brink of the canal and his troops fell back with the others. The charge began at six: at half past eight, the fire of the musketry ceased and at two the cannonade ended.[13]

---

[13]For the details of the British charge see Lambert's report, James, *Military Occurrences,* II, Appendix, number 96; also the testimony of Majors Tylden and McDougal quoted in the same, pages 375 to 379; *Subaltern,* chapter 21; Gleig, *Campaigns in America,* 323–7; Latour, *Historical Memoir,* 154–164; and Reid and Eaton, *Jackson,* 365–70. *Subaltern,* alone, mentions Keane's oblique movement, but he does it so explicitly that it is impossible to ignore him.

But for the confusion in Gibbs's column the British charge was made splendidly. It was received by the Americans with equal courage and without confusion. All night they lay on their arms in two equal shifts which relieved one another at the ramparts. The first clearing of the horizon at dawn revealed the enemy drawn up in line more than four hundred yards in front of the ditch. The American batteries opened at once, while the British gave the signal for the charge. With grim determination and some admiration the backwoods riflemen saw the red line narrow itself into a compact column sixty men broad and start at double quick for that part of the works which was defended by Carroll and Adair. They had ample time for preparations and concentrated their forces at the danger point in several ranks which fired and loaded alternately. At easy musket range the American infantry delivered a murderous fire, shaking the column, while the batteries, loading with grape and canister, ploughed wide lanes through the compact mass. The roll of musketry was like continuous peals of thunder. The first onslaught lasted twenty-five minutes, when the column recoiled to its original position, where it was reformed and brought back. Again the Tennesseeans and Kentuckians received it with a hail of musket-balls and grape-shot. A few of the attackers crossed the canal, probably two hundred, and endeavored to climb the slippery sides of the parapet. Some succeeded, only to be killed or captured on the top, and others remained in comparative safety at the bottom till they rejoined their retreating colleagues. When the smoke of battle cleared away, a broad space before the seventh battery was red with the prostrate forms of British soldiers. "The ground," says *Subaltern,* "was literally covered with dead; they were so numerous that to count them seemed impossible."[14] They were counted, however, the dead and wounded on the east bank, and the number was 1,971. Jackson's loss on this side was six killed and seven wounded. Among the British casualties were one lieutenant-general, two major-generals, eight colonels and lieutenant-colonels, six majors, eighteen cap-

---

[14]Edition 1833, page 262.

tains, and fifty-four subalterns. This excessive proportion of the officers engaged shows the excellence of the frontier marksmanship.

On the west bank the battle went otherwise. Jackson was accustomed to concentrate his energies on one thing at a time. While he gave himself to driving the British from Pensacola, he neglected New Orleans, although he might have done much good by riding thither at least once while he waited for Coffee. In the same manner he gave his attention to the east bank and left the west side to others. It does not appear that he was once on that side during the sixteen days that the British were pushing their way toward the city. He left the defense there to Maj.-Gen. David Morgan, of the Louisiana militia, a man of little military experience or ability, and gave him a body of militia who had never seen service of any kind. And although the river was only three-quarters of a mile wide at this place no boats were provided for crossing so as to allow means of quick reinforcements. On January 7th, Morgan had 550 militia, when it was known that he would be attacked during the night. To reinforce him Jackson in the afternoon ordered 500 of the unarmed Kentuckians to proceed to the west bank by way of the city, where they were expected to get some arms which the mayor was retaining for an emergency. In the city they learned that Adair got these arms earlier in the day, but after some delay they got seventy muskets at the naval station which, with some inefficient arms they had before, made 170 who had guns. The rest did not feel called upon to hurry into danger without arms and went into camp a little south of the city. The armed ones, under command of Colonel Davis, proceeded and came to Morgan's lines at four o'clock in the morning of the eighth. They had marched in twelve hours from Dupree's line to Morgan's line, a distance of eight miles, not enough to exhaust them, but under such conditions that they were tired and discouraged. Morgan received them gladly, and keeping the larger part of his Louisiana troops in his line sent the Kentuckians at once farther down the river to meet the enemy. It was not a cheerful detail to men who were expecting an opportunity to rest, but they departed without protest.

Earlier in the night Morgan sent Major Arnaud, with 100 militia, down the river road to prevent the landing of the British. Finding no enemy on the bank he bivouacked his command at midnight three miles from Morgan and placed a single sentinel on the road southward from it. At dawn Thornton with 600 men and three gun-barges on the river manned by about a hundred sailors moved northward as rapidly as possible. They soon came upon Arnaud's faithful sentinel, who gave his comrades fair warning of their danger and enabled them to escape in safety. A mile from Morgan they joined the Kentuckians under Colonel Davis, who took command of both bodies, formed them on a canal, and awaited Thornton's attack. It came promptly with an attempt to turn the right, where Arnaud was placed. The Louisianians were thrown into confusion and fled incontinently, so demoralized that very few of them saw further service during the day. Davis was forced to fall back, and he joined Morgan who assigned him to a place on his right flank. Thornton followed aggressively, annoying the Americans both on land and from his three gun-barges, which continually raked the bank with grape-shot.

Morgan's line, on the opposite side of the river and a mile southward of Jackson's line, was badly located. It began at the southern end of Patterson's batteries, which covered nearly a mile of the bank, and ran with a canal from the river to the swamp, a distance of 2,000 yards. To hold such a line properly would require 2,000 men. It was selected against the advice of Jackson's engineer, who pointed out a position half a mile northward where the plain was only half as wide. But that position would leave half of Patterson's batteries south of the line; and since Morgan decided after conferring with Patterson, it is not unfair to assume that the desire to protect the batteries had something to do with Morgan's decision. Entrenchments were thrown up on the line for 200 yards from the river, and in this part were placed one twelve-pounder and two six-pounders with that part of the militia which remained after Arnaud's flight. This left 1,800 yards undefended, and when Davis arrived about eight o'clock, hard pressed by Thornton, he was ordered to take position upon it. Between him and the militia was an interval of 200 yards, his own command of less than 200 men was stretched out to cover 300 yards, and the rest of the line to the swamp was without defense except for a picket guard of eighteen men. The whole force was a little over 600, some of whom were badly armed.

Thornton was as quick as he was energetic. Seeing Morgan's exposed right he determined to turn it. He sent a part of the 85th regiment to make this flank movement by way of the woods and out of range of any guns which Patterson or Morgan could bring to bear on them. With another part of his force he made a feint along the road, and with still another sought to enter the gap between Davis and the militia. The Kentuckians stood well for a time, but realizing that they were about to be surrounded, withdrew from their position, leaving the militia exposed on their right with the result that these also retreated. Both Morgan and Patterson expected that the batteries of the latter would protect the line, but in the actual conflict it was seen that the defenders of the line so obstructed the fire that they could not be used on an enemy approaching from the south. Thornton's success on the line forced Patterson to withdraw. He had time merely to spike his long-range guns, which had served so well in annoying the enemy on the east bank, and to withdraw his gunners. Thus it happened that about the time the attack on the east side was a failure that on the west was completely successful. Thornton pursued the retreating Americans for two miles. Holding the west bank for a mile above Jackson's line the British were now in a position to force him out of his position, had they been disposed to follow Thornton's success.

Fortunately for the Americans, the British were satisfied with the situation. They had suffered too much on the east bank to utilize their success on the west, and Major-General Lambert, who was now in command, after finding that it would take 2,000 troops to hold what Thornton had won—which Jackson tried to hold with 600—ordered the left column to recross the river during the night. Thus ended an engagement in which Jackson lost six killed and wounded, sixteen pieces of artillery, and the key to his first line of defense. It cost the enemy seventy-three killed and wounded, and Thornton was among the latter. The entire losses for the day were for the British 2,137 and for the Americans seventy-one, fifty of which were sustained in a sortie from Jackson's line.[15]

Responsibility for the disaster on the west bank rests on Morgan and Patterson, who adopted an impossible line of defense, and on Jackson, who was ignorant of the conditions there and who failed to send enough troops to hold it. For two weeks 1,000 of Carroll's men had lain on the Chef Menteur road in the unwarranted expectation that the enemy would divide his force and carry that approach before it could be strengthened from the American lines on the river. Had these Tennesseeans been ordered to join Morgan on the afternoon of the seventh, the story of the battle would probably have been different.[16]

Jackson did not recognize this responsibility and, with both Morgan and Patterson, placed it on the detachment of Kentuckians. In the moment when Gibbs and Keane were repulsed, the commander-in-chief, standing on the levee by his line, saw through the mists the maneuvers of Thornton a mile and a half away. Events immediately in front of him gave him confidence and he waited to see a like success on the west bank. To his disappointment the flashes of the guns through the fog revealed the retreat of the Kentuckians and Louisianians. "At the very moment," runs his report, "when the entire discomfiture of the enemy was looked for, with a confidence amounting to certainty, the Kentucky reinforcements, in whom so much reliance had been placed, ingloriously fled, drawing after them, by their example, the remainder of the forces." This was his official indignation. His unofficial wrath burst out in violent abuse that morning on the levee, as he saw the men falling back. He ordered General Humbert, distinguished in the French Army of Napoleon but now serving as a volunteer private in the American ranks, to take 400 men, cross the river,

---

[15]For the battle of the west bank see Latour, *Historical Memoir,* 164–176, Reid and Eaton, *Jackson,* 373–378, Gayarre, *Louisiana,* IV, 478–496, Smith, *The Battle of New Orleans,* (Filson Club Publications, number 19), 89–121, Jackson's and Patterson's reports in Latour, *Historical Memoir,* Appendix, number 29, Thornton's and Lambert's reports, *Ibid,* number 66, and in James, *Military Occurrences,* Appendix, numbers 96 and 97.

[16]Gayarre, *Louisiana,* IV, 422, and Jackson's fragmentary *Journal,* December 23, Jackson's assertion that only sixteen hundred of Carroll's men had arms seems doubtful, but even if it is correct, he still had six hundred of Carroll's men, whom he could have spared to Morgan. See Jackson to Monroe, December 24, 1814 and February 17, 1815, Jackson Mss.

and recover the lost position at any cost. Humbert obeyed with pleasure, but on the other side found that some of Morgan's officers objected to serving under a man who was not a citizen, and as Jackson had neglected to give him written authority for assuming command he returned in disgust. The withdrawal of Thornton made it possible for the Americans to reoccupy their former position, where a better line was established and Patterson's batteries were remounted in a better location.

At noon of the eighth there was a Bengal from the enemy on the east bank and a flag of truce approached with a letter asking for an armistice to bury the dead. Desiring to conceal the loss of the three senior officers, Lambert signed the request without naming his rank. Jackson desired to gain time and replied with explicit terms, which he hardly expected Lambert to accept. The latter took it under consideration, promising to answer by ten o'clock on the ninth. Lambert hesitated, because Jackson insisted that operations should not cease on the west bank and that neither party should reinforce his troops there.[17] By next morning, Thornton's command was safe on the east bank, and Lambert accepted the armistice. The dead and the severely wounded, left on the field during the night, were now removed. Gleig, a British officer who rode out to the scene, tells us what he saw. "Of all the sights," he says, "I ever witnessed, that which met me there was beyond comparison the most shocking and the most humiliating. Within the small compass of a few hundred yards were gathered together nearly a thousand bodies, all of them arrayed in British uniforms. Not a single American was among them; all were English; and they were thrown by dozens into shallow holes, scarcely deep enough to furnish them with a slight covering of earth. Nor was this all. An American officer stood by smoking a segar, and apparently counting the slain with a look of savage exultation; and repeating over and over to each individual that approached him,

---

[17]See Jackson's report, January 9, 1815, Latour, *Historical Memoir,* Appendix number 29, and Reid and Eaton, *Jackson,* 383. But Jackson's fragmentary *Journal* and a letter from Lambert to Jackson, January 8, both in the Jackson Mss, seem to show that the armistice was accepted on the eighth. Jackson thought that Lambert was frightened by the demand that neither side should reinforce the west bank, and delayed till he could bring Thornton over.

that their loss came only to eight men killed, and fourteen wounded."[18]

From the eighth till the eighteenth the armies were inactive except for a desultory cannonade from the American line and a spiritless British bombardment of Fort St. Philip, on the Mississippi. Major Hinds, whose conduct in this campaign marks him for a man of singular ability, asked permission to attack with the cavalry. Jackson refused, lest Hinds should do something which would bring on an engagement in the open field. He advised with Adair and Coffee, both of whom urged him not to attack in the open. The former said: "My troops will fight when behind breastworks or in the woods, but do not hazard an attack with raw militia in the open plain: they cannot be relied on. The officers are inexperienced, the soldiers without subordination or discipline. You would hazard too much by making an attack with them in the open plain against well-disciplined troops."[19]

On the fifteenth, signs of activity in the camp showed that the British were about to depart: on the morning of the nineteenth their lines were deserted. They had constructed fortifications at the mouth of Bayou Bienvenue and withdrawn behind them till the army could be carried slowly to the fleet riding in deep water sixty miles away. Hinds with 1,000 men was sent to cut up their rear, but found them so well defended in the narrow passes of the swamps that he considered it unwise to attack.[20] On the twenty-seventh, the difficult work of embarking was completed; but bad weather detained the fleet at its anchorage until February 5th, when it was at last able to stand away to the east. Two days later it came to a halt off Dauphine Island, where the army was disembarked for a period of rest after a most exhausting and demoralizing experience. Its total loss, by the British account, since December 23rd, was 2,492, while its opponents lost only 333.[21]

On the morning of the nineteenth, Jackson and his staff rode to the abandoned camp. They were met on the way by a British surgeon with a letter from Lambert announcing his departure

---

[18]Gleig, *Campaign at Washington and New Orleans*, 332.
[19]Jackson's fragmentary *Journal*, Jackson Mss.
[20]*Ibid.*
[21]Latour, *Historical Memoir*, Appendix, number 29; James, *Military Occurrences*, II, 388.

from Louisiana and asking considerate treatment for eighty wounded who could not be moved. Jackson received the messenger with courtesy and sent his chief medical man to aid in caring for the wounded men, and later he visited them himself. On the ground the enemy left fourteen pieces of artillery so disabled as to be useless. On the twenty-first, the major part of the American Army was withdrawn from the lines and entered the city amid demonstrations of joy by the inhabitants. On the twenty-third a *Te Deum* was sung in the cathedral with great pomp. As the general proceeded across the square to the edifice he passed under a triumphal arch under which two maidens presented him with laurel wreaths; farther on other maidens strewed flowers in his path; at the door the Abbé Dubourg delivered a laudatory address to which Jackson replied in studied moderation; and a guard of honor escorted him to his lodgings.

In his address the abbé referring to the recent victory said: "The first impulse of your religious heart was to acknowledge the signal interposition of Providence." A "religious heart" has rarely been considered one of Jackson's possessions, yet in this case the priest's words were appropriate. Several of the grim warrior's letters witness his conviction that his success, marvellous to himself, was partly due to Divine intervention. To his friend, Colonel Robert Hays, he wrote: "It appears that the unerring hand of providence shielded my men from the shower of Balls, Bombs, and Rockets, when every Ball and Bomb from our guns carried with them a mission of death. Tell your good lady and family God bless them."[22] Nor did he hesitate to give the same opinion in his official dispatches. To Monroe he wrote: "Heaven, to be sure, has interposed most wonderfully in our behalf, and I am filled with gratitude when I look back to what we have escaped; but I grieve the more that we did not, with more and more industry use the means with which she had blessed us. Again and again I must repeat, we have been always too backward with our preparations. When the enemy comes we begin to think of driving him away; and scarcely before."[23]

---

[22]Jackson to Hays, January 26, 1815, Jackson Mss.
[23]Jackson to Monroe, February 17, 1815, Jackson Mss.

It is true that Jackson realized the military situation slowly. It was not till the British were actually at hand that he realized the importance of guarding New Orleans: it was not till the gunboats were taken that he realized that he ought to concentrate his forces: it was not till December 29th that he ordered New Orleans to be searched for entrenching tools;[24] it was not till the British held Bayou Bienvenue that he realized its importance: it was not till the militia were about to arrive without arms that he realized how few muskets he had: it was not till Jean Lafitte suggested that the extreme left of his line ought to be bent backward so as to rest on an impassable swamp that this position was made secure;[25] and it was not till Thornton held the left bank that he realized fully its importance in the general scheme of defense.

A serious embarrassment in this campaign was the lack of arms. Jackson tried to throw the responsibility on others. His apologists say[26] he asked for a supply in the summer of 1814, but no reference to this is made in his extensive preserved correspondence in the summer and early autumn. He even drew 500 stands from New Orleans to Mobile in September.[27] The first specific reference to the subject in the correspondence is in a letter to Governor Blount, October 27th.[28] Coffee had just arrived without a full equipment and that seems to have aroused his interest for the first time. Up to that time he seems to have overlooked the fact that his division was without arms, which was quite in keeping with his failure to give attention to detail. He was now, however, urgent enough. Monroe, at last aroused to the necessity, ordered the commandant at Fort LaFayette, near Pittsburg, to send a supply immediately. November 8th 5,000 stands were sent by sail boats from that place with the expectation that they would arrive in twenty days. The time was ample, but the captains loitered to trade and the delay was fatal. One of the boats was fast enough to fall in with Carroll on his way to the place of danger, and he took the responsibility of taking 1,100 stands to make up the deficiency in his command;

---

[24]Livingston to Mayor Girod, December 29, 1814, Jackson Mss.
[25]Livingston to Jackson, December 25, 1814, Jackson Mss.
[26]Latour, *Historical Memoir*, 66.
[27]Captain Humphrey to Jackson, September 6, 1814, Jackson Mss.
[28]Jackson Mss.

the rest arrived at their destination after the battle of the eighth.[29]

Nor was Jackson quite correct in saying that he had had only 3,200 stands at the time of the battle. The regulars, Carroll's men, Coffee's men, the Louisiana militia, and 1,000 of the Kentuckians, over 6,000 in all, must have had arms. Besides, the returns of his ordnance department show that 2,404 stands were issued from December 18th till January 8th.[30]

Deficient as he sometimes was in the science of warfare, he was nevertheless an excellent fighter. Wherever he fought, fighting was good. Mutiny frequently appeared in his camp because of the great exertion he demanded of his men, but neither in the Creek nor in the New Orleans campaign did the soldiers directly under his authority ever flinch on the field of battle. Had he been present on the west bank on the morning of January 8th, the result, doubtless, would have been less humiliating. Good officers, as he wrote down in his journal, will make good soldiers:[31] his own influence showed the truth of the statement.

General Jackson's qualities made a good impression on his opponents. James, the British historian of the day, says: "He proved himself at New Orleans, not only an able general for the description of country in which he had to operate, but, in all his transactions with the British officers, both an honorable, and a courteous enemy. In his official despatches, too, he has left an example of modesty, worthy of imitation by the generality of American commanders, naval as well as military."[32] The characterization is correct. Jackson had a strong sense of dignity. When his antipathy was aroused, he was most perverse, stickling over punctilios, blustering, and absolutely wrong-headed, but under normal conditions he treated his antagonist with the consideration of a brave man, who is not afraid to be generous. An illustration of this quality is the cordial manner in which in the following note he restored the sword of General Kean who requested to be allowed to redeem it:

---

[29]Jackson to Carroll, October 31; Jackson to Monroe, October 31, 1814; Woolesley to Jackson, November 8, 1814; Monroe to Blount, November 3, 1814; Jackson Mss.
[30]Jackson Mss.
[31]Jackson's fragmentary *Journal,* January 18, 1815. Jackson Mss.
[32]James, *Military Occurrences,* II, 390.

"The general commanding the American forces, having learned that Major-General Kean of the British Army had expressed a wish for the restoration of his sword, lost in the action of the eighth of January in consequence of a wound, feels great satisfaction in ordering it to be returned to him. Mr. Livingston, one of his volunteer aids, is charged with the delivery of it. The undersigned, feeling for the misfortune of the brave, begs that General Kean will be assured of his wishes for his speedy restoration."[33]

---

[33]Jackson to General Kean, February 4; G.M. Ogden to Jackson, February 3, 1815; Jackson Mss.

CHAPTER VII

THE AMERICAN CIVIL WAR, 1861-65

Robert E. Lee (1807–70) led the Confederate armies during the American Civil War. His distinguished career prior to the war included distinction in the Mexican War, from which he emerged as a colonel. Between 1852 and 1855, he was the superintendent at West Point and later served in Washington. As the Civil War approached, he rejected an offer by President Lincoln to lead the field command of the Union armies. Instead, he accepted the command of the Virginia forces and was later appointed by Secessionist President Davis to lead the Confederate armies. After the war he served as the head of Washington and Lee college in Virginia, to become an idol of both sides of the American Civil War.

Ulysses Simpson Grant (1822–85) graduated from West Point in 1843 and served in the Mexican War. At President Lincoln's request he created the Illinois Volunteers and raised an army that drove the Confederacy from western Kentucky. He did badly at the Battle of Shiloh but gained an impressive victory at Vicksburg. In 1864 he was appointed overall commander of the Union armies by President Lincoln. Grant's brilliant planning eventually crushed Lee and the Confederacy. He became the 18th president of the United States in 1868.

George Gordon Meade (1812–72) graduated from West Point in 1835. He became a civil engineer, working mostly as a surveyor in the Mississippi delta and in harbor engineering. He served in the Mexican War. During the Civil War he distinguished himself for his leadership capacities in the Peninsula campaigns, at Bull Run, at Antietam and at Chancellorsville. Taking over the Army of the Potomac from General Hooker, he won the crucial Battle of Gettysburg. In his later years he commanded various areas in the South during the Reconstruction period.

The author of the first selection, James Ford Rhodes (1848–1927), was an American historian. After making money in the iron and coal business in Cleveland, he devoted himself to the study of American history. He wrote many books, including *The History of the United States from the Compromise of 1850 to 1877.* He lived abroad but eventually moved to Boston and wrote books about presidents Hayes, McKinley and Theodore Roosevelt. His most famous book is *The History of the Civil War,* from which the "Battle of Gettysburg" is extracted.

The distinguished military historian Major General John Frederic Charles Fuller was introduced in an earlier chapter as the author of the selection on the Spanish Armada. In this chapter we include an extract from his classical study of Grant and Lee.

The Battle of Gettysburg, 1863
by
James Ford Rhodes

Meade can best tell the story of his promotion. "It has pleased Almighty God," he wrote to his wife on June 29, "to place me in the trying position that for sometime past we have been talking about. Yesterday morning at 3 A.M. I was aroused from my sleep by an officer from Washington entering my tent, and after waking me up, saying he had come to give me trouble. At first I thought it was either to relieve or arrest me. . . . He handed me a communication to read, which I found was an order relieving Hooker from the command and assigning it to me. . . . As it appears to be God's will for some good purpose—at any rate as a soldier, I had nothing to do but accept and exert my utmost abilities to command success. . . . I am moving at once against Lee. . . . A battle will decide the fate of our country and our cause. Pray earnestly, pray for the success of my country (for it is my success besides)."

Frank Haskell, a staff officer in the Second Corps, who wrote during July, 1863, a graphic account of the Battle of Gettysburg, recorded his belief that "the Army in general, both officers and men, had no confidence in Hooker, in either his honesty or ability." When the change of command became known, he wrote: "We breathed a full breath of joy and of hope. The Providence of God had been with us—General Meade commanded the Army of the Potomac. . . . The Army brightened and moved on with a more elastic step." General Reynolds at once went to see Meade and assured him of his hearty support.

The president conferred upon his general full power. Meade advanced northward in his aim "to find and fight the enemy." He had been prompt to command, his subordinates zealous to obey. The officers, sinking for the moment all their rivalries and jealousies, were careful and untiring in their efforts, while the soldiers showed extraordinary endurance in their long and rapid marches in the hot sun and sultry air of the last days of June.

Meade's advance northward caused Lee to concentrate his army east of the mountains; he called Ewell back from his projected attack on Harrisburg to join the army at Cashtown or Gettysburg "as circumstances might require." In the meantime Hill and Longstreet had been ordered to Cashtown, which was eight miles west of Gettysburg. Both Lee and Meade hoped and expected to fight a defensive battle and their maneuvers were directed to this end.

The circumstances that led to a collision at Gettysburg on July 1 between a number of the Confederates and Reynolds commanding the left wing need not be detailed. Reynolds was killed and afterwards his troops met with a serious reverse. When Meade heard of his death, which was for him as great a disaster as the loss of Stonewall Jackson had been to Lee, he sent forward to take command Hancock, who restored order out of the existing confusion. Nevertheless, the first day of the Battle of Gettysburg was a decided Confederate success.

By six o'clock on the afternoon of July 1, Meade had arrived at the opinion that "a battle at Gettysburg is now forced on us"; and he issued orders to all of his corps to concentrate at that point. He himself arrived on the battlefield about midnight, pale, tired-looking, hollow-eyed, and worn out from loss of sleep, anxiety and the weight of responsibility.

At about eight o'clock on the morning of July 2, accompanied by a staff-officer and orderly, he rode forth on a visit to his right wing. Schurz, who spoke with him on this occasion, was struck with "his long-bearded, haggard face, his care-worn and tired" look, "as if he had not slept that night." "His mind was evidently absorbed by a hard problem," Schurz went on. "But this simple, cold, serious soldier with his business-like air did inspire confidence. The officers and men as much as was permitted crowded around and looked up to him with curious eyes and then turned away not enthusiastic but clearly satisfied. With a rapid glance he examined the position of our army and . . . nodded seemingly with approval. After the usual salutations I asked him how many men he had on the ground. I remember his answer well, 'In the course of the day I expect to have about 95,000—enough I guess for this business.' After another sweeping glance over the field, he added, as if reflecting something to himself, 'Well we may fight it out here just as well as anywhere else.' "

By the afternoon of July 2, Lee and Meade had their whole forces on the field, Lee mustering 70,000, Meade 93,000, less the losses of the first day, which had been much greater on the Union than on the Confederate side. The armies were about a mile apart, the Confederates occupying the eminence concave in form called Seminary Ridge, whilst the Federals were posted in a convex line on Cemetery Ridge—a position admirably adapted for defense. Meade decided to await attack, and if he had studied closely the character and record of his energetic adversary, he must have been almost certain that it would come. Longstreet, however, differed with his commander. In a conversation at the close of the first day's fight, he expressed his opinion that their troops should be thrown round Meade's left; they would then be interposed between the Union Army and Washington and Meade would be forced to take the offensive. Lee, in the anxiety and excitement of the moment, was somewhat irritated at this suggestion of a plan contrary to the one he had already determined and said, "No, the enemy is there and I am going to attack him." From the beginning of his invasion he made no secret of the poor esteem in which he held his foe. While recognizing in Meade a better general than Hooker, he believed that the change of commanders at this critical moment would counterbalance the advantage in generalship; and impressed as he was by the rapid and efficient movements of the Army of the Potomac since Meade had taken command, he must on the other hand have felt that he and his army were almost invincible—a confidence shared by nearly all his officers and men, for his success on his own soil had been both brilliant and practically unbroken. "There were never such men in an army before," Lee said. "They will go anywhere and do anything if properly led."

Lee was up betimes on the morning of July 2, but, owing to the slow movements of his soldiers, he lost much of the advantage of his more speedy concentration than Meade's. He did not begin his attack until the afternoon was well advanced when the last of the Union Army, the Sixth Corps, was arriving after a march of thirty-two miles in seventeen hours. He told accurately the result of the tremendous fighting and heavy loss that afternoon on both wings of each army. "We attempted to dislodge the enemy, and, though we gained some ground, we were unable to get possession of his position." The Confederate assaults had been disjointed: to that mistake is ascribed their small success.

Meade claimed the victory. "The enemy attacked me about 4 P.M. this day," he telegraphed to Halleck on July 2, "and after one of the severest contests of the war was repulsed at all points." That Meade in this despatch was not consciously resorting to the time-honored device in war by stretching the claim beyond the fact is to be inferred from the note to his wife written at 8:45 on the following morning, "We had a great fight yesterday, the enemy attacking and we completely repulsing them: both armies shattered."

From the reports of the several corps commanders at the council of war which Meade called on the night of July 2, it was evident that the Union Army, having incurred a loss of 20,000 men, was indeed seriously weakened, but the generals had not lost spirit and all voted to "stay and fight it out." As the council broke up, Meade said to Gibbon, who was in temporary command of the Second Corps, "If Lee attacks to-morrow it will be in *your front.*" Why, asked Gibbon. "Because he has made attacks on both our flanks and failed, and, if he concludes to try it again it will be on our center." I hope he will, replied Gibbon. If he does we shall defeat him.

In the early morning of July 3, there was fighting on the Union right. "At it again," wrote Meade to his wife, "with what result remains to be seen. Army in fine spirits and everyone determined to do or die." On the other side, after Lee and Longstreet had made a reconnaissance of the Union position, Lee said that he was going to attack the enemy's center. "Great God," said Longstreet. "Look, General Lee, at the insurmountable difficulties between our line and that of the Yankees—the steep hills, the tiers of artillery, the fences, the heavy skirmish line—and then we'll have to fight our infantry against their batteries. Look at the ground we'll have to charge over, nearly a mile of that open ground there under the rain of their canister and shrapnel." "The enemy is there, General Longstreet, and I am going to strike him," said Lee in his quiet, determined voice.

All the events of the past month—invasion and answering maneuver, marching and countermarching, the fighting of two days —were the prelude to a critical episode; three or four terrible hours were now imminent which should go far toward deciding the issue of the war. "From 11 A.M. until 1 P.M. there was an ominous stillness." Suddenly from the Confederate side came the reports of two signal guns in quick succession. A bombardment from one hundred and fifty cannon commenced and was replied to by eighty guns of the Union Army whose convex line, advantageous in other respects, did not admit of their bringing into action a large part of their artillery. The Confederate fire was chiefly concentrated upon the Second Corps where Hancock had resumed command. It was, he wrote in his report, "the heaviest artillery fire I have ever known." But it did little damage. The Union soldiers lay under the protection of stone walls, swells of the ground, and earthworks, and the projectiles of the enemy passed over their heads, sweeping the open ground in their rear. Hancock with his staff, his corps flag flying, rode deliberately along the front of his line and, by his coolness and his magnificent presence, inspired his men with courage and determination. One of his brigadiers, an old neighbor, said to him, "General, the corps commander ought not to risk his life in that way." Hancock replied, "There are times when a corps commander's life does not count." For an hour and a half this raging cannonade was kept up, when Meade, knowing that it was preliminary to an assault and desiring to lure the Confederates on, gave the order to cease firing, in which action he had been anticipated by Hunt, chief of the Union artillery, because his ammunition was running low.

Meade's ruse was successful. Longstreet was inclined to think that the Confederate fire had been effective, and Alexander, who commanded the Confederate artillery, "felt sure that the enemy was feeling the punishment." Pickett, who was to lead the attack, rode up to Longstreet for orders. "I found him," Pickett wrote, "like a great lion at bay. I have never seen him so grave and troubled. For several minutes after I had saluted him he looked at me without speaking. Then in an agonized voice he said: 'Pickett, I am being crucified at the thought of the sacrifice of life which this attack will make. I have instructed Alexander to watch the effect of our fire upon the enemy, and when it begins to tell he must take the responsibility and give you orders, for I can't.' "

Alexander had confidence in the attack because Lee had ordered it, although he shrank from the responsibility now thrust upon him; yet, having seen Pickett and found him cheerful and sanguine, he played his part. And when he dared wait no longer he sent a note to Pickett, who was still with Longstreet: "For God's sake come quick. Come quick or my ammunition will not let me support you properly." Pickett read it, handed it to Longstreet, and asked, Shall I obey and go forward? Longstreet, so Pickett wrote, "looked at me for a moment, then held out his hand. Presently clasping his other hand over mine, without speaking, he bowed his head upon his breast. I shall never forget the look in his face nor the clasp of his hand when I said, 'Then, General, I shall lead my division on.'

"My brave boys," wrote Pickett, "were full of hope and confident of victory as I led them forth, forming them in column of attack [at about 3:15] though officers and men alike knew what was before them. . . . Over on Cemetery Ridge the Federals beheld . . . an army forming in line of battle in full view, under their very eyes." Hancock, who expected the attack and was prepared to meet it, wrote in his report, The enemy's "lines were formed with a precision and steadiness that extorted the admiration of the witnesses of that memorable scene."

Pickett's 15,000 had nearly a mile to go across the valley; with banners flying they marched forward "with the steadiness of a dress parade." Haskell of the Second Corps, against which the charge was directed, wrote: "Every eye could see the enemy's legions, an overwhelming resistless tide of an ocean of armed men sweeping upon us! Regiment after regiment and brigade after brigade move from the woods and rapidly take their places in the line forming the assault. Pickett's proud division [5000] with some additional troops hold their right. The first line at short intervals is followed by a second, and that a third succeeds; and columns between support the lines. More than half a mile their front extends; more than a thousand yards the dull gray masses deploy, man touching man, rank pressing rank and line supporting line. The red flags wave, their horsemen gallop up and down; the arms of eighteen thousand men [15,000], barrel and bayonet, gleam in the sun, a sloping forest of flashing steel. Right on they move, as with one soul, in perfect order, without impediment of ditch or wall or stream, over ridge and slope, through orchard and meadow and cornfield, magnificent, grim, irresistible." The Union artillery, which had been put in entire readiness to check such an onset, "opened fire upon the advancing column at 700 yards and continued until it came to close quarters." Still the Confederates advanced steadily and coolly. Their artillery had reopened over their heads in an effort to draw the deadly fire at them from Cemetery Ridge; but the Union guns made no change in aim and went on mowing down Pickett's men. A storm of canister came. The slaughter was terrible; but, nothing daunted, the remnant of Pickett's division of 5000 pressed on in the lead. The other brigades followed. Now the Union infantry opened fire and the Confederates replied. General Garnett, just out of the sick ambulance and commanding a brigade in Pickett's division, "rode immediately in the rear of his advancing line" with great coolness and deliberation, and endeavored, so wrote Major Peyton, "to keep his line well closed and dressed. He was shot from his horse while near the center of the brigade within about 25 paces of the stone wall." But "our line much shattered still kept up the advance until within about twenty paces of the wall when, for a moment, it recoiled under the terrific fire that poured into our ranks both from their batteries and from their sheltered infantry. At this moment General Kemper came up on the right and General Armistead in rear, when the three lines joining in concert, rushed forward with unyielding determination and an apparent spirit of laudable rivalry to plant the Southern banner on the walls of the enemy." Armistead, wrote Colonel Aylett, was "conspicuous to all. Fifty yards in advance of his brigade, waving his hat upon his sword, he led his men upon his enemy with a steady bearing. . . . Far in advance of all he led the attack till he scaled the works of the enemy and fell wounded in their hands, but not until he had driven them from their position and seen his colors planted over their fortifications." The enemy's "strongest and last line was gained," wrote Major Peyton; "the Confederate battle flag waved over his defences and the fighting over the wall became hand to hand and of the most desperate character; but more than half having already fallen, our line was found too weak to rout the enemy." "The advancing mass was so deep and wide as to raise doubt whether the Union line could stand against its weight and momentum, but a brief contact with bayonets crossed and muskets clubbed solved this doubt. The Confederates threw down their arms as if they simultaneously realized that the battle was lost. Many surrendered while others who escaped the pursuing shots fled across the field to Seminary Ridge."

"I have never seen a more formidable attack," wrote Hancock to Meade on the day of the battle, "with worse troops I should certainly have lost the day." Haskell's detailed account confirms this judgment, as does the study of Colonel Thomas L. Livermore, who was in the battle. Meade, "his face very white, the lines marked and earnest and full of care," rode up to Haskell and "asked in a sharp eager voice, 'How is it going here?' 'I believe,

General, the enemy's attack is repulsed,' was the reply. '*What! Is the assault already repulsed?*' 'It is, sir.' 'Thank God!' exclaimed Meade."

Lee, entirely alone, rode forward to encourage and rally his broken troops. His earlier excitement had passed and he betrayed no bitterness in his disappointment; his composure was really extraordinary and the spirit in which he spoke of the disaster was nothing short of sublime. "*All this has been my fault,*" he said. "It is I that have lost this fight."

Again he said, "this has been a sad day for us, a sad day." The fate of two of Pickett's brigadiers has been recorded; the third, Kemper, was "desperately wounded." "Seven of my colonels were killed," wrote Pickett, "and one was mortally wounded. Nine of my lieutenant colonels were wounded and three were killed. Only one field officer of my whole command was unhurt and the loss of my company officers was in proportion." Two of the three brigades were under the command of majors when the battle was over. The casualties of the division of 5000 were nearly 2900.

Pickett was unhurt and no one of his staff appears in the list of killed and wounded. He set forth at the head of his troops but did not go forward to the Union line; he stopped part way. The words he wrote to his betrothed on the following day have the ring of sincerity, "your soldier lives and mourns and but for you, he would rather, a million times rather, be back there with his dead to sleep for all time in an unknown grave." Nevertheless the question was naturally raised in the South whether he might share in the glory won by his division that day. History answering must follow the judgment of General Lee, who knew all the circumstances and was a preeminently truthful and impartial man. On July 9 Lee wrote to Pickett, "No one grieves more than I do at the loss suffered by your noble division in the recent conflict or honors it more for its bravery and gallantry." In a later, undated letter, he said, "You and your men have crowned yourselves with glory."

Pickett's charge, though a hazardous enterprise, was by no means a hopeless one and might well have succeeded had not Meade and Hancock been thoroughly prepared for it and had they not shown generalship of a high order. With Hooker in command

—the irresolute Hooker of Chancellorsville—there would have been a different story to relate. A comparison of the management of the two battles will confirm Halleck's judgment that Hooker "would have lost the army and the capital."

Moreover, Lee had to decide between an attack and an inglorious retreat. Divided, his army could live upon the country, but during a prolonged concentration it could not be fed. His decision was in keeping with his aggressive disposition, and his mistake seems to have been in underrating Meade's ability and in overestimating both the physical and moral damage done by his artillery fire. If the Confederates, who made the breach in the Union line could have held on, adequate support would undoubtedly have been given and Lee's idea of "one determined and united blow" delivered by his whole line might have been realized. And if he could have thoroughly beaten the Army of the Potomac, Baltimore and Washington would have been at his mercy. Perhaps the risk was worth taking.

Whether Meade should at once have made a countercharge across the valley, or attacked the Confederate right before dark on July 3, or occupied Lee's line of retreat that afternoon and made a general advance early the next morning are questions frequently discussed by military writers. Meade's own idea is disclosed in these words of July 5 to his wife. The Confederates "awaited one day expecting that flushed with success, I would attack them when they would play their old game of shooting us from behind breastworks."

"Under the cover of the night and heavy rain" of July 4, Lee began his retreat. Meade followed. The strain on a commanding general during such a campaign is shown by these words to his wife on July 8: "From the time I took command till to-day, now over ten days, I have not changed my clothes, have not had a regular night's rest and many nights not a wink of sleep and for several days did not even wash my face and hands, no regular food and all the time in a great state of mental anxiety. Indeed I think I have lived as much in this time as in the last thirty years." In this letter, which was written from Frederick, he said, "I think we shall have another battle before Lee can cross the river."

The heavy rains and resultant high water prevented Lee from

crossing the Potomac at once and, by July 11, Meade in his pursuit had come within striking distance of the Confederate Army. While proceeding with great caution, he had determined to make an attack on July 13; but as he was wavering in mind and feeling oppressed by his great responsibility he called a council of war. Five out of six of his corps commanders were opposed to the projected attack, which caused him to delay giving the orders for it. Meade devoted July 13 to an examination of the enemy's position, strength, and defensive works; and the next day, advancing his army for a reconnaissance in force, or an assault if the conditions should be favorable, he discovered that the Confederate Army had crossed the Potomac in the night. "The escape of Lee's army without another battle has created great dissatisfaction in the mind of the President," telegraphed Halleck [July 14]. Meade asked to be relieved of the command of the army: his application was refused.

During July 12 and 13, Lincoln was anxious and impatient and when, about noon of the 14th, he got word that Lee and his army were safely across the Potomac he was "deeply grieved." "And that, my God, is the last of this Army of the Potomac!" he said. "Meade has been pressed and urged, but only one of his generals was for an immediate attack, was ready to pounce on Lee; the rest held back. What does it mean, Mr. Welles? Great God! what does it mean?" "We had them within our grasp," he said. "We had only to stretch forth our hands and they were ours. And nothing I could say or do could make the army move." In a later private letter he developed this opinion. "I was deeply mortified," he said, "by the escape of Lee across the Potomac, because the substantial destruction of his army would have ended the war and because I believed such destruction was perfectly easy. . . . Perhaps my mortification was heightened because .I had always believed— making my belief a hobby possibly—that the main rebel army going north of the Potomac could never return, if well attended to; and because I was so greatly flattered in this belief by the operations at Gettysburg."

No one should accept this judgment of Lincoln's without considering Meade's defense. "Had I attacked Lee the day I proposed to do so," the General wrote, "and in the ignorance that then existed of his position, I have every reason to believe the attack would have been unsuccessful and would have resulted disastrously. This opinion is founded on the judgment of numerous distinguished officers after inspecting Lee's vacated works and position. . . . I had great responsibility thrown on me. On one side were the known and important fruits of victory, and, on the other, the equally important and terrible consequences of a defeat."

In the end it was Lincoln himself who suggested the sanest possible view of the episode. In a letter of July 21 he wrote, "I am now profoundly grateful for what was done without criticism for what was not done [at Gettysburg]. General Meade has my confidence as a brave and skilful officer and a true man." The change in Northern sentiment between July 1 and 4 reveals unmistakably the sense of a great deliverance.

The Generalship of Grant and Lee, 1864–65
by
Major General J. F. C. Fuller

Plans for the 1864 Campaign

Once established at Chattanooga, the situation became clear; clear to Grant, if not to his government, and, on December 7, 1863, he wrote as follows to Halleck:

". . . I take the liberty of suggesting a plan of campaign that I think will go far towards breaking down the rebellion before spring. . . . I propose . . . to move by way of New Orleans and Pascagoula on Mobile. I would hope to secure that place or its investment by the last of January. Should the enemy make an obstinate resistance at Mobile, I would fortify outside and leave a garrison sufficient to hold the garrison of the town, and with the balance of the army make a

campaign into the interior of Alabama and possibly Georgia.
. . . It seems to me that the move would secure the entire
States of Alabama and Mississippi and part of Georgia, or
force *Lee* to abandon Virginia and North Carolina. Without
his force the enemy have not got army enough to resist the
army I can take. . . ."

This plan was not, however, adopted, and after a brief campaign
in the Meridian area, in which Sherman did great damage to
the railroads, Grant was called to Washington on March 3, and
on the 9th was promoted to the rank of lieutenant-general and
placed in command of the entire military forces of the United
States.

In all Grant had eight weeks to prepare in; that is from March
10 to May 4, when his great combined campaign began. Not only
was he unknown in the East, but was acquainted with few of the
officers of the Army of the Potomac, only once before had he
visited Washington, and Lincoln he had never as yet met. The
situation which confronted him is described by Badeau [historian]
as follows: "A score of discordant armies; half a score of contrary
campaigns; confusion and uncertainty in the field, doubt and de-
jection, and sometimes despondency at home; battles whose object
none could perceive; a war whose issue none could foretell—it was
chaos itself before light had appeared, or order was evolved"—and
only eight weeks to evolve it in! . . .

Considering the possibilities of a coastal move, such as McClellan had carried out in 1862, he soon discarded his idea in favor
of an overland advance, for such a movement would cover Washington. To effect this operation he decided to move direct upon
Lee, whilst from Chattanooga Sherman maneuvered against Lee's
rear; the object of the Army of the Potomac, the immediate command of which he left to General Meade, being to hold Lee by
constant attack. On April 9 he wrote to Meade: *"Lee's* army will
be your objective point. Wherever *Lee's* army goes you will go
also." The Army of the Potomac, supported by the Ninth Corps
under Burnside, was to constitute the fulcrum of his strategy; on
it Sherman's lever at Chattanooga was to work.

Soon after assuming supreme command he sent Sherman a
letter and a map, which were received by that general on April 2.

Unfortunately the letter has been lost, but the map clearly explains its contents, for on it are drawn a series of blue lines showing the proposed operations. Sherman answered this letter on April 5 saying: "From that map I see all, and glad am I that there are minds now at Washington able to devise; and for my part, if we can keep our counsels I believe I have the men and ability to march square up to the position assigned to me and to hold it. . . ." Again, on April 10, he wrote: "Your two letters of April 4th are now before me and afford me infinite satisfaction. That we are now all to act in a common plan on a common center, looks like enlightened war." . . .

Whilst Sherman was advancing, Meade's army was to be supported by two flanking armies—Sigel's operating in the Shenandoah Valley, and Butler's based on Fortress Monroe. Sigel was to move on Staunton and threaten the Virginia and Tennessee and the Virginia Central railroads . . . whilst Butler was to move on Petersburg and Richmond. Realizing that the command of the sea was the backbone of his strategy, and well aware that efficient strategy is based upon adequate supply, Grant decided to move Meade's army as close to the coast as possible, for though on account of the nature of the country this was tactically a disadvantage, strategically it was essential, as the sea coast would enable him to change his base of supply at will; further, no troops would be required to protect this line of supply.

On April 29 he sent the following dispatch to Halleck, now Chief of Staff at Washington:

> "The Army will start with fifteen days' supplies; all the country affords will be gathered as we go along. This will no doubt enable us to go twenty-five days without further supplies, unless we should be forced to keep in the country between the Rapidan and the Chickahominy, in which case supplies might be required by way of the York or the Rappahannock Rivers. . . . When we get once established on the James River, there will be no further necessity of occupying the road south of Bull Run." . . .

Having elaborated his strategic plan, Grant turned to tactics: What was to be his method of fighting? He knew full well Lee's liking for maneuver, he also knew that the Confederate cause was on the wane, and what Lee dreaded most of all was a heavy casualty list. He decided, therefore, that his tactics must be offensive; that Lee's army must be reduced in strength by constant attack; that it must be thrown on the defensive, and that once it was reduced to defend itself freedom of movement would be denied to it.

Whilst this plan was being thought out and prepared for, what was happening in the Confederate camp? In September, 1862, Longstreet had pointed out to Lee that the next campaign should be fought in Tennessee, and that a defensive attitude should be assumed in Virginia. Lee regarded such a campaign with doubt, and all that came of this suggestion was that Longstreet was sent to reinforce Bragg at Chattanooga.

In December Beauregard sketched out a comprehensive plan of campaign which was forwarded to Richmond. He pointed out that the total available forces were 210,000, and that unless the Government ordered the army to concentrate against one decisive point, the war would end by it being beaten in detail. He suggested withdrawing 40,000 men from the East and creating an army of 100,000 strong in the West to operate against Grant by moving against his communications from about Knoxville. Nothing came of this plan though Lee also saw the danger in the West. On December 3 he pointed out to Davis "that the enemy may penetrate Georgia," and "I think that every effort should be made to concentrate as large a force as possible under the best commander to ensure the discomfiture of Grant's army." To which Davis answered: "Could you consistently go to Dalton?" To which Lee replied: "I can if desired, but of the expediency of the measure you can judge better than I. Unless it is intended that I should take permanent command, I can see no good that will result, even if in that event any could be accomplished." . . .

The winter of 1864 was one of great anxiety to Lee. The army was in rags, half-starved, and lacking in supplies, in clothing, shoes, and equipment. Desertions were frequent, for life in the bivouacs on the Rapidan was all but unbearable; yet as Chesney says, at this period the Confederacy was not so short of men as of discipline, not because the men were indifferent soldiers, they were superb soldiers, but because the administration of the army was so utterly rotten that even the staunchest soldiers succumbed to it. Added to these anxieties, as we have seen, was the doubt in Lee's mind as to what Grant would do. At length this uncertainty ended, for on April 5, 1864, Lee wrote to Davis that it is apparent that Richmond is Grant's object, and the same day he issued a general order—"The army will be immediately placed in condition to march." His opinion was that "a great battle would take place on the Rapidan," and his thoughts were at once attracted towards their old center—a distracting raid down the Valley. . . .

From the Wilderness to Cold Harbor

Grant's army, that is the Army of the Potomac and Burnside's corps, numbered about 115,000 officers and men of all arms "equipped for duty." Sheridan's Cavalry Corps (13,287) covered the front from northwest of Culpeper Court House on the right to near Richardsville on the left; Army headquarters and the Fifth Corps, under Warren (25,663), were at and around Culpeper Court House; the Second Corps, under Hancock (28,333), south of Brandy Station; the Sixth Corps, Sedgwick (24,213) north of this place, and the Ninth Corps, Burnside (22,762), stretched from a little north of Rappahannock Station to within a few miles of Manassas Junction. South of the Rapidan stood Lee, as already described.

On May 4 and 5 all the Federal armies moved forward, on a common plan and towards a common center: Grant on Lee, Sherman on Johnston, Sigel up the Valley, and Butler towards Richmond. It was a wonderful object lesson in cooperative effort when compared to the individual and unconnected operations which had hitherto characterized Federal strategy.

Strategically Grant's immediate problem, namely, the movement of the Army of the Potomac, was not difficult once the Rapidan was crossed, but tactically it was a plunge into a jungle in which numbers were of little account, and local knowledge of the highest value, where cavalry were virtually dismounted and artillery spiked, and where every extra wagon was an encumbrance. In the Wilderness of Virginia Hooker had met his fate, and Meade, who, in 1863, had penetrated its fringes, had rapidly withdrawn from them and sought safety in more open ground. Here the clash took place on the 5th, and of the fighting Badeau says: it was "a wrestle as blind as midnight, a gloom that made manoeuvres impracticable, a jungle where regiments stumbled on each other and on the enemy by turns, firing sometimes into their own ranks, and guided often only by the crackling of the bushes or the cheers and cries that rose from the depths around."

Tactically, Grant was not prepared for this type of fighting—Indian warfare. His formations were far too heavy, his lines of attack too cumbersome, and his tactics too rigid. He had hoped, yet scarcely expected, to traverse the Wilderness without a battle; he should, therefore, on the 4th have pushed on as far as he could; but he did not do so, apparently because he was afraid of uncovering his trains. Had he, in place of attacking Lee, or rather counterattacking Lee when *Lee* attacked, entrenched his position, let Lee attack it, and under its protection had he continued his movement forward, throwing up entrenchments on his right flank as he advanced, it is possible that he might have got through the Wilderness at considerably less loss, and yet have inflicted an equal loss on the Army of Northern Virginia, the tactics and very deficiencies in the organization of which made it more adaptable for forest warfare.

On the 5th, as Swinton [a historian] says: "The action . . . was not so much a battle as the fierce grapple of two mighty wrestlers suddenly meeting." On the 6th it was the same, both sides were fought to a standstill, and under cover of night, Lee withdrew his army behind its entrenchments.

Tactically this battle was indecisive; the losses were heavy, Grant's numbering 17,666, and Lee's, though unknown, cannot have been less than 7,750. Strategically it was the greatest Federal victory yet won in the East, for Lee was now thrown on the defensive—he was held. Thus, within forty-eight hours of crossing the Rapidan, did Grant gain his object—the fixing of Lee.

In this the first battle of the campaign, Grant's will to succeed, cost what it might, soon revealed to Lee that, in spite of the forest and the shelter it afforded, numbers in the end would count. Again

Hannibal on horseback. After a painting by Ferris. THE BETTMANN ARCHIVE

Alfred von Schlieffen, Prussian general and military writer, chief of the general staff. THE BETTMANN ARCHIVE

Painting of Sir Francis Drake. WIDE WORLD PHOTOS

Marlborough leading his troops at the Battle of Blenheim, August 13, 1704. Engraving. THE BETTMANN ARCHIVE

John Trumbull's painting of General Burgoyne surrendering at Saratoga. WIDE WORLD PHOTOS

Duke of Wellington. Painted by
Goya, 1812. THE BETTMANN
ARCHIVE

Painting of President Andrew
Jackson by Samuel Wald. WIDE
WORLD PHOTOS

Painting of Napoleon long before
Waterloo. WIDE WORLD PHOTOS

General Robert E. Lee on his horse, Traveller. WIDE WORLD PHOTOS

General Ulysses S. Grant during the Civil War. WIDE WORLD PHOTOS

Marshal Joffre, hero of The Marne. WIDE WORLD PHOTOS

General Erwin Rommel in North Africa. WIDE WORLD PHOTOS

General Douglas MacArthur wading ashore at Leyte. WIDE WORLD PHOTOS

Field Marshal General F. Paulus after his surrender at Stalingrad. WIDE WORLD PHOTOS

General V.I. Chuikov after Stalingrad. WIDE WORLD PHOTOS

General A.I. Yeremenko, leader of 4th Ukranian Army. WIDE WORLD PHOTOS

Admiral William F. Halsey before the Leyte operations. WIDE
WORLD PHOTOS

*Four Allied generals confer in a hayfield in France
after Normandy. From left they are: Lieutenant General Omar N. Bradley, 12th Army Commander; General Sir Bernard L. Montgomery, Allied Field Commander in Western France; Lieutenant General M.C.
Dempsey, Commander British Second Army and Lieutenant General Courtney H. Hodges, U.S. First Army
Commander.* WIDE WORLD PHOTOS

and again throughout this campaign he writes: "Thanks to a merciful Providence our casualties have been small." It was remarkable also in that, as Colonel Lyman says: "The great feature of this campaign is the extraordinary use made of earthworks. . . . When our line advances, there is the line of the enemy, nothing showing but the bayonets, and the battle-flags stuck on the top of the works. It is a rule that when the Rebels halt, the first day gives them a good rifle pit; the second a regular infantry parapet with artillery in position; and the third a parapet with an abattis in front and entrenched batteries behind. Sometimes they put this three days' work into the first twenty-four hours. Our men can, and do, do the same; but remember, our object is offense—to advance. You would be amazed to see how this country is intersected with field works, extending for miles and miles in different directions and marking the different strategic lines taken up by the two armies, as they warily move about each other." . . .

As was so often the case, Lee's staff duties were muddled; nevertheless, on the morning of the 7th he ordered Anderson, now in command of Longstreet's corps, for, like Jackson, this general had been wounded by his own men, to move to Spottsylvania on the morning of the 8th; but as Anderson could find no place to bivouac, he did so that night, and as it happened short-headed Grant by a few hours.

In spite of his losses and the confusion which such a battle rendered inevitable, Grant was in no way dismayed. A lesser man would have halted and reorganized, but Grant determined to push on. To a staff officer he said: "To-night *Lee* will be retreating South," and within twenty-four hours of the battle being drawn, the Army of the Potomac was heading for Spottsylvania. There he found Anderson blocking his way, and there he learned that Sherman's and Sigel's advances were progressing, but that Butler was in difficulties. In order to relieve the pressure on Butler's army he ordered Sheridan and the whole of the Cavalry Corps to "cut loose" and to proceed on a raid against the north of Richmond.

At Spottsylvania Lee ably entrenched himself between the rivers Po and Ny, his entrenchments taking the form of an inverted V. This enabled him to place the bulk of his men in line, and to use the garrison of one face of the V to reinforce the other as occasion demanded. The weak point was the apex, and this was not unnoticed by Grant, who, on the 10th, launched an attack under Colonel Upton against its western face and captured some 1,200 prisoners. This attack was so successful that he decided to employ the whole of Hancock's corps in an assault upon the apex of the salient. At 4:35 A.M. on the 12th Hancock moved forward through the mud and mist, marching on a compass bearing, and in massed formation struck the Confederate entrenchments and surged over them; but his assault formations were so dense that the mass of his men at once melted into an uncontrollable mob. "You could see," says General Barlow, "men of all commands intermingled and lying, in some places forty deep, on the other side of the captured works, and on the slope which ran down from them." At 5:45 A.M. came the first Confederate counterattack; then the struggle for the "Bloody Angle" began, in which Lee lost between 9,000 and 10,000 officers and men, and Grant 6,820.

Grant has been blamed for these persistent attacks, and mainly because it is not realized that had he attempted to maneuver Lee out of his position, which he might have done, he would have forced Lee back towards Butler. This was the very thing he did not want to do, for by holding him as far away from Butler as he could, he facilitated his advance along the James River, which was causing as great a consternation in Richmond as Jackson's in the Valley had to Washington two years before, which shows the wisdom of this distracting movement. . . .

Thus far Grant's central idea had been that wherever Lee went Meade should follow; for this he now substituted a bolder one, namely, wherever Meade went *Lee* should be compelled to follow. On the 20th Hancock's corps was moved south to Guinea's Station, and the next day Lee discovering this move began to withdraw from his entrenchments; but he was too wary a general to get involved with Hancock; instead he placed himself between Richmond and his enemy by falling back on a position in the neighborhood of Hanover Junction immediately south of the North Anna River. . . .

On the afternoon of the 25th Grant withdrew his forces across the North Anna, and directed Meade to move on Hanover Town. This movement, which was a complex one on account of the proximity of the two armies, was carried out successfully, and a new battle front was established on Totopotomoy Creek. Lee followed suit, both armies drifting southwards, Lee covering Richmond and Grant hoping against hope to compel Lee to come out of his trenches. By June 1 both armies confronted each other in the vicinity of Old and New Cold Harbor; Lee's right flank resting on the Chickahominy and his left extending north of Gaines's Mill, the locality in which McClellan was repulsed in 1862.

On this ground was fought the battle of Cold Harbor, a battle which in the history of the Civil War has been given a prominence it does not deserve. It was not a great battle or a decisive one, Lee's losses were slight and Grant's not excessive, for they amounted to 5,617, of which 1,100 were killed and 4,517 wounded; by most historians these losses have been grossly exaggerated. Its notoriety may be traced to political reason. The North was growing weary; intrigue was rife; the presidential election was approaching, and Lincoln's position was by no means secure. All hoped for speedy victory, and as battle followed battle Grant's stock fell in terms of public opinion.

Grant was not blind to this situation. He realized the urgency of an early success; but he also realized that if he now refrained from attacking Lee, politically this would be construed as the failure of the entire campaign. The alternative was a frontal assault, and rightly, so I think, he decided on one, but his method was faulty in the extreme.

First he postponed his attack twenty-four hours, timing the assault for 4:30 A.M. on June 3, which gave Lee ample time to strengthen his position. Secondly, he ordered an attack *all along the line* in place of massing his guns opposite a fraction of Lee's front, and then after a heavy bombardment assaulting this fraction. As it happened, each of his divisions was taken in enfilade as well as decimated by frontal fire, and all were so severely handled that the attack was decided in less than an hour. General McMahon says that the time taken in the actual advance was not more than eight minutes; Swinton says ten.

Grant's military excuse for fighting this battle was that as Lee refused to assume the offensive he considered him "whipped," and though afterwards he regretted ever having fought it, he undoubtedly believed that the morale of Lee's army was spent, and remembering the successful assaults at Missionary Ridge and Spottsylvania, he considered that one tremendous blow would overthrow his antagonist. Of Grant's offensive tactics Badeau says: "I have often heard him declare that there comes a time in every hard-fought battle when both armies are nearly or quite exhausted, and it seems impossible for either to do more; this he believed the turning-point; whichever after first renews the fight, is sure to win." Unfortunately for Grant, though he expected the highest heroism from his own men, he failed to realize that his enemy was of the same stock.

The Petersburg Campaign

Grant was checked but not checkmated; to a lesser man Cold Harbor would have been a death blow, but to Grant it was to prove the stepping-stone of one of the most audacious and difficult operations of war ever attempted. Halleck suggested that Grant should invest Richmond from the north bank of the James; but as its most important lines of supply lay on its southern side, Grant saw that this suggestion was worthless. As Lee's front could no longer be attacked, he decided to attack Lee's rear—"to move the army to the south side of the James River by the enemy's right flank," in order to "cut off all his sources of supply except by the [James River] canal."

Meanwhile, as Beauregard had foreseen, Lee had been forced back to the defenses of Richmond, and even now in place of concentrating, as Beauregard suggested, he dispersed his forces. Not only did he send Breckinridge's division back to the Valley, but, on June 11, Early was ordered to proceed to this same locality and threaten Washington. It was his old game, now a little worn by constant application. This time there was no panic; at Fort Stevens outside the Northern capital General Wright, in command of the reinforcing Sixth Corps which Grant had sent back from the James, met General McCook, who pointing out Early's pickets a few rods from the work said: "Well, Wright, there they are; I've nothing here but quartermaster's men and hospital bummers; the enemy can walk right in if he only tries; let's go down below and get some lager beer." Early could have walked in, but had he done so he would never have walked out again; so, wisely, he retired.

The detachment of Early seems to have had a curious psychological influence upon Lee. On June 7 Beauregard had telegraphed Bragg: "Should Grant have left Lee's front, he doubtless intends operations against Richmond along James River, probably on south side." He pointed out the extreme danger Petersburg was in. Two days later he writes: "The present movements of Grant's army have a significance which cannot have escaped your observation. He clearly seeks to move around Lee's forces, by an advance upon his left flank, in the direction of the James River, with a view to operate between that river and the Chickahominy, and in case of his meeting with no adequate resistance to plant himself on both sides of the former, throwing across it a pontoon bridge, as close to Chaffin's Bluff as circumstances may permit, and failing in this scheme, he may continue his rotary motion around Richmond, and attack by concentrating the whole of his army on the south side of the James River, using the fortified position at Bermuda Hundred Neck as a base for his operations." . . .

Grant's plan entailed the seizing of Petersburg before Lee could come to the support of Beauregard, who held the city with a small garrison. General Smith and the Eighteenth Corps were detailed for this operation. This corps was withdrawn from the Chickahominy on the 12th, and on the 14th Smith reported to General Butler, who strongly reinforced him. On the morning of the 15th he set out, and at about 10:00 A.M. came under range of the guns of Petersburg. From this hour until 5:00 P.M. he reconnoitered the position, and at length ordering his artillery up, discovered that the horses had been sent to water; this delayed the attack until 7:00 P.M. By 9:00 P.M., hearing that the first position was carried, he deemed "it wiser to hold what we had than . . . to lose what we had gained. . . ."; these are his own words.

Smith must have known that Beauregard's force was a weak one, actually it consisted of 2,200 artillery and infantry, and Smith had 18,000 troops. His delay and caution were inexcusable, he "feared to run any risk" and "preferred to sleep on his arms that night."

The importance of Petersburg to Richmond and the Confederate forces was so great, and its occupation so vital to the fulfilment of Grant's strategy that General Smith's lack of energy may well be considered one of the most serious errors of the entire campaign. Though a highly educated soldier, this failure proved him to be totally unfitted for command. Muddle now followed muddle; Hancock, who should have followed Smith's corps at short interval, lost hours of invaluable time in awaiting an issue of rations, and when he caught up with Smith, this general made no proper use of his corps.

Meanwhile, on the 13th, Lee discovered that Grant had left his front and simultaneously Early began his northern movement. In place of recalling Early, the next day he wrote to Davis: "I think the enemy must be preparing to move south of the James," and further: "I apprehend that he may be sending troops up the James River with the view of getting possession of Petersburg before we can reinforce it." He repeated this apprehension on the following day, and also wrote to Davis saying that "Early was in motion this morning at 3 o'clock and by daylight was clear of our camp. . . . *If you think it better to recall him,* please send a trusty messenger to overtake him to-night. I do not know that the necessity for his presence to-day is greater than it was yesterday. His troops would make us more secure here, but success in the Valley would relieve our difficulties that at present press heavily upon us." . . .

Fortunately for Lee, Beauregard played his part with consummate skill. He was in fact so weak that he was compelled to call in the garrison of the works at Bermuda Hundred. This unbottled Butler, and enabled him to advance and place his army between Petersburg and Richmond, which must inevitably have resulted in the fall of the capital. Once again he blundered, and lost the opportunity of a life's time. Meade, meanwhile, persisted in attacking Petersburg at its strongest point, and in consequence wrecked Grant's strategy.

On the 15th Beauregard reported his position at Petersburg to be critical, and Lee answered that he did "not know the position of Grant's army." Beauregard was attacked on the 15th, 16th, and 17th, and sent message after message asking for support; Lee, however, did nothing until the 17th, when he ordered A. P. Hill to move to Chaffin's Bluff. Not until the 18th would he believe Beauregard's reports, when he telegraphed Early, "Grant is in front of Petersburg. Will be opposed there. Strike as quickly as you can, and if circumstances authorize, carry out the original plan, or move upon Petersburg without delay."

Between June 13 and 18 no impartial critic can doubt that Lee's generalship was of a low order. General Alexander writes: "Thus the last, and perhaps the best, chances of Confederate success were not lost in the repulse at Gettysburg, nor in any combat of arms. They were lost during three days of lying in camp, believing that Grant was hemmed in by the broad part of the James below City Point, and had nowhere to go but to come and attack us." Grant's constant attacks had hypnotized Lee into believing that his adversary had no other cards to play. He sees that Grant may cross the James, then he doubts that he will do so, and stakes all on his old bluff—a Valley raid. When he arrived at Petersburg at 11:30 A.M. on the 18th, Beauregard urged him to order Hill's and Anderson's corps to attack Grant's left flank and rear. "Lee refused his assent, on the ground that his troops needed rest, and that the defensive having been thus far so advantageous to him against Grant's offensive north of the James, and to Beauregard, at Petersburg, he preferred continuing the same mode of warfare." This meant the assumption of a passive defensive, and Lee knew it, for, on June 21, he wrote to Davis: "I hope your Excy will put no reliance in what I can do individually, for I feel that will be very little. The enemy has a strong position, and is able to deal us more injury than from any other point he has ever taken. Still we must try and defeat them. I fear he will not attack us but advance by regular approaches. He is so situated that I cannot attack him."

From the date of this dispatch, that is from the date Grant began to lay siege to Petersburg, the end of the Confederacy, like a gathering storm cloud, loomed over the horizon of the war, daily growing greater and more leaden. Some reckoned on a Northern political collapse, a refusal to renominate Lincoln, and the consequent abandonment of the war; but Lee knew that as long as Grant held him at Richmond and Petersburg this was an event so unlikely as to be beyond practical politics. Grant's tactics of attrition were telling, and during the siege of Petersburg they continued to tell for his shuttle-cock operations of feinting here and striking there, says Lee, "fatigue and exhaust our men, greatly impairing their efficiency in battle." The only hope was to break this stranglehold, to cut loose from Richmond and transfer the struggle to some other area. Lee looked furtively at Early. On June 29 he wrote to Davis: "I still think it is our policy to draw the attention of the enemy to his own territory. It may force Grant to attack me"; and then, on July 11: "I fear I shall not be able to attack him to advantage, and if I cannot I think it would be well to reinforce General Early"; but where from?

Turning to Grant, we find no recrimination, no excuses, no blame. His plan had been wrecked by the incompetence of his subordinates. He once again had failed, but he refused to accept failure, and instead modified his strategy without changing its central idea, which was to hold on to Lee. As he could not destroy Lee he would invest Petersburg, and then work round to the south of the city against Lee's lines of supply, the chief of which were the Weldon, the South Side, and the Danville railroads. . . . Though means vary, his idea remains constant, to hold fast to Lee so that Sherman's maneuver may continue.

Between June 18 and the end of October Grant waged incessant war on these railways, ever threatening Petersburg and so compelling the Confederate Government and Lee to concentrate on its protection. He realized that as long as Petersburg was in danger Richmond was threatened; not only would Lee be compelled to maintain a powerful force in its neighborhood, but by doing so it would be most difficult for him to detach troops to oppose Sheridan now operating in the Valley, or to reinforce Johnston.

The Campaigns of Sheridan and Sherman

Whilst Grant was moving southwards through the Wilderness, attacking at Spottsylvania and on the Chickahominy, crossing the James and besieging Petersburg, it must be remembered that two other campaigns were in progress, namely, one in the Valley of Virginia and the other in Georgia, and that these two campaigns were as closely linked to his own as his was to them. These three were in fact essential parts of one grand campaign, and can only be correctly appreciated when related to each other.

In the Valley, on May 15, General Sigel had been badly defeated at Newmarket, and was replaced by General Hunter who, on June 17, advanced to within five miles of Lynchburg. . . . The next day meeting with Early's corps, sent north by Lee as already related, he retired into the Kanawha Valley, leaving the Shenandoah Valley open to Early, who forthwith advanced down it, and on July 11 threatened Washington. Foreseeing what was likely to happen, on the 5th Grant had already sent the Sixth Corps to Washington; in consequence, on the 14th, Early recrossed the Potomac and retired towards Strasburg. In order to close the Valley Grant determined systematically to devastate it, and to carry out this work General Sheridan was given the command of the troops in that area on August 7.

At first Sheridan got into difficulties with the politicians at Washington, which necessitated Grant visiting him. Then he got into his stride, and decisively defeated Early at Opequon Creek on September 19. Following him up he again defeated him at Fisher's Hill on the 22nd, and again at Cedar Creek on October 19. These victories had a most encouraging influence on the political situation.

Meanwhile Sherman's lever was moving forward on Grant's fulcrum—the Army of the Potomac; it consisted of 100,000 men and 254 guns, and was opposed by Johnston at the head of 43,000 men at Dalton. Imaginative and fertile in resources, Sherman saw clearly that in spite of his numerical superiority every mile he advanced would lengthen his communications and so reduce his strength. He determined, therefore, not to do what Johnston wished him to do, namely, attack him in strongly fortified positions; but instead, by constant maneuver, to keep a grip on him whilst Grant was hammering Lee in the East. On May 4 he advanced his united forces, the Army of the Cumberland, under Thomas, in the center, the Army of the Tennessee, under McPherson, on the right, and the Army of the Ohio, under Schofield, on the left; his tactical idea being: to advance on his enemy, gain contact with him, pin him down, and then, by outflanking him, compel him to abandon his position and fall back. This he successfully did at Dalton, again on the Oostanaula River, at Etowah, Allatoona, New Hope Church, and Marietta. At Kenesaw Mountain, on June 18, he attacked his enemy but with no great success; nevertheless Johnston, on July 2, withdrew to the Chattahoochee River, where, on the 17th, the Confederate Government, not understanding his able tactics and disapproving of his constant retreats, replaced him by General Hood.

Hood, who was of an impetuous nature, attacked Sherman three times, and on each occasion was repulsed with heavy losses. Being compelled to fall back on Atlanta, Sherman followed him up; there Hood's position became untenable, and on September 1 "the gate city of the South" was in Sherman's hands. . . .

Five Forks and Appomattox Court House

On January 11, 1865, Lee wrote to Seddon: "We have but two days' supplies"; on the 19th: "There is great suffering in the Army for want of soap"; on the 27th he mentions the "alarming frequency of desertions"; on February 4 he acknowledged his "confirmation by the Senate as General-in-Chief of the Armies of the Confederate States"; and then, on the 22nd, he hinted to Breckinridge, the new secretary of war, that he can do nothing until he abandons the James River. The date of this announcement coincides with that of the fall of Wilmington, and without Wilmington Richmond was throttled. Lee seems to have realized this, for again on this same day, February 22, he wrote to Longstreet: If forced to withdraw, "I propose to concentrate at or near Burkeville. . . . We might also seize the opportunity of striking at Grant, should he pursue us rapidly, or at Sherman, before they could unite."

On this same day, in spite of the fact that he was now commander-in-chief, he suggested to Breckinridge that General Johnston should be sent south to command against Sherman, adding, "if he was ordered to report to me I would place him there on duty." This wise move appears to have originated out of two suggestions made to Davis by General Beauregard, one on February 3, and the other on February 21, that the only policy to adopt was to stop

Sherman. On February 22 Johnston was detailed to do so, but it is Lee who should have gone south, for a general-in-chief should always face the position of greatest danger and importance. With Sherman in North Carolina, Richmond had become a theater of secondary value. Lee should have realized this for directly Fort Fisher, the key to Wilmington, fell on January 15. Perhaps he did, but his subservience to Davis was so complete that he refused to move; he was paralyzed by his theory that duty demanded that he should suggest and must obey but should never decide.

General Gordon informs us that during the first week in March he saw Lee, and placed before him three suggestions, which in order of precedence were:

(1) To make the best possible terms with the enemy;
(2) To abandon Richmond, join Johnston, and strike at Sherman;
(3) To strike at Grant.

Lee's answers were typical of the man: As regards the first he said: "that he scarcely felt authorized to suggest to the civil authorities the advisability of making terms." As regards the second, "he doubted whether the authorities in Richmond would consent to the movement," besides his men were in a starving condition, and he could not move half his artillery or trains. Whereupon Gordon urged him to assume his powers as commander-in-chief, and to point out to the government the absolute necessity of securing favorable terms of peace while the army was still organized and resisting. Then Gordon says: "His long training as a soldier and his extreme delicacy were still in his way—a barrier against even apparent interference in any department not his own and against any step not in accord with the strictest military and official ethics. He said as much, but then added: 'I will go, and will send for you again on my return from Richmond.' . . ." On his return "he said nothing could be done at Richmond. The Congress did not seem to appreciate the situation. Of President Davis he spoke in terms of strong eulogy: of the strength of his convictions, of his devotedness, of his remarkable faith in the possibility of still winning our independence, and of his unconquerable will power. The nearest approach to complaint or criticism were the words which I can never forget: 'You know that the President is very pertinacious in opinion and purpose.' . . . 'What then is to be done, General?' He replied that there seemed to be but one thing that we could do—fight. To stand still was death. It could only be death if we fought and failed."

Grant's plan for 1865 was to draw the net closer and closer round his antagonist. His first problem was to occupy the remaining seaports—Charleston, Mobile, and Wilmington, of which the last was by far the most important. Its entrance was protected by Fort Fisher which, as I have already noted, fell on January 15. The capture of this fort was, says Vice-President Stephens, a blow equal to the loss of Vicksburg.

Hood disposed of, and Fort Fisher in Federal hands, Grant, fearing that Lee might attempt to break away and unite with Johnston, decided to watch him rather than attack him, holding his army in readiness to spring upon Lee should he abandon Richmond. Next he decided to close four columns in on Lee: Sherman to advance on Branchville, Columbia, and eventually on Raleigh; Schofield to be transferred from Tennessee to North Carolina, secure Wilmington, and then occupy Goldsboro, in order to open a base of supplies for Sherman; Sheridan to move on Lynchburg; Thomas to move on Selma, sending a strong force of cavalry under General Stoneman towards Columbia; and Canby to take and occupy Mobile.

Thomas's movement, on account of his extreme slowness, failed; Schofield, however, occupied Wilmington on February 22, and Sherman, advancing north on February 1, after a march of 425 miles joined hands with Schofield at Goldsboro on March 23. Meanwhile Sheridan set out towards Staunton, annihilated the remnants of Early's army, occupied Charlottesville, and then turning south rejoined the Army of the Potomac on March 19.

Lee's situation was now a desperate one. On February 19 he warned his government that Richmond might have to be abandoned, and on March 23 hearing from Johnston that Sherman had joined hands with Schofield, two days later, apparently to disengage himself, he assumed the offensive, attacked Fort Steadman and failed hopelessly on account of faulty staff arrangements. The initiative was now Grant's absolutely, and not waiting for Sherman, who was unable to advance on the Roanoke River until

April 10, Grant decided to strike, and on the 24th issued his orders.

His plan was to hold the trenches north of the James with one corps—the Twenty-fifth; mass two, the Ninth and the Sixth, in the Petersburg area ready to break the enemy's front should Lee strip it; the remainder, in all 66,000 men, preceded by Sheridan and 14,000 cavalry, to move west and turn Lee's right flank.

Hearing that Lee was concentrating on his right, in spite of the rain which in many places had rendered the ground impassable for wheeled traffic, Grant, on the 30th, ordered Sheridan to seize the road junction at Five Forks. . . . This he did on April 1, decisively beating General Pickett. The result of this battle was that the South Side railroad was now at Grant's mercy, consequently the fate of Petersburg was sealed.

Learning of this success, in order to prevent a concentration against Sheridan, and to enable him to advance on the South Side railroad, Grant ordered an assault along the whole of the Petersburg front. This took place at 4:00 A.M. on April 2, the Confederate works west of Petersburg being penetrated and Lee's army cut in two. All west of Lee's center was now being driven by Sheridan beyond the Appomattox, and all east of it was forced into Petersburg by Grant wheeling his left flank inwards. Early on the 3rd Petersburg was occupied, and Richmond was at last in Federal hands.

Correctly surmising that Lee would follow the Danville railroad in order to gain the Roanoke, Grant decided not to follow him and become involved with his rear guards, but instead to get ahead of him and intercept his line of retreat. On the 3rd, before leaving Petersburg, Grant had written to Sheridan saying: "The first object of present movement will be to intercept Lee's army and the second to secure Burkesville"; consequently Sheridan continued his movement westwards, intercepting Lee's retreat on Danville; whereupon Lee decided to march upon Farmville. He was now to all intents and purposes hemmed in; on his left was Sheridan and the Sixth Corps, on his right the Fifth Corps, and in rear of him the Second; nevertheless he pushed on, deciding to cross to the left bank of the Appomattox at Farmville and gain Danville by the road leading through Appomattox Court House.

On April 2 Lee had turned the head of his army towards Amelia

Court House, his one idea now being to join up with Johnston. Not only was this move weeks, if not months, too late, but as he advanced, his half-starved army began to dissolve, men deserting by hundreds and thousands. Yet, on the 1st, at Richmond, or within easy call of this city, were stored up 4,000,000 rations of meat and 2,500,000 of bread, without counting considerable supplies of tea, coffee, and sugar. Lee could have drawn on these immense supplies not only before the evacuation of Richmond but during it; this is made abundantly clear by Jefferson Davis; but he issued no orders concerning them, and when asked at what point on the railroad he would like supplies sent, he replied "that the military situation made it impossible to answer." The final dictum of history must be that whatever excellence Lee possessed as a strategist or as a tactician, he was the worst quartermaster-general in history, and that, consequently, his strategy had no foundations, with the result that his tactics never once resulted in an overwhelming and decisive victory.

As the Army of Northern Virginia straggled onwards to its doom, Grant ordered the Second and Sixth Corps to move north of the Appomattox and press the enemy's rear, while Sheridan, the Fifth and Ord's Corps, were directed on to Appomattox Station, as information had been received that Lee intended to resupply his army at that place. On the evening of the 8th Sheridan reached Appomattox Station, from where he pushed Lee's advanced troops back towards the Court House. On the morning of the 9th Lee advanced to attack him, when Sheridan's cavalry, "parting to the right and left," disclosed the Fifth and Ord's Corps in line behind them. Simultaneously the Second and Sixth Corps arrived in rear of Lee's men. The white flag was then raised, and a little later, at McLean's house, in "a naked little parlour containing a table and two or three chairs," Robert E. Lee at the head of 7,892 infantry with arms, 2,100 cavalry, 63 guns and not a single ration, surrendered to Ulysses S. Grant.

CHAPTER VIII

THE FIRST BATTLE
OF THE MARNE, 1914

The first battle of the Marne, lasting but three days, took place between September 6 and 9, in 1914, a month after the German armies had invaded France and were poised to take Paris. The German armies had several advantages—besides the advantage of surprise—in the continuity of their leadership. The elder Count Bernhard von Moltke had led the Prussian armies into France in 1870. His nephew, Count Ludwig von Moltke, had been along with him in the Franco-Prussian War, becoming his adjutant later. Now Ludwig von Moltke, heading the German armies, was putting into action the much-studied Schlieffen Plan, after a fashion.

Marshal Joffre and General Gallieni led the French armies. The British were commanded by Sir John French. The German defeat at the first battle of the Marne was due to the combined tactical brilliance and execution that both Joffre and Gallieni initiated during the three days that might have won the war for Germany. Instead, on September 10, the Germans were in full retreat.

General Joseph Simon Gallieni (1849–1916) had been appointed the military governor of Paris after the war began. It was Gallieni who created a new form of transport, the 2000 Parisian taxis that took 50,000 soldiers to the front—a major factor in winning the battle. Military historians have argued ever since about whether it was Joffre or Gallieni, or both men, who created the plans and inspired the French victory. Gallieni had a long history as an able commander, soldier and executive in the French colonies of Tonkin, the Sudan and Madagascar. In 1915 Gallieni became the minister of war under the Briand government, but he resigned, partially because of ill health, when his plans to reorganize the French command were not backed up by the Briand cabinet. Like Joffre, despite their differences, he is considered a hero of the Marne.

Marshal Joseph Jacques Cesaire Joffre (1852–1931) had a distinguished career as a military engineer in the French colonies, especially in Timbuktu. After serving as a professor at the War College, he was appointed commander-in-chief of the French forces in 1911. When World War I broke out, he became the supreme commander. This includes a selection from his book *The Personal Memoirs of Joffre,* a vivid distillation of the armies at battle and the brilliant maneuvering during those early days of September.

Following Joffre's account is a piece called "Nach Paris!" written by Georges Blond, the French historian. And to round out the full picture of the First Battle of the Marne, the chapter concludes with an appreciation of Gallieni, taken from the book *The Poilus,* by Joseph Delteil.

The Battle of the Marne
by
Field Marshal Joffre

At the moment when the battle on which the fate of the country depended was about to open, the military situation had taken on an aspect infinitely more favorable than anything I could have dared to hope for a few days before.

The French Third, Fourth, Ninth and Fifth Armies, with their right resting on the entrenched camp of Verdun, were deployed along a front of about 125 miles, roughly marked by Sermaize, Vitry-le-François, Sommesous, the Saint-Gond Marshes, Esternay and Courtacon. Thrown forward on their left in an advanced echelon were the British Army and the French Sixth Army; the first southwest of Coulommiers, the second northwest of Meaux, covered on its left by Sordet's Cavalry Corps. The line, in its general aspect, presented the form of a vast pocket, into which five German armies seemed bent upon engulfing themselves. For all the information gathered during the day of September 5th went to show that the enemy was vigorously pursuing his march to the south. His general dispositions appeared to be as follows:

Von Kluck's army (the First) had reached the vicinity of Coulommiers, having left a few elements on the right bank of the Ourcq; these were entrenching themselves facing west.

Von Bülow's army (the Second) had crossed the Marne between Dormans and Epernay on the morning of September 5th. At noon the heads of its columns were reported to be on a line running through Champaubert, Etoges, Bergères, Vertus.

Von Hausen's army (the Third) had been identified only by its XII Corps, which, on September 4th, was reported to be at Condé-sur-Marne, between Epernay and Châlons.

The Prince of Würtemberg's army (the Fourth) had reached the line Châlons, Francheville, Bussy-le-Repos, on September 5th.

The Army of the German Crown Prince (the Fifth) was moving southwards on both sides of the Argonne.[1] . . .

But however advantageous the general situation appeared—above all, now that I could count upon the cooperation of the British—it can well be conceived that I was none the less beset by grave preoccupations. For in spite of the assurances which Generals Foch and Franchet d'Esperey had given me, I could not blind myself to the fact that this offensive, suddenly undertaken with armies worn out by an exhausting retreat, presented a problem bristling with uncertainties. . . .

The army corps which had been sent to reinforce the sensitive points in our line of battle were still in course of movement. These were, notably, the XV Corps, destined for the Third Army, the XXI Corps destined for the Fourth Army, and a division of the IX Corps which was intended for the Ninth Army. This fact had

---

[1]Information Bulletins of G.H.Q. dated September 5th and 6th.

its influence in increasing the regret I felt at having been obliged to start the battle on September 6th.

Ever since the 4th, combats had been raging with great violence on the Lorraine front. Here the enemy was seeking to get possession of Nancy, while at the same time, by an action in the Woëvre, he was menacing the rear of the Third Army. On the front of the First Army, he fortunately showed less activity; but as General Dubail had had his effectiveness considerably reduced, all he could do was to hold on to his positions.

The German attacks began on the afternoon of the 4th, and during the whole of the 5th they continued in the region of Gerbéviller and the Forest of Champenoux. That evening General de Castelnau reported that the enemy's numerical superiority, added to the power and range of his artillery—whose siege batteries had now made their appearance—rendered it improbable that the Second Army would be able to resist for any length of time. "If I am strong pressed," he wrote, "I can either defend myself as long as possible where I am, or else I can slip away in good time and take up a position first along the Forest of Haye, Saffais, Belchamps and Borville, then fall back to another line and so try to hold out and continue to cover the right flank of the group of armies."

Now, if the maneuver I was about to undertake was to succeed, I had to be sure that our two armies on the right flank would hold their ground, and it will be seen, as events are related, how grave a source of apprehension the Second Army continued to be for me during the whole Battle of the Marne.

All of our forces, as I wrote to the Minister of War, were now either in line or on the point of arriving. The only unit which remained available was the Second Moroccan Division; one of its brigades (General Cherrier) had just reached France, and the other (General Gouraud) would not be able to complete disembarking before September 12th.

From the point of view of reinforcements, the Germans were in an even more precarious situation than ourselves. Their deployment had long since been completed, and our air service reported that there was no sign of any forces following up the advancing armies; this confirmed me in my idea that the enemy could not have any fresh body of troops available. What was even more encouraging, information which I have previously referred to as indicating that important movements of German troops were taking place from west to east across Belgium gave rise to the hope that the enemy had weakened the forces opposed to us. But we little guessed to what an extent this weakening of his line would be to our advantage—for it was not until later that we learned that the troops the Germans had withdrawn had been taken from their right—precisely the point against which I was preparing to make my strongest effort.

It has often been said that during a modern battle a commander-in-chief, having once put his forces into position and given his initial orders, has nothing further to do; all he can do is to await the results of a contest whose development he is powerless to control.

The Germans had inherited this theory from Marshal von Moltke. History shows that while the victor of Sadowa and Sedan conducted his troops methodically and with painstaking care up to the eve of battle, once the engagement began, he renounced all idea of directing it, and made no effort to impose his decisions during its progress. This method reflected the marshal's temperament, disliking as he did to direct events which necessarily escaped all predetermination: he, therefore, admitted that the conduct of a battle was the affair of subordinate commanders. The wars in which he had been a chief actor brought no contradiction to this doctrine, von Moltke having had the rare good fortune to meet as adversaries only generals such as Benedek and Bazaine, whose inertia and passivity, one might say, were absolute.

Having observed that the results obtained by this method were excellent, the Germans decided that it was the right one to follow, and they continued to apply it. The younger von Moltke, nephew of the marshal, and the general who commanded the German armies during the first weeks of the war, was not the sort of man, as far as one can judge, to modify a formula which accorded so well with the irresolution of his nature and which in his secret moments he must have found particularly satisfactory. In fact, documents now available make it perfectly clear that the German High Command, from its headquarters in distant Luxembourg, knew almost nothing of what was happening on the battlefield of the Marne; as a consequence, its action upon army commanders was only spasmodic: it did not keep them informed as to the general situation, its instructions to them were incomplete and arrived too late.

Quite another conception prevailed amongst us in France. We agreed that sudden inspiration had no place in a modern battle; we recognized that the extent of its front, the size of its masses, and the length of time it might last necessitated a more minute preparation than was the case in battles whose successive phases the commander-in-chief could follow with a spy-glass. Nevertheless, we believed that, in spite of all the difficulties, a battle could and should be directed. However intelligent and energetic the various army commanders might be, each one of them would know only what was happening over a small fraction of the line, and the events taking place in his immediate front would assume an importance to his eyes which would distort their perspective; the commander-in-chief alone could have a general view of the whole battle and assign its true value to each event. Moreover, as new situations would constantly present themselves, no one but the commander of the whole front could give the orders required to meet each one as it arose.

The Battle of the Marne brought out in strong relief the ideas I have just expressed. It began as soon as we had succeeded in concentrating around the German right a mass sufficiently heavy to give us on this part of the strategic field the double advantage of position and numerical superiority. In spite of this situation, if we had tried to apply inflexibly a formula of envelopment at any price—which, moreover, was never my intention—we would have been playing into the enemy's hands. But our forces were sufficiently strong and our system sufficiently flexible to prevent the inevitable reaction of the enemy from catching us unawares. Von Kluck could only ward off the menace which threatened his right by creating between his army and that of von Bülow a breach which continued to widen progressively. In this way, beginning with the second day, the battle of the Marne took on the characteristics of a rupture of the enemy's line, a rupture which the German commander-in-chief had neither the time nor the means to avoid.

This conception of how a battle should be conducted, when it is fought under the conditions presented by the wide extension of modern fronts, presupposes not only the existence of a complete unity of doctrine between the commander-in-chief and his subordinates, but also implies that sure and rapid communication between them can be effected through the telegraph and telephone and by means of staff officers, who are, properly speaking, exponents of the very brain and will of the commander-in-chief. The task which fell to these liaison officers was extremely delicate, and they have sometimes been accused of assuming to themselves an authority out of all proportion to their rank. It is possible that errors were committed by these men; it is also likely that they at times became victims of the enmity aroused by pitiless decapitations which the interest of the country had induced me to make.

Be all this as it may, the fact remains that although I was obliged to stay at my headquarters during the whole of this battle,[2] in order to make the decisions which circumstances at any hour of the day or night might require, I was able, nevertheless, to command a deployment whose right rested on the Vosges and whose left, if we include d'Amade's divisions, extended as far as Rouen.

The courage and tenacity of our men being granted, it was the French system of command which triumphed at the Marne. . . .

Manoury's army was established during the day of September 5th between the Ermenonville Forest and the Marne, from Meaux to Vers. On its right some collisions occurred that day with the enemy, notably at Penchard, Monthyon and Saint-Soupplets. For September 6th, its objective was the Ourcq, from Lizy to Neufchelles. But it immediately encountered the German IV Reserve Corps, which put up a desperate resistance and was soon after supported by the whole of the II Corps; the latter had been recalled by forced marches from Coulommiers, and now endeavored to outflank our left around Etavigny. On September 6th at night-

---

[2] I forced myself throughout the battle of the Marne and during the delicate phase which followed it (to be precise, from September 5th to the 20th) to remain at my headquarters. I went out of my office only for the purpose of taking a daily walk of a mile or two and eating my meals. I slept at night in the Château de Marmont, which Colonel Maitre had placed at my disposal.

fall, the Sixth Army was halted on the line Chambry-Marcilly-Puisieux-Betz, that is to say, a long way from its first objective. Nevertheless, the earliest results of the entrance into action of this army soon became apparent to my eyes.

The Fifth Army had advanced on the morning of the 6th from the front Sézanne-Villers-Saint-Georges-Courchamps, and towards noon had encountered the enemy. Conneau's Cavalry Corps, to the north of the Jouy forest, covered its left and assured its liaison with the British Army. The latter had started that morning, not from the front Changis-Coulommiers, as was indicated for it in General Orders No. 6, but from a line situated nine miles to the southeast, running from Pézarches to Lagny; but that evening its left had reached the west bank of the Grand Morin without difficulty, while its right, thrown back, lay in the region of Pézarches.

At 11:00 A.M. on the 7th Franchet d'Esperey reported to me that the German First Army "on the front Esternay-Courtacon was in full retreat towards the north" . . . and that the Fifth Army was pursuing its advance. During the evening, while the X Corps, on its right, was supporting Foch's left division (the 42nd) towards Loizy-au-Bois, its center and left had reached the line Marsains-Tréfoils-Moutils, and Conneau's cavalry had arrived at La Ferté-Gaucher. By the close of the day the British Army had attained the line Choisy-Coulommiers-Maisoncelles, without meeting serious resistance.

On the other hand, our Sixth Army attempted in vain to reach the Ourcq; the enemy in front of it continued to receive reenforcements and von Kluck parried all the efforts which Maunoury made to effect an envelopment of his right in the direction of Betz.

On the evening of the 7th the situation of the German armies in front of our left appeared to me to be as follows:

To meet Maunoury's attack, which manifestly had surprised him, von Kluck had constituted on the Ourcq a detachment composed of the IV Reserve Corps, the II Active Corps and the 4th Cavalry Division, while with the rest of his army he was fighting, facing the south, against Franchet d'Esperey's left. Between these two main portions of the German First Army, a gap had been produced, opposite the British; this breach was masked by German cavalry forces, large, indeed, but not strong enough to hold up our Allies.

My idea, therefore, was for Franchet d'Esperey with his left to attack that part of the German First Army which faced him; to push the British Army into the gap I have just mentioned (crossing successively the Grand Morin, the Petit Morin and the Marne); and at the same time to accentuate Maunoury's enveloping movement by directing it, no longer upon Château-Thierry but farther north on the right bank of the Ourcq. This was the basis of the instructions I issued to our three armies on the left during the afternoon of September 7th.[3]

While this was happening on our left, the battle was developing less favorably on our center and right. The left of Foch's army, strongly supported by Franchet d'Esperey's left, resisted all the assaults of the enemy in the region of Loizy-au-Bois and Mondemont, but its right had been forced to give ground ever since the opening of the battle. Fère-Champenoise had been lost and on the evening of the 8th the line ran through Semoine-Gourgancon-Carroy, which represented a loss of eight miles. This retirement derived additional gravity from the fact that it opened still further the wide interval which separated Foch's right from the Fourth Army's left. As early as the 6th, I had already called General de Langle's attention to the need of keeping strong reserves in rear of his left ready to counterattack enemy forces which might seek to turn Foch's right, and it was for this purpose that I had placed the XXI Corps at de Langle's disposal. This corps was supposed to arrive in the region of Wassy, Montierender, on the 7th.

Unfortunately, ever since the morning of the 7th the Fourth Army had been at grips with the German Fourth Army reinforced by a part of the Third (von Hausen), and by a combination of circumstances for which de Langle was in no way to blame, the left of his army, contrary to anticipations, had become precisely

---

[3]In order better to coordinate the movements of the Sixth Army, which was now getting farther and farther away from the Capital, I sent a telegram on the morning of the 7th to the military governor of Paris to inform him that hereafter I would send my orders direct to General Maunoury, a copy being addressed to the governor. This decision was essential, and, for the purpose of gaining time, I had already been obliged to send orders direct to the Sixth Army—notably General Orders No. 6 of September 4th for the resumption of the general offensive.

the weakest point of his line. The infantry of the XII Corps, which it had been necessary to send by rail to the region of Chavanges during the preceding days, could as yet put only a few battalions in line to the south of Vitry-le-François; these supported as best they could the corps artillery. Then the main body of the XVII Corps, also much fatigued, had only reached the Aube near Ramerupt and had hardly started its advance east of Mailly.

What made it all the more difficult for General de Langle to reinforce his left flank during the first days of the battle was the fact that a gap existed (marked by the forest of Trois Fontaines) between his right and Sarrail's left, and the fighting on this wing was extremely severe. Sarrail complained violently of the situation, demanding an energetic action on the part of the II Corps (right of the Fourth Army) against Revigny or Contrisson, while waiting for the XV Corps (sent by the Second Army) to get into line northwest of Bar-le-Duc, between the Saulx and the Ornain.

It was thus that for a moment I was assailed by the fear of seeing the center of my line broken by a double rupture, one on each wing of the Fourth Army.

Fortunately, nothing of the sort took place. Von Hausen's army, engaged partly against Foch's right and partly against de Langle's left, was unable to penetrate into the 25-mile gap which lay between the two armies, and which was most inadequately masked by our 9th Cavalry Division. Beginning on September 8th the infantry of the now reconstituted XII Corps brought new strength to the front of the Fourth Army, while that same evening the XXI Corps arrived at Sompins, ready to support the left of this army; its entry into action, however, was too late to obtain any tangible results that day.

Turning now to the Third Army, I sent on September 7th two orders[4] to General Sarrail. In these I directed him to do all in his power to help the Fourth Army, just as the latter was bending every effort towards supporting the Ninth. Moreover, when evening arrived on September 8th, the XV Corps, after being at first forced back between the Saulx and the Ornain by the enemy's pressure, had finally succeeded in gaining ground, thus assuring the liaison between the Third and Fourth Armies.

---

[4]The first at 8:30 A.M. and the second at 4:15 P.M.

But now a new danger arose in front of Sarrail: enemy detachments were marching towards the Meuse in the neighborhood of Saint-Mihiel, and the fort at Troyon had been vigorously bombarded by the Germans on the evening of the 8th. To parry this threat General Sarrail caused the bridges over the Meuse to be destroyed and had the river guarded by the 7th Cavalry Division.

As a matter of fact the situation of the Third Army had become delicate, largely because its commander considered himself obliged to maintain contact with the fortress of Verdun. At 8:00 P.M. on September 8th I sent him an order authorizing him, if the need arose, to draw back his right so as to assure his communications and thus give greater power to the action of his left wing. In this way I showed Sarrail that I attached more importance to having the Third Army keep in touch with the Fourth than I did to its liaison with Verdun; indeed, in case of necessity, that fortress was quite capable of taking care of itself. To reassure Sarrail and bring some help to his task, I had directed Castelnau, the preceding day, to send the 2nd Cavalry Division on September 8th towards the Woëvre, so as to protect the rear of the Third Army. On the 8th, with the same idea in view, I also approved the despatch by rail to Commercy of a mixed brigade taken from the garrison of Toul.

Although the battle had increased in violence along the whole front and now reached beyond the Meuse and well into the Woëvre, I did not lose sight of the armies which were operating between Nancy and the Vosges. I had already taken very important forces from these armies and I proposed to take more if the situation required it. Nevertheless, I had to make sure that such a step would not compromise their power of resistance; for in that case the enemy would regain the initiative which we had just snatched from him.

I have related at the opening of this chapter that on the evening of September 5th, General de Castelnau had manifested his intention of abandoning the Grand Couronné and Nancy if he could not maintain his army on its positions without compromising its future. On the 6th, at 1:10 P.M., I sent him a telegram informing him that while his intentions, in case he was forced to abandon the Grand Couronné, met with my approval, I considered it preferable that he hold on to his present positions until a decision was obtained in the battle just commenced.

As it turned out, the commander of the Second Army succeeded that day in checking the enemy's attacks and he was even able to assume the offensive. But on the 7th the situation on his front again became threatening, and General de Castelnau, deeply affected by the death of one of his sons and learning that the battalion charged with defending Mount Sainte-Geneviève had abandoned that position, gave orders to his chief of staff, General Anthoine, to have the retreat begun, while at the same time he made ready to inform the civil authorities of Nancy that they must evacuate the town.

The decision was a grave one. This was no moment for giving the Germans the chance to trumpet to the world that they had taken Nancy. Moreover, from a strategic point of view, the retreat of the Second Army would place the First in a serious dilemma. Either that army would imitate the Second and fall back in liaison with it, thus abandoning the Franche-Comté and making probable the envelopment of the right flank of our armies, or else it would continue its resistance, basing itself for that purpose on the fortified towns of Belfort and Epinal. But this would mean the rupture of our two right armies, with the additional prospect of seeing Dubail's army shortly backed up against the Swiss frontier.

Fortunately, before sending out these orders, General Anthoine, fully appreciating their gravity, telephoned to G.H.Q. to announce the decision just taken. I immediately had de Castelnau called to the telephone. I remember this incident all the more exactly as I very rarely used the telephone myself during the whole campaign. The general drew a very dark picture of the situation of his army. There had been serious lapses in one of the corps; whole bodies of troops had become disbanded. "If I try to hold on where I am," he added, "I feel that my army will be lost. We have got to face the idea of immediately retreating behind the Meurthe."

"Do nothing of the kind," I replied. "Wait twenty-four hours. You do not know how things are going with the enemy. He is probably no better off than you are. You must not abandon the Grand Couronné and I give you formal orders to hold on to your present positions."

I then gave Major Bel instructions to proceed immediately to General de Castelnau, confirm the verbal order I had just given him, delay the execution of the retreat that was in preparation, and have him hold on in front of Nancy at any cost.

As it turned out, moreover, if Mount Sainte-Geneviève had been evacuated, it was in no sense due to the enemy's action but because of a misunderstanding of orders, and the position had been immediately reoccupied. The German attacks diminished in violence little by little from this day forward, and on September 11th, abandoning his attempt against Nancy at the very moment that our victory on the Marne was being concluded, the enemy marked a considerable retirement in Lorraine; and this was continued during the following days.

During all this period General Dubail had maintained an unshakable confidence, not once did his morale weaken and he never failed punctually to execute my orders.

We will now return to the armies on the left, which we last saw on the evening of September 7th oriented in the directions I had prescribed for them. On the 8th Maunoury found himself at grips with an enemy who had become still further reinforced during the night and who by a daring maneuver sought to recover the initiative by attempting to envelop our extreme left.

Fortunately, the IV Corps, which I had previously withdrawn from the Third Army, had begun to detrain at Paris on the 5th, and General Gallieni during the night of the 7th/8th sent one of its divisions (the 7th) to Maunoury. To accelerate its movement and enable the troops to reach the Sixth Army in as fresh a condition as possible, Gallieni made use of every available means of transport—railways, requisitioned motorcars, etc. The other division of the IV Corps (the 8th), the governor of Paris, in full agreement with Maunoury, thought himself obliged to engage south of the Marne, in order to support closely the movement of the British Army. As a matter of fact, this division was wholly useless in this region, and on the morning of the 8th it was still on the Petit Morin, where it was doing nothing at all. For this reason, about 9:00 A.M. of that day, I suggested to Maunoury that it would be advantageous to withdraw this division from his right and move it to his left, where there was work for it to do and where it could join the other elements of its corps.

During the morning of this same day, the 8th, I received the distressing news that Maubeuge had fallen the previous day. I had just cited in orders its governor, General Fournier, for his gallant defense of the piace, but the radio did not reach the besieged town until after its surrender. This event came at a bad moment; for it would free at least one army corps, which the Germans could move rapidly to Montdidier or Anizy. Therefore, when I informed Maunoury of this news I directed him to send out Sordet's cavalry to cut the enemy's communications, especially in the direction of Soissons and Compiègne.

At the end of the day, the Sixth Army, far from having succeeded in moving forward, was painfully resisting on its positions, at the same time making ready to refuse its left, which von Kluck was pressing vigorously. Fortunately, the Fifth Army continued its victorious advance. Its right gave a firm point of support to Foch; its center, overcoming the resistance of the enemy's rearguards, was arriving on the Petit Morin; while its left corps (XVIII) had Marchais-en-Brie.

Between Maunoury and Franchet d'Esperey, the British Army was not advancing as rapidly as I could have wished, although it had already attained appreciable results. On September 7th I had requested the minister of war to express to Lord Kitchener my warmest thanks for the constant support which the British forces had brought to our armies, and I also sent a personal letter to Sir John French to tell him of my gratitude. He answered the same day, thanking me for my message and adding that the situation now presented itself very favorably; he also congratulated me upon the "happy combination" I had just achieved.

All this did not prevent me from being impatient to see the British Army get forward more rapidly. Three times during the day of September 8th I urged upon its commander-in-chief the importance I attached to its action; I insisted upon the need of marching as fast as possible to the assistance of the Sixth Army, which now had to bear the whole brunt of the German First Army's attack; and I expressed the hope that I would see the British emerging on the other bank of the Marne before the day was over. But Sir John replied that German rear-guards had checked him on the Petit Morin; that same evening he had only reached the heights which lay to the north of this river.

When night arrived on the 8th, the situation, on the whole, appeared very promising—very different, indeed, from what a few days before I had thought it possible to anticipate.

All the German attacks between the Vosges and the Meuse had been mastered, in spite of the heavy withdrawals I had made from the First and Second Armies; in the center, the frontal attacks being conducted by the Fourth and Ninth Armies now gave me a right to hope that the enemy would not succeed in breaking this portion of our front. De Langle's right was at last buttressed by the XV Corps which had just come into action on Sarrail's left. It is true that Foch's right had again yielded ground, a fact which greatly disturbed me; for de Langle was not yet in a position to give him efficient help. But the splendid courage and unshakable confidence of the man at the head of the Ninth Army made me feel certain that the yielding of his line was only a local accident, whose influence upon the engagement as a whole would not be greatly felt.

It is simple justice to do honor here to the exceptional qualities displayed by General Foch during this battle; for throughout its course he gave the full measure of his ability. Admirably assisted by his chief of staff, Colonel Weygand, at no instant did his activity slacken or the inspiration of his morale abate.

On our left wing, the maneuver I had at first prepared was now becoming wholly changed in character. General Maunoury had been obliged to renounce the envelopment of his energetic adversary; but the latter had only succeeded in parrying our attack against his right by opening between his left and von Bülow's army a breach into which Franchet d'Esperey's left was pushing like a wedge, and into which I was making my strongest efforts to thrust the British. The information sent in by air reconnaissances, and that furnished by identifications secured during the battle, made me realize the extraordinary possibilities of action which this new situation opened up. Therefore, at 7:00 P.M., I sent to the three armies on our left a Special Instruction whose object was to explain to them the maneuver I desired to accomplish. The following are its most essential passages.[5]

---

[5]Special Instruction No. 19.

The combined efforts of the Allied armies composing our left wing have obliged the German forces to fall back; this they have done in two distinct groups.

The first group which appears to be composed of the IV Reserve Corps and the II and IV Active Corps, is fighting on the Ourcq, facing west, against our Sixth Army; it is even trying to outflank this army on the north.

The other group, comprising the rest of the German First Army (III and IX Active Corps), and the entire Second and Third Armies, continues to oppose, facing south, the French Fifth and Ninth Armies.

The connection between these two groups appears to be maintained solely by several cavalry divisions supported by detachments of all arms; these are opposite the British forces.

It seems essential to crush the German extreme right before it can be reinforced by troops which will be made available by the fall of Maubeuge.

I therefore requested:

(a) The Sixth Army to hold in check the enemy forces facing it;

(b) The British Army to cross the Marne between Nogent l'Artaud and La Ferté-sous-Jouarre and attack the left and rear of von Kluck's army;

(c) The Fifth Army, while covering with its left the right flank of the British (aided in this task by Conneau's cavalry), and also continuing to support with its right the left flank of Foch's army, which was making ready to assume the offensive, to move forward with its main body, faced to the north, and drive the enemy across the Marne.

The first paragraph of this Instruction described the situation in a way which would now be recognized as exact, except in one particular: the III and IV German Corps had been identified during the day's fighting, and the Special Instruction places them as being still facing the Fifth Army; in reality they were already on the move towards the Ourcq front.[6] The breach opened up

---

[6]The following radio, sent by von Kluck at 6:30 P.M., September 8th, was deciphered a few days later by the Code Section of French G.H.Q.: Today the Army fought a hard engage-

between von Kluck and von Bülow was therefore even wider than I had imagined.

The 9th of September seems to have marked the culminating point in the effort made by the enemy to extricate himself from the situation in which he had become involved.

Our Sixth Army succeeded at first in holding on to its positions; in the neighborhood of Betz the enemy had even marked a slight withdrawal and had evacuated this village. But during the afternoon the German III and IX Corps, debouching from the northeast and from the north, caused the French left to yield and forced it back to the line Chèvreville-Silly-le-Long. Maunoury immediately recalled the 8th Division, as I had directed him to do, and pushed it by a night march towards the left of his army. On my side, I had occupied myself during the morning with the selection of an infantry division to be furnished by the Fifth Army and which I caused to be sent by rail with the utmost speed towards Dommartin-en-Goële. In notifying General Maunoury of the despatch of this division, I explained the attitude I expected him to observe: "While waiting for the arrival of reinforcements intended to enable you to resume the offensive, you must avoid any decisive action, by retiring your left wing, if necessary, in the general direction of the Entrenched Camp of Paris."

However, in spite of the violence of the attacks delivered against him, Maunoury never for a moment lost sight of his mission or gave up the idea of resuming the offensive. This is shown in the telegram he sent me after his left had effected its withdrawal: "I will place the 8th Division near Silly-le-Long, and I will then give orders to attack. Heavy losses during the four days' fighting. Morale good. Have sent cavalry well forward."

The stubbornness of the combats delivered by the Sixth Army, the effort demanded of the men, the tenacity and coolness of their chief secured to us the immense result of making the victorious advance of Sir John French and Franchet d'Esperey compara-

---

ment against superior enemy forces west of the Ourcq, on the line Antilly (2 miles east of Betz)—Cougis (south of Lizy). The III and IX Corps, sent during the night to the right wing, will make an enveloping attack tomorrow morning. On the Marne, the line Lizy-Nogent l'Artaud will be defended by the II Corps of Cavalry and a reinforced brigade of infantry against attacks coming from the direction of Coulommiers.

tively easy. I personally expressed my satisfaction to General Maunoury and to his army, and the Grand Cross of the Legion of Honor marked the high price I placed upon the services just rendered our country by the commander of the Sixth Army.

In the report from which a few lines have just been quoted, Maunoury referred to a new task which had been confided to the Cavalry Corps. This force, composed of three divisions, was admirably placed on our extreme left and it should have done most useful work. Unfortunately, although the war had been going on scarcely a month, Sordet's cavalry had arrived at a most distressing state of exhaustion. The more or less useless raid it had made into Belgium, followed by a retreat which only came to an end to the southwest of Paris, had resulted in enormous wear and tear; but the operations alone were not responsible for ruining this corps—the generals and their staffs had a large share in the matter. It thus came about that on September 7th General Sordet, after having put his corps into action in the vicinity of Betz, decided that night, under pretext that the region where he was operating was short of water, to recall his divisions to Nanteuil-le-Housouin, where they arrived only at midnight. Upon learning of this retirement, General Maunoury ordered Sordet to move again to the front, and in this way the corps, after a rest of barely one hour, had to go all the way back over the same road.

Upon the recommendation of the commander of the Sixth Army, I decided to relieve General Sordet of his command and replace him by General Bridoux who was then commanding the 5th Cavalry Division. I had great esteem for Sordet, and before hostilities broke out he gave evidence of qualities which justified my confidence. Most probably he was a victim of the fact that during the years which preceded the war the cavalry arm had not kept sufficiently abreast of the times. General Bridoux was an officer full of dash and with him at its head the Cavalry Corps would have rendered us the greatest services; but unfortunately he had been in command hardly a day when he was killed. While making a journey one night by motor-car, a mistaken direction caused him and his staff to run into an enemy outpost; General Bridoux was mortally wounded and several of his officers were either killed or wounded at his side. His death was a calamity.

As I had directed him to do on September 8th, General Maunoury tried to push out the Cavalry Corps for the purpose of threatening the right and rear of von Kluck and delay the entry into action of the enemy forces which the fall of Maubeuge had set free; unfortunately the condition of men and horses made it impossible to fulfill this mission. The only thing accomplished was by the division commanded by General Cornulier-Lucinière, which succeeded in creating some confusion in von Kluck's rear and came near capturing (so it seems) the commander of the German First Army and all his staff.

After having been halted in the neighbourhood of La Ferté-sous-Jouarre by a broken bridge, the British Army, on the evening of September 9th, succeeded in gaining a foothold on the north shore of the Marne between La Ferté and Château-Thierry, held by the Fifth Army. This advance menaced the rear of the left wing of von Kluck's army which was now furiously assailing Maunoury.

Franchet d'Esperey's left had continued its forward progress. His XVIII Corps was moving towards Viffort, halfway between the Petit Morin and Château-Thierry. At 2:00 P.M. I had an order telephoned urging him to push to the Marne: "It is imperative that the XVIII Corps cross the Marne this evening in the vicinity of Château-Thierry, so as to support energetically the British columns." That night, September 9th, this corps did succeed in installing its advanced posts on the northern side of the river. On its left, Conneau's cavalry had also pushed over a brigade. When night arrived the rest of the Fifth Army found itself south of Surmelin, between Condé-en-Brie and Baye. The corps on the right (X), placed at Foch's disposal by Franchet d'Esperey, brought needed relief to the Ninth Army, at that time seriously pressed along its whole front. In his evening report of the day's operations, the commander of the Fifth Army announced himself quite ready to begin an action against the flank of the German forces which were assailing the Ninth Army.

Taken all in all, while the maneuver which I had prescribed for September 9th in Special Instruction No. 19 had not as yet been fully executed, its development was proceeding satisfactorily. The retirement of the Sixth Army's left wing was not a serious matter.

General Maunoury was cool and confident and he would soon have new forces at his disposal which would permit him to resume his offensive. The British Army and the left of our Fifth were commencing to debouch on the other side of the Marne and, like a wedge, were now penetrating into the space between the German First and Second Armies.

In a new Special Instruction[7] issued during the evening of the 9th, I announced the results so far obtained and the movements to be effected: the Sixth Army, its right resting on the Ourcq, was to push von Kluck towards the north, whilst the British, supported by the Fifth Army, would march to Clignon and thus complete the separation of von Kluck from the army on his left.

Meantime the frontal engagement continued uninterruptedly. The maneuver effected by General Foch on September 9th is well known. In response to his request for assistance, Franchet d'Esperey had placed at his complete disposal the X Corps and the 51st Reserve Division. Foch sent the X Corps to the west of Champaubert, between the Petit Morin and Fromentières and relieved the 42nd Division, forming the left of his army, by the 51st Reserve Division. Having thus provided himself with a reserve, he moved the 42nd Division in rear of his center with orders to make ready to attack in the direction of Fère-Champenoise; then at 4:00 P.M. he gave orders for his whole line to advance. The II Corps was only able to make a commencement of the movement; the 42nd Division arrived too late to get into action before night fell; the X Corps alone, moving to the north of the Saint-Gond marshes, began to drive the enemy back, while at the same time the 77th Infantry Regiment retook the important point of support constituted by the Château de Mondemont.

In the Fourth Army, the situation likewise improved. The violence of the German attacks on its right and center weakened visibly; west of the Marne, the entrance into action of the XXI Corps and elements which General de Langle had taken from his two right corps was destined to render it possible on the following day to make an attack facing northwest for the purpose of aiding Foch.

---

[7]Special Instruction No. 20, September 9, 1914, 8:00 P.M.

In Sarrail's army the fighting went on without the enemy being able to gain any ground; on the left of this army, the XV Corps was moving in close conjunction with de Langle's right. During the night of September 9th/10th the Germans launched a violent attack against the front of the VI Corps; this offensive, definitely checked the next morning, marked the end of their efforts against the Third Army.

On the Meuse the enemy vainly continued his attempts. Troyon did not allow itself to be intimidated by the German bombardment, while the screen furnished by the 7th Cavalry Division, the presence of the 2nd Cavalry Division on the right bank near Saint-Mihiel as well as the provisional brigade which Castelnau had sent from Toul towards Commercy, proved sufficient to cover the rear of Sarrail's army.

By the evening of September 9th, therefore, I was justified in considering the situation as favorable: on the left our success had become pronounced while in the center and on the right the enemy's rush appeared to be definitely checked. But victory was closer than I had dared to hope for.

On the morning of the 10th, as the Sixth Army moved out to make the attack prescribed in my Instruction of the preceding evening, all of a sudden it felt the enemy's resistance give way and during this day it advanced over nine miles almost without firing a shot.

On its right, the British Army reached Clignon without meeting resistance, and at the close of the day it halted south of the Ourcq, from La Ferté-Milon to Neuilly-Saint-Front.

The Fifth Army was across the Marne from Château-Thierry to Dormans, and General Franchet d'Esperey reported to me that in front of him the enemy's retreat was becoming precipitate, part of his forces moving towards the north, part towards the east.

On the line of the Ninth Army likewise, our success began to be manifest. The general advance which Foch had undertaken to effect the day before was now gaining impetus and all went to show that, here also, the enemy had effected a precipitate retreat during the night. For the evening of the 10th, Foch established his headquarters at Fère-Champenoise which the Prussian Guard had held that very morning.

In front of the Fourth and Third Armies the situation still remained stationary. Instead of de Langle's left being able to work for the benefit of the Ninth Army, as I had hoped would be the case, it was the latter which found itself in a position to aid the army on its right. Opposite Sarrail the enemy's activity lessened still further, and the XV Corps, having finished the cleaning up of the forest of Trois Fontaines, now held position abreast of the right corps of the Fourth Army.

What now remained to be done was to follow up the success achieved by our left and center and at the same time overcome the resistance which continued to hold up our two armies on the right. To this effect I sent out a series of orders on September 10th with the object of giving a fresh impetus to the battle.

To French and Maunoury I made the request that they push straight to the north on each side of the Ourcq; on their extreme left, Bridoux's Cavalry Corps was to endeavor constantly to threaten the enemy's lines of retreat, and on their right the Fifth Army was so to place itself as to be able to act, *facing east,* in the direction of Rheims, against the columns which were retreating before the Ninth Army.[8]

To General Foch I pointed out that the result of the battle would depend in a large measure on the action of his army against the corps facing our Fourth Army.[9]

To General de Langle I urged the necessity of a vigorous advance, especially on his left.[10]

To General Sarrail I telegraphed that I only expected him to hold fast where he stood.[11]

In addition to this, I made every effort to threaten the two flanks of the retreating enemy—his right, by sending a radio message to General Coutanceau, military governor of Verdun, to attack with all his forces any enemy convoys which crossed the Meuse north of Verdun, and his left, by pushing General d'Amădés' Territorial Divisions to the region of Beauvais.[12]

---

[8]Special Instruction No. 21 of September 10th, afternoon.
[9]Special Order of September 10th, morning.
[10]Special Order of September 10th, 10:00 A.M.
[11]Special Order of September 10th, 10:10 A.M.
[12]Special Order of September 9th.

I also telegraphed the First Army to entrain the XII Corps at Epinal and send it to the north of Paris; for my whole attention was now concentrated upon the necessity of preventing the enemy from recovering himself, and to ensure this I desired to reinforce still further General Maunoury's army, which I considered to be the principal factor in our maneuver.

That evening I had the certainty of victory, although I was as yet unable to measure its full extent. I reported to the minister of war the first results, namely, on my left, the enemy in full retreat having already yielded more than 37 miles; his center weakening in front of Foch; his left, while not yet beaten, at the end of their resistance.

On September 11th, our victory became confirmed along the whole of the line. The Sixth Army had reached the front Pierrefond-Chandun; the British were crossing the upper Ourcq; Franchet d'Esperey, driving before him the weak rear-guards of the enemy, had pushed the heads of his columns south of the Vesle between Chéry and Ville-en-Tardenois; his right corps, the X, which had so powerfully contributed to Foch's success, was moving from Vertus towards Epernay, while the Ninth Army itself was on the Marne between Sarry and Tours. The Fourth Army also was now advancing. Its left, during the night, had reached the Marne below Vitry, its right, the Colonial Corps, occupied the bridges over the Saulx and the II Corps those over the Ornain, in close touch with the left of the Third Army, which itself was in the act of crossing the last-named river. The remainder of Sarrail's army was not making any headway, but at the close of the day a report from his staff stated that an "impressive calm" reigned along the whole of their front.[13]

That afternoon I telegraphed as follows to the minister of war: "The Battle of the Marne is an incontestable victory for us." Before writing out this bulletin, the question arose as to the name which should be given to the battle we had just won.

In former times an engagement drew its name from the place near which it had been fought or the spot where the decisive action

---

[13]. . . I immediately gave orders for this army to commence an energetic pursuit of the enemy.

had taken place. But in modern battles, extending as they do over immense fronts, on which numerous actions of equal importance take place simultaneously, the name of some one locality is no longer sufficiently characteristic.

During the fighting in Manchuria the belligerents had several times been led to give a battle the name of the river whose valley had been the scene of the encounter. The battle which the Allied forces had just fought on the front running from Verdun to Paris had taken place in the Valley of the Marne and its affluents—the Ourcq, the Grand Morin, the Petit Morin, the Saulx, and the Ornain. It was this fact which decided me to call it the Battle of the Marne; for this term evoked both the idea of a front and of an extensive region.

As I have already said at the opening of this chapter, the Battle of the Marne, which began on our side with a maneuver that sought to envelop the enemy's right wing, was brought to a finish by the rupture of the adverse formation, in which two breaches had been opened, one between the German First and Second Armies, the other between the Second and Fourth Armies—the Third Army itself having become broken into two factions, which had united with von Bülow's left and the Prince of Württemberg's right respectively. It was this unexpected situation of which we took advantage; and this fact confirms what I have said above, that a doctrine which consists in abandoning to subordinate commanders the strategic direction of a battle is a most dangerous one.

On the other hand, if we compare the Battle of the Marne with the Battle of the Frontiers, it will be seen that the two had a close relation to each other. If, on the Ourcq, Maunoury's army had faltered as did our armies of the left on the 22nd of August, if Foch had given way at Fère-Champenoise, as did our Third and Fourth Armies at Audun-le-Roman and at Paliseul, my plan would have crumbled to pieces a second time.

If our success on the Marne responded to my expectations, the reason in great part lies in the fact that our armies at the commencement of September were no longer what they were during the first days of the war. Taught by the hard experience of the battles on the frontier, our infantry, although it had lost many of its officers, employed the ground to better advantage and more willingly used its entrenching tools whose value the men now fully comprehended; and it no longer went into action without being supported by artillery. It is also true that many of the generals whose incapacity the war had suddenly revealed had been replaced by other and more capable men. Between the day when the army was mobilized and the 6th of September, I had been obliged to remove two army commanders (the Third and the Fifth), nine army corps commanders (out of a total of twenty-one), thirty-three infantry division commanders,[14] one cavalry corps commander, and five cavalry division commanders (out of a total of ten divisions). Even if I did not go so far as to adopt the radical measures contemplated by M. Messimy and have the incapable shot, it can at least be said that these changes weeded out the higher commands and rejuvenated the list of general officers.

The British, like ourselves, had also profited by the hard lessons of the opening days of the struggle. With the exception of the Crimean War, they had never fought in Europe since Waterloo, and the gap was a huge one. If, during the Battle of the Marne, they did not advance as fast as I would have liked—and as they doubtless could have done in view of the weak forces the Germans had left in front of them—their conduct in this battle was in every way worthy of their military traditions, and the role they played in it was what I would have expected of them.

Now that our maneuver on the Marne had been crowned with success, Sir John French, loyal soldier that he was, showed in every way his confidence. Unfortunately, he was rent between two influences: the one was represented by General Wilson, a man of the keenest intelligence, with a sound appreciation of every situation, and, in addition, accustomed to French methods and thoroughly knowing France—for which country, indeed, he had a profound sentiment; the other was represented by General Murray, chief of staff of the Expeditionary Forces, who spent his time exhorting the field marshal with counsels of extreme prudence. It was a great relief to us when, a few months later, General Murray was called back to England. . . .

---

[14]Twenty-three generals commanding active divisions out of forty-seven (including the two colonial divisions), and ten commanding reserve divisions, out of twenty-five.

Although the Battle of the Marne did not bring as much as I expected of it, I nevertheless think I am justified in briefly pointing out the main results obtained.

The month of August had given the first game of the rubber to the Germans; with the Belgians thrown back upon Antwerp, the British and French towards the Seine. Our left wing threatened with envelopment and Paris with capture; there can be small doubt that at this moment the Germans were looking forward to another Sudan repeated on an enormous scale. Our adversaries' plan had as its foundation a rapid victory in the West. The need of winning the war before the resources of Russia could be brought into play was now all the more imperative, since the British Empire had thrown itself into the conflict on our side. As I have said several times in the preceding pages, it would have been playing into the enemy's hands if I had risked the destinies of our country at a moment when the essential thing for us was above all to hold out and avoid destruction. It was this consideration which justified me in waiting for an always possible turn of fortune. I paid for this delay by sacrificing—temporarily, as I hoped—a considerable part of our territory. Although a total defeat of the Germans was not accomplished, nevertheless the occasion we had so patiently waited for did enable us to drive them back along the whole line, and our victory forced them to bury themselves in trenches. What a disappointment for men in a hurry!

But, it can well be said, the result achieved was the primary cause of the final defeat of the Germans, although it was not assigned its true value at the time. Amongst the Allies, and especially in France, after the first immense relief experienced when the menace of dire catastrophe that had hung over the country during the first days of September was seen to be lifted, public opinion, a few days after the victory of the Marne, was conscious of only one thing, and that was that the German Army was firmly fastening itself upon our soil. Instead of emphasizing to the public the happy reversal of the situation, the minister of war softened down the communiqués which I sent him at the close of the battle, before giving them to the press. When I expressed to M. Millerand the pain I felt at seeing these changes, he wrote to me on September 15th as follows:

I alone am guilty; but I do not wish to leave the shadow of a doubt in your mind as to the reasons which induced me to put the soft pedal upon the expression of our joy.

I thought it wise to save the nerves of this country, and I preferred the risk of understating the truth to that of exaggerating it.

M. Millerand's patriotism was too sincere and his feeling for me too genuine for it to be possible to attach to him any suspicion of ungenerous intention; but I cannot help thinking that the minister of war was, under the circumstances, too modest in the terms he used to announce our victory. The enemy's propaganda drowned with the tongue of brass the voice of victorious France, not only in neutral countries, but even in our own. For many people, the Marne came to be considered as a sort of miracle; for others, as a happy and unexpected piece of luck. For those persons who received their inspiration from the enemy press, the battle reduced itself to a maneuver undertaken by the German Supreme Command, which, in the absence of the strategic results it had failed to achieve, from now on invariably pointed to the "war map" as being the argument most easy to comprehend.

Fortunately, the essential fact remained that the enemy had been driven back to a line fifty miles north of Paris and it could be said that he was definitely halted. People breathed once more, and confidence revived.

"Nach Paris!"
by
Georges Blond

The offices of the O.H.L. (*Oberste Heeresleitung,* General Headquarters) were in a state of quite unusual activity. All departments were under orders to leave Coblenz and to be in operation the following morning (August 30th) in Luxembourg, capital of the Grand-Duchy. Secretaries and orderlies were hurriedly packing up files and documents, under the supervision of their impatient officers.

The whole German population had just been thrilled by the communiqué of August 27th: "After a series of successful engagements the German armies on the Western Front have entered French territory. From Cambrai to the southern Vosges the enemy has been everywhere defeated and is now in full retreat. On account of the vast area of the battlefield, part of which is wooded and mountainous, it is not yet possible to assess the losses of the enemy in killed, in prisoners and in war material."

General von Kluck's 1st Army had defeated the British at Mons on August 23rd. On the same day von Bülow's 2nd Army had defeated the French on the Sambre, in the region of Charleroi. The 4th Army, under the duke of Wurtemberg, had advanced in the Ardennes, and the 5th Army, under the Imperial Crown Prince, in the Woevre district of Lorraine. On the 20th and 21st the 6th Army, under Prince Ruprecht of Bavaria, and the 7th Army, under von Heeringen, had defeated the French in Lorraine, and on August 26th the 1st Army had again defeated the British, at Le Cateau, east of Cambrai. On the 27th, General Helmuth von Moltke, chief of the General Staff, had submitted to his supreme commander, the emperor, the proposed directive for the continuation of operations. The document ended with these words: "His Majesty orders the German Armies to advance on Paris."

The staff officers at the O.H.L. considered that their headquarters should have been moved much further forward than Luxembourg. They would have preferred to follow more closely behind the irresistible advance of the armies so that they themselves would be able to hurry forward and join the victorious troops entering Paris.

No one doubted that such a triumphant entry was imminent, and the General Staff officers felt, in common with all other officers of the German armies, that they were entitled to take part in it. The remarkable victory now within their reach was not due to good luck or to the futility of the opposing forces. An army of more than a million Frenchmen was in full retreat after only a few days' fighting; and this for the simple reason that the German High Command had shown crushing superiority in every branch: discipline, training, use of weapons, organization, tactics, and strategy. The German officer corps had labored for years to achieve this victory. And von Schlieffen, the brilliant strategist who had planned it, was the archetype of the military caste that was looked upon with pride as the élite of the German nation.

The role of the High Command in peacetime is (clearly) to prepare for war. Political developments on the Continent of Europe after 1875 had led the German High Command to envisage the possibility of war on two fronts. Marshal Moltke, the aged victor of the 1870 campaign, had declared that, in such conditions, the attack should first be opened against the Russians, a defensive front being maintained, meanwhile, against the French. The German fortified positions along the line, Thionville-Metz-Strasbourg, and thence along the Rhine from Strasbourg to Basle were considered an insuperable barrier against any French attack. Once Russia was defeated the offensive would be switched to France. Marshal Moltke's successor, Waldersee (1838–1891), had held the same view.

But as soon as von Schlieffen came on the scene he declared the Moltke Plan to be obsolete, useless, and quite unsuited to the necessities and potentialities of modern warfare. "The Russian railway system" (he said) "is lamentable. It would take the Russian staff six weeks to transport an army up to our frontier and several months to mount a major offensive. We, however, can crush France in less than two months, and that must be our primary task. In the meantime, we should establish a weak defensive front against Russia.

"It would be foolish to look upon our operations against France as a sort of battering-ram applied to the restricted area of the Franco-German frontier. Our modern army masses require ample space for their effective deployment; what is more, frontal attack is an outmoded, rudimentary conception. Our objective should be, not the enemy's front, but its flanks. The encirclement of the Roman Army by Hannibal at Cannae still remains the classic masterpiece of military strategy and tactics.

"There are geographical reasons preventing us from turning

both flanks of the French forces, but we can clamp down their right wing in the fortified areas and turn their left flank by marching through Belgium."

To which certain critics had replied: "Belgian neutrality has been guaranteed since 1839 by Great Britain, France, Russia, Prussia, and Austria. That treaty is still in force. Any violation of Belgian territory will mean war with Great Britain."

"No plan is without its risks," was the answer. "It is quite possible that England will declare war; but her intervention will be slow and at first ineffective. Once France has been crushed, England—for economic reasons—will be ready to make peace."

"Our object will be to turn the French left flank by attacking it with our strongest striking force, which, having crossed Belgium, will march on Paris ahead of the French forces, cutting them off from Paris and later falling upon their rear. The French armies will finally be brought to bay in the Jura region."

Such (originally) was the gigantic plan. Von Schlieffen was ready to subordinate everything to this vast turning movement of the German right wing, which was to be made irresistible. The attacking force of thirty-five army corps and eight further divisions of infantry would turn the French left wing somewhere beyond Lille. "The German soldier on the extreme right of the line will be brushing his sleeve against the English Channel." Paris would in fact be outflanked from the lower Seine and be attacked *from the west.*

But another objection had been raised: "We cannot mobilize the number of men required for such an operation."

"We can certainly mobilize them if we get rid of the outdated notion that reservists cannot be used in the front line. They can, if they are well led. By using them as front-line troops we gain twenty divisions."

Such was the second of von Schlieffen's revolutionary ideas; and it was kept even more secret than the famous Plan. Von Schlieffen had retired in 1905 and died in 1913 at the age of eighty. According to members of his family his last words were: "Above all, strengthen the right wing."

But time brings inevitable change. Between 1906 and 1914, a number of factors, including the improvement of the Russian railway system and the raising of military service in France to three years, had led General von Moltke, nephew of the famous marshal and successor to von Schlieffen, to make slight amendments to the Schlieffen Plan. In order to stiffen the defense against Russia and strengthen the German forces on the Franco-German frontier the colossal right wing had been trimmed a little; even so, it was still very impressive. It would consist of a force of three armies, totaling sixteen army corps, or about 600,000 men; in the center, eleven army corps, about 400,000 men, and on the left, to cover the Alsace-Lorraine front, 320,000 men.

The Marne
by
Joseph Delteil

(Translated by Jacques Le Clercq)

On September 5th, at six o'clock in the morning, Gallieni observed the enemy from the top of the Eiffel Tower. Soon he saw the enemy columns stop, all together, concentrate under the oak trees, then describe a fantastic turn to the left, and abandoning the capital, Paris, march straight to the south, straight on the French Army.

A smile spread over Gallieni's old goat face. His eyes shone out from the secure regions of problems that are solved. The great soldier's heart beat, that old heart of his, full of Madagascar campaigns and of black suns.

He ran down the steps of the Eiffel Tower, four at a time. A ray of sunlight rose over the tower, innocent and graceful, playing with the steel and the general.

The general was figuring his business. The point was to fall on Kluck's flank lickety-split, to throw him into confusion in five seconds flat, to surround the entire German right wing and to destroy the enemy on the Marne.

For this purpose speed was essential. It was the genius of Gallieni, of that impotent and crippled old man, to be quick.

In those days there were neither garrisons of microbes, nor chemical artillery, nor aviation-transports, nor any of the wonders of modern war. They still used big guns and railways. Gallieni invented the taxi.

Then and there he ordered a general commandeering of all the taxis in Paris. On September 6th, at noon, two thousand taxis, with their chauffeurs at the helm, stood at Porte de Pantin. In the evening they were filled with gasoline and oil. All of the Avenue Jean Jaurès was swimming in oil.

On the following day, September 7th, from four o'clock on, they embarked. An entire army of fifty thousand men took their places in the taxis. The soldiers carried neither their packs nor any sort of impedimenta. Three things were essential: gasoline, men, rifles. Overboard with the rest! Gallieni came to inspect them. He arrived, very tall in an old military coat, thin as a drawn sword, solitary, taciturn, without dash, almost without a body, something crystalline, a glass skeleton, a soul of mountain-flax. He was as shabby as an umbrella.

He strolled philosophically in front of the taxis, without a word. Then he made a sign.

And the army of taxis started forward.

Very early in the morning, in columns of two, they rolled in the phantasmagoria, cleaving the fog, inhaling the wind. They ran over dogs baying at the moon; they ran over the toes of the villagers. The shadows stank of axle-grease. No honks, no horns. A hoarse breath issued from these machines in the animal dawn. The motors snored. The soldiers snored. Night snored.

In his Hotel des Invalides, a man was watching: Gallieni.

His brow bowed over a map, a telephone at his ear, he was watching. Motionless in his ugly red plush armchair, coughing, his feet cold, with ever those precious pearls in his liver, he bounded along the roads of Ile-de-France. "Hello, Vaujours! Not there yet?—*Ah, merde alors!*—What in hell are they doing?" He grumbled, and, from time to time, the ashes of a cigarette fell over the map, less burning than the thin hand of the general.

Hello! The general had three eyes: one eye on the Ourcq; one eye on the taxis; one eye on Kluck. His mind ran ten minutes ahead of the taxis at first, then a quarter of an hour, then an hour. It was a speed test between mind and reality. "What! You're passing through Claye-Souilly? Go twice as fast, God damn it!" —"Hello? The Ourcq? General, you must stand your ground three hours, watch in hand. The 34th has lost three hundred men? Well, then, shoot them!"

An orderly officer entered. Gallieni did not move. The officer waited five minutes, a half hour, an hour. Gallieni did not move. The officer, pale with fear, turned right-about-face and ran for his life. "Hello! The taxis are at Neufchelles? No, no, no. Not a moment's stop! I forbid it! On the pain of death! General, you will be answerable to me for every minute!"

It was eight o'clock in the morning. On the Ourcq, the Tenth Army Corps, exhausted, was giving way. The enemy stormed Bouillancy. The taxis bowled along, black with mist and mud. Occasionally, one of them toppled into the ditch, dirty, dry. They ran over its body. Now they moved at a fantastic pace. The soldiers had awakened. They gazed at this countryside of cabbage-fields, stubble and alder-trees, all bathed in the light of earliest morning. A long cloud of dust rolled between the fields of the dew. The oil rose to your throat. The chauffeurs, panting, forced on more speed incessantly.

About nine o'clock, the taxis reached the Ourcq. All the army disembarked. The fifty thousand fresh men threw themselves into the fray. There blew a great draught.

The Battle of the Marne was won. . . .

CHAPTER IX

THE SECOND BATTLE
FOR TOBRUK, AND
EL ALAMEIN, 1941–1942

Field Marshal Erwin Rommel (1891–1944), son of a schoolmaster, was born at Heidenheim, Germany. In 1910 he was a military cadet. Between 1914 and 1918 he had a distinguished career as an infantry officer. Between wars he was a military instructor and wrote a well-known infantry manual. When World War II broke out, Rommel commanded a battalion protecting Hitler. In May 1940, he led the 7th Panzer Division to the English Channel.

The "Desert Fox," Rommel, commanding the German armies in the African campaigns, threw the British back into Egypt, but eventually he was forced to evacuate Africa. Later, accused of participating in the 1944 plot to kill Hitler, Rommel was forced to take poison on October 14, 1944.

The two battles for Tobruk and El Alamein are classics of Rommel's methods with men and tanks.

The British historian, B. H. Liddell Hart, with the help of Rommel's widow, Lucia-Maria Rommel, her son, Manfred, and General Fritz Bayerlein, collected, edited and translated *The Rommel Papers,* from which the two selections in this chapter are taken.

The papers themselves have a unique history, for Hitler wanted them destroyed and thus the hiding places used by the Rommel family were constantly being changed. In the process, many documents were lost or stolen. When the American Army took the town of Herrlingen, where the family lived, the Rommels were given a receipt for some of Rommel's letters to his wife—and off they were sent to some military archive in Washington. The same thing happened to a chest and a trunk—a receipt, for Rommel's excellent photographs of various campaigns, especially "notes and sketches from the First World War—the material he had used in his book, *The Infantry in Attack,*" as his son Manfred wrote in the story of *The Rommel Papers.*

Eventually, with Liddell Hart's intervention, Washington finally returned the papers, and the massive job of putting them together into a book was undertaken. Rommel was a natural letter writer and diarist, and the two selections in this anthology show the virtues of his exactness both as a writer and a military strategist.

As Liddell Hart says in his introduction: "The impact that Rommel made on the world with the sword will be deepened by the power of his pen. No commander in history has written an account of his campaigns to match the vividness and value of Rommel's. . . . No one else has so strikingly conveyed in writing the dynamism of *Blitzkrieg* and the pace of *panzer* forces. . . . All Great Captains possessed in high degree this faculty of grasping instantly the picture of the ground and the situation; of relating one to the other, and the part to the whole. . . . Exasperating to staff officers, he was worshipped by the fighting troops, and what he got out of them in performance was far beyond any rational calculation."

The Second Battle for Tobruk
by
Field Marshal Erwin Rommel

Tobruk was one of the strongest fortresses in North Africa. In 1941, with magnificent troops in its garrison, it had presented us with immense difficulties. Many attacks had collapsed in its defenses and much of its outer perimeter had literally been soaked in blood. Often the battle had raged round a square yard at a time. We were no strangers to Tobruk. . . .

To every man of us, Tobruk was a symbol of British resistance and we were now going to finish with it for good.

On the morning of the 16th June, I drove up to the Via Balbia and then along it to the west. Fighting at Gazala had finally ceased and another 6,000 British troops had found their way into our prison camps. Evidence of the British defeat could be seen all along the road and verges. Vast quantitites of material lay on all sides, burnt-out vehicles stood black and empty in the sand. Whole convoys of undamaged British lorries had fallen into our hands, some of which had been pressed into service immediately by the fighting troops, while others were now awaiting collection by the salvage squads. Apparently the British had taken off some of their units by sea. Soon we met our troops advancing eastwards from the Gazala line. They received orders to push on as fast as they could up to the western edge of Tobruk and were provided with lorry columns to carry their men up to the front by shuttle service. Quick regrouping for the investment of Tobruk was now the most urgent necessity.

One of the first lessons I had drawn from my experience of motorized warfare was that speed of maneuver in operations and quick reaction in command are decisive. Troops must be able to carry out operations at top speed and in complete coordination. To be satisfied with norms is fatal. One must constantly demand and strive for maximum performance, for the side which makes the greater effort is faster—and the faster wins the battle. Officers and N.C.O.s must continually train their troops along these lines. . . .

The Indians were still holding on in El Hatian. On the 16th June, the 90th Light Division, despite all the courage they displayed, were again unable to extend the wedges in the defense system which assault teams had made the evening before. As with all other British defense systems in the Marmarica, this position had been constructed with great technical skill and according to the most up-to-date ideas. Following the example of Bir Hacheim, a part of the garrison (consisting of the 29th Indian Brigade) broke out during the night and withdrew to the south. The Indians simply concentrated their weight on one sector, opened fire with every weapon and then broke out, thus showing once again the difficulty of effectively enveloping a fully motorized enemy whose structure of command has remained intact.

The remainder of the Indians in El Hatian surrendered on the evening of 17th July. Some 500 prisoners and considerable quantities of war material fell into our hands.

The powerful forts of El Duda and Belhammed had already been captured the day previously by the Afrika Korps. The moment that El Hatian fell I sent the 90th Light Division against several other British strong points which were still holding out in that area. They were surrounded and stormed.

The whole of the Afrika Korps with the Ariete were now put on the march to Gambut and the area to its south. We wanted, as I have already said, to divert British attention from Tobruk and at the same time gain the necessary freedom of movement in our rear for the Tobruk attack. Primarily, however, this advance was directed against the R.A.F. who, with their short time of flight from neighboring bases, were being unpleasantly attentive. We intended to clear them off their airfield near Gambut and keep them out of the way during our assault on Tobruk.

So now my army was moving east again. The Ariete, who had instructions to maintain touch with the Afrika Korps, fell behind from the start and lost contact. I went off to look for them but very soon ran into a tank battle. Shells whistled backwards and forwards and we were not sorry to escape from that unfriendly neighborhood. Soon afterwards we succeeded in making contact with the Ariete by radio and moved them up to the main body.

At about 19.30 hours that evening [the 17th] I switched the 21st Panzer Division to the north and rode with my *Kampfstaffel* about two miles in front of the van of the division. A slight fracas blew up south of Gambut and a few Foreign Legionaires were taken prisoner. Finally, after some trouble with extensive British minefields, we arrived at Gambut with the leading troops at around 22.00 hours. The main body remained lying before the minefields all night.

At dawn on the 18th June, British aircraft again appeared over the 21st Panzer Division, which was moving on northwards. The road and railway were reached shortly before 04.30. This railway, which the British had built during the past few months, ran from Mersa Matruh to the outer perimeter of Tobruk. We crossed it, demolishing some of the track on the way. The 4th Rifle Regiment had already taken 500 prisoners on the road during the night and this figure was now steadily increasing. On the airfields, which the British had not evacuated until the last moment, we captured 15 serviceable aircraft and considerable quantities of oil and petrol, which we found very useful.

On arriving back that night at Army H.Q., we found life being made unpleasantly hazardous by the activities of a British 25-pounder battery, which began to shell our position. I sent Captain Kiehl with the *Kampfstaffel* to drive it off, which he did, but the British promptly selected another site and began to honor us with their attentions again. I soon became bored with this and shifted my H.Q. back to El Hatian, where the staff of British XXX Corps had formerly been housed.

Mopping up of the area between Tobruk and Gambut was completed on 18th June and the necessary moves carried out to close in Tobruk. An excellent piece of organizational work was now done in building up supplies for the assault. During our advance we had found some of the artillery depots and ammunition dumps, which we had been forced to abandon during the Cunningham offensive in 1941. They were still where we had left them, and were now put to good use.

The Afrika Korps moved into its new position on the afternoon of 19th June, while the 90th Light Division thrust east to take possession of British supply dumps between Bardia and Tobruk. The movement of this division was particularly important to increase still further British uncertainty about our true intentions. In addition the Pavia Division and Littorio Armored Division, units of which were just arriving, were to screen the attack on Tobruk to the west and south.

We had the impression that evening that our movements had only been partially and inaccurately observed by the enemy, and there was therefore every chance that our attack would achieve complete surprise. Outside the fortress of Tobruk, there was no

British armor of any consequence left in the Western Desert and we could therefore look forward with great hopes to the forthcoming enterprise.

In spite of the hard time we had been through, the army was on its toes and confident of victory. On the eve of the battle every man was keyed up and tense for attack.

The Conquest of Tobruk

The Tobruk garrison was of approximately the same strength as it had been in 1941, and consisted of the following troops of the British Empire:

2nd South African Infantry Division, reinforced.
11th Indian Brigade.
2nd Battalion, Guards Brigade.
Several infantry tank regiments, under command 32nd
    Army Tank Brigade.
Artillery strengthening to the extent of several artillery regiments.

[This is not quite correct. The 2nd South African Division had only two infantry brigades instead of three. On the other hand, the 201st Guards Brigade had two battalions and part of a third under its command. The 32nd Army Tank Brigade had two battalions of infantry tanks. There was no additional artillery apart from the 4th Anti-Aircraft Brigade.]

—Basil Liddell Hart

Although this force corresponded in numbers to the 1941 garrison, it could not be expected to put up such a stubborn and well-organized resistance, for the bulk of the troops had already given us battle and were tired and dispirited. The British command, moreover, which never was very quick at reorganizing, had been given no time to build up its defensive machine.

Besides this force in Tobruk, Ritchie still had available five infantry divisions of which three had been very badly mauled; the other two had been freshly brought up. His two armored divisions had been virtually wiped out in the recent fighting, but were now receiving reinforcements and replacements from the Nile Delta.

One more word about the Tobruk defenses.

Tobruk, hemmed in on its eastern and western sides by rocky and trackless country, extends out to the south into a flat and sandy plain. It had been extremely well fortified by the Italians under Balbo, and full account had been taken of the most modern weapons for the reduction of fortifications. The numerous defense positions running in a belt round the fortress were sunk in the ground in such a manner that they could only be located from the air. Each defense position consisted of an underground tunnel system leading into machine and antitank gun nests. These nests, of which most of the defense positions had a considerable number, waited until the moment of greatest danger before throwing off their camouflage and pouring a murderous fire into the attacking troops. Artillery could not take them under direct fire because of the lack of apertures on which to take aim. Each separate position was surrounded by an antitank ditch and deep wire entanglements. In addition the whole fortified zone was surrounded at all points passable to tanks by a deep antitank ditch.

Behind the outer belt of fortifications, most of which was several lines in depth, were powerful artillery concentrations, field positions and several forts. The majority of the defense works were protected by deep minefields.

The feint attack in the southwest was to be executed by XXI Italian Corps, who were provided with several tanks in support. The group making the main attack consisted of the Afrika Korps and XX Italian Corps. Before the attack was opened, the main attack sector, southeast of the fortress, was to be bombed by the entire German-Italian Air Force in Africa. Once the infantry had succeeded in reducing the fortified lines, the Afrika Korps was to press on over the crossroads to the harbor and open up the Via Balbia to the west. Following up the Afrika Korps, XX Italian Corps was to capture the British defense works and thrust through to the Ras el Madauer in the rear of the South Africans. . . .

My assault force moved into its assembly areas on the night of the 19th June. At 05.20 hours several hundred aircraft hammered their bombs on the break-in point southeast of the fortress. I watched the effect of this attack. Great fountains of dust plumed up out of the Indian positions, whirling entanglements and weapons high into the air. Bomb after bomb tore through the enemy wire.

As soon as the aircraft had finished, the infantry of the Afrika Korps (15th Rifle Brigade) and XX Italian Corps moved forward to the assault. Lanes had been cleared through the mines the night before. Two hours later the German storming parties had succeeded in driving a wedge into the British defenses. One position after another was attacked by my "Africans" and captured in fiercest hand-to-hand combat.

The engineers had the antitank ditch bridged by 08.00 hours. The exploits of the engineers that day merited particular praise. It is difficult to conceive what it meant to do work of this kind under heavy British fire. Now the way was open and we unleashed the armor.

At about 08.00, I drove with my *Gefechtsstaffel* through the Ariete's sector and into the 15th Panzer Division's. Riding in an armored troop-carrier, I went through as far as the lanes through the minefields, which lay under heavy British artillery fire. Considerable traffic jams were piling up as a result of this fire and I sent Lieutenant Berndt up immediately to organize a smooth flow of traffic. Half an hour later, I crossed the antitank ditch with Bayerlein and examined two of the captured positions. Meanwhile, the Afrika Korps was becoming the target of British tank attacks from outside the fortress and a violent tank battle flared up, in which the artillery on both sides joined. Towards 11.00 hours, I ordered the Ariete and Trieste, who, after overcoming the antitank ditch, had come to a halt in the British defended zone, to follow up through the Afrika Korps's penetration. The German attack moved steadily on and the Afrika Korps, after a brief action in which 50 British tanks were shot up, reached the crossroad Sidi Mahmud at about midday. We held the key to Tobruk.

I now accompanied the Afrika Korps's advance onward from the crossroad. A furious fire beat into the attacking troops from the Fort Pilastrino area and several nests on the Jebel descent. Several British ships weighed anchor and made as if to leave harbor, apparently attempting to get their men away by sea. I at once directed the A.A. and artillery on to this target and six ships were sunk. Most of the men aboard them were picked up.

The advance continued and we soon reached the descent into the town, where we came up against a British strong-point which fought back with extraordinary stubbornness. I sent Lieutenant von Schlippenbach with a summons to the garrison of 50 men to surrender. Their only answer was a withering fire on our vehicles. Eventually, our outrider, Corporal Huber, covered by six antiaircraft men, succeeded in approaching the strong-point and putting the garrison out of action with hand grenades.

Pilastrino offered to capitulate in the evening and a Stuka attack on the fort was called off. Fort Solaro was stormed by my men and another gunboat sunk in the harbor. By nightfall two-thirds of the fortress was in our hands; the town and harbor had already been captured by the Afrika Korps in the afternoon.

At 05.00 hours on the 21st of June, I drove into the town of Tobruk. Practically every building of the dismal place was either flat or little more than a heap f rubble, mostly the result of our siege in 1941. Next I drove off along the Via Balbia to the west. The staff of the 32nd British Army Tank Brigade offered to surrender, which brought us 30 serviceable British tanks.[1] Vehicles stood in flames on either side of the Via Balbia. Wherever one looked there was chaos and destruction.

At about 09.40 hours, on the Via Balbiaoabout four miles west of the town, I met General Klopper, G.O.C. 2nd South African Infantry Division and garrison commandant of Tobruk. He announced the capitulation of the fortress of Tobruk. He had been unable to stave off the defeat any longer, although he had done all he could to maintain control over his troops.

I told the general, who was accompanied by his chief of staff, to follow me in his car along the Via Balbia to Tobruk. The road was lined with about 10,000 prisoners of war.

On arrival at the Hotel Tobruk, I talked for a while with General Klopper. It seemed that he had no longer been in possession

---

[1]These must have been tanks under repair in the workshops, and were not surrendered by the brigade staff proper. Only a few tanks remained in action with the brigade after its desperate fight the previous day, and the brigade commander ordered these to be destroyed that night prior to an attempt to escape on foot in small parties.—*Basil Liddell Hart*

of the necessary communications to organize a break-out. It had all gone too quickly. I instructed the South African general to make himself and his officers responsible for order among the prisoners, and to organize their maintenance from the captured stores. . . .

The capture of Tobruk, which had taken place without interference from outside, marked the conclusion of the fighting in the Marmarica. For every one of my "Africans," that 21st of June was the high point of the African war. I had the following Order of the Day issued by the Panzer Army:

Soldiers!

The great battle in the Marmarica has been crowned by your quick conquest of Tobruk. We have taken in all over 45,000 prisoners and destroyed or captured more than 1,000 armored fighting vehicles and nearly 400 guns. During the long hard struggle of the last four weeks, you have, through your incomparable courage and tenacity, dealt the enemy blow upon blow. Your spirit of attack has cost him the core of his field army, which was standing poised for an offensive. Above all, he has lost his powerful armor. My special congratulations to officers and men for this superb achievement.

Soldiers of the Panzer Army Afrika!

Now for the complete destruction of the enemy. We will not rest until we have shattered the last remnants of the British Eighth Army. During the days to come, I shall call on you for one more great effort to bring us to this final goal.

ROMMEL.

Next day Rommel heard by wireless from Hitler's headquarters that in reward for his victory he had been made a field marshal. He was 49. He was so busy in the days that followed that he quite forgot to change his shoulder badges to those of his new rank— two crossed batons. It was only after he had reached El Alamein that he was reminded of this by Field Marshal Kesselring, who gave Rommel a pair of his own badges. Rommel received his actual baton when he saw Hitler in Berlin in September. He remarked to his wife at the time: "I would rather he had given me one more division."

—Basil Liddell Hart

Alamein in Retrospect

We had lost the decisive battle of the African campaign. It was decisive because our defeat had resulted in the loss of a large part of our infantry and motorized forces. The astonishing thing was that the authorities, both German and Italian, looked for the fault not in the failure of supplies, not in our air inferiority, not in the order to conquer or die at Alamein, but in the command and troops. The military career of most of the people who aimed these accusations at us was notable for a consistent absence from the front, on the principle of *"weit vom Schuss gibt alte Krieger"*—"far from the battle makes old soldiers."

It was even said that we had thrown away our weapons, that I was a defeatist, a pessimist in adversity and therefore largely responsible. My refusal to sit down under this constant calumny aimed at my valiant troops was to involve me later in many violent arguments and rows. Our old ill-wishers particularly—men who had always resented our success—drew from our defeat the courage to vilify us, where previously they had had to keep silent. The victim of it all was my army, which, after my departure from Tunis, fell to a man into British hands, while highly qualified armchair strategists were still entertaining ideas about operations against Casablanca.

The fact is that there were men in high places who, though not without the capacity to grasp the facts of the situation, simply did not have the courage to look them in the face and draw the proper conclusions. They preferred to put their heads in the sand, live in a sort of military pipedream and look for scapegoats whom they usually found in the troops or field commanders.

Looking back, I am conscious of only one mistake—that I did not circumvent the "Victory or Death" order 24 hours earlier. Then the army would in all probability have been saved, with all its infantry, in at least a semibattleworthy condition.

To leave future historians in no doubt as to the conditions and circumstances under which both troops and command had to labor at El Alamein, I give the following summary:

The first essential condition for an army to be able to stand the strain of battle is an adequate stock of weapons, petrol and ammunition. In fact, the battle is fought and decided by the quartermasters before the shooting begins. The bravest men can do nothing without guns, the guns nothing without plenty of ammunition, and neither guns nor ammunition are of much use in mobile warfare unless there are vehicles with sufficient petrol to haul them around. Maintenance must also approximate, both in quantity and quality, that available to the enemy.

A second essential condition for an army to be able to stand in battle is parity or at least something approaching parity in the air. If the enemy has air supremacy and makes full use of it, then one's own command is forced to suffer the following limitations and disadvantages:

By using his strategic air force, the enemy can strangle one's supplies, especially if they have to be carried across the sea.

The enemy can wage the battle of attrition from the air.

Intensive exploitation by the enemy of his air superiority gives rise to far-reaching tactical limitations (already described) for one's own command.

In the future the battle on the ground will be preceded by the battle in the air. This will determine which of the contestants has to suffer the operational and tactical disadvantages detailed above, and thus be forced, throughout the battle, into adopting compromise solutions.

In our case, neither of the conditions I have described were in the slightest degree fulfilled and we had to suffer the consequences.

As a result of British command of the air in the Central Mediterranean, and of other reasons I have already given, the army's supplies were barely sufficient to keep life going, even on quiet days. A build-up for a defensive battle was out of the question. The quantity of material available to the British, on the other hand, far exceeded our worst fears. Never before in any theater of war had such a vast quantity of heavy tanks, bombers and artillery, with inexhaustible supplies of ammunition, been engaged on so short a front as at El Alamein.

British command of the air was complete. On some days they flew 800 bomber sorties and 2,500 sorties of fighters, fighter-bombers and low-flying aircraft. We, on the other hand, could fly at the most 60 dive-bomber and 100 fighter sorties. And this number continually decreased.

The principles of British command had on the whole not altered; method and rigid adherence to system were still the main feature of their tactics. But on this occasion, the British principles actually helped the Eighth Army to victory, for the following reasons:

(a) There was no open desert fighting, as our motorized forces were drawn to the front to support the frontally engaged infantry divisions.

(b) The British had such superiority in weapons, both in quality and quantity, that they were able to force through any and every operation.

The methods which the British employed for the destruction of my force were conditioned by their overwhelming material superiority. They were based on:

Extreme concentrations of artillery fire.

Continuous air attacks by powerful waves of bombers.

Locally limited attacks, executed with lavish use of material and manifesting an extremely high state of training, fully in line with previous experience and the conditions under which the battle was fought.

For the rest, the British based their planning on the principle of exact calculation, a principle which can only be followed where there is complete material superiority. They actually undertook no operations but relied simply and solely on the effect of their artillery and air force. Their command was as slow as ever in reacting. When we embarked on our retreat on the night of the 2nd November, a long time elapsed before the British forces started their pursuit—and, but for the intervention of that unfortunate order, we would probably have been able to escape to Fuka with the bulk of our infantry. Their command continued to show its customary caution and lack of resolute decision. Thus they repeatedly allowed their armored formations to attack separately, instead of throwing in the 900 or so tanks, which they could safely have committed on the northern front, in order to gain a quick decision with the minimum of effort and casualties. In fact, only half that number of tanks, acting under cover of their artillery and air force, would have sufficed to destroy my forces, which frequently stood immobile on the battlefield. These piecemeal tactics also caused the British themselves very high casualties. In all probability their command wanted to hold back its armor for the pursuit, as their assault formations could not apparently be regrouped quickly enough to follow up.

In the training of their armored and infantry formations the British command had made excellent use of the experience they had gained in previous actions with the Axis forces—although, of course, the new methods they used were only made possible by their vast stocks of ammunition, material and new equipment. These methods are described in detail in the following:

Tank Tactics

Here the new British methods were made possible by the use of new tanks, more heavily gunned and armored than ours (including the Grant, Lee and Sherman; the heavy Churchill is also said to have put in an appearance), and their inexhaustible supplies of ammunition.

With the light tanks sent out in advance, the heavier, gun-carrying tanks remained more and more in the rear. The task of the light tanks was to draw the fire of our antitank and antiaircraft guns and armor. As soon as our guns and tanks have given away their positions, the heavier British tanks opened a destructive fire on all the targets they had located, from a range of up to 2,700 yards and, if possible, from the rear slope of a hill. Their fire seemed always to be directed by the commander of the squadron. The vast quantities of ammunition which this system needed were continually fed forward in armored machine-gun carriers. By this means the British shot up our tanks, machine-gun nests and antiaircraft and antitank gun positions at a range at which our own guns were completely incapable of penetrating their heavier tanks and could not, in any case, have afforded the ammunition they would have needed to shoot themselves in.

Artillery Tactics

The British artillery once again demonstrated its well-known excellence. A particular feature was its great mobility and tremendous speed of reaction to the needs of the assault troops. The British armored units obviously carried artillery observers to transmit the needs of the front back to the artillery in the shortest possible time. In addition to the advantage given by their abundant supplies of ammunition, the British benefited greatly from the long range of their guns, which enabled them to take the Italian artillery positions under fire at a range at which the Italian guns, most of which were limited to 6,000 yards, were completely unable to hit back. As by far the greater part of our artillery was made up of these obsolete Italian guns, this was a particularly distressing circumstance for us.

Infantry Tactics

When our defense had been shattered by artillery, tanks and air force, the British infantry attacked.

With our outposts pinned down by British artillery fire—their positions had been located long before by air reconnaissance—highly trained British sappers, working under cover of smoke, cleared mines and cut broad lanes through our minefields. Then the tanks attacked, followed closely by infantry. With the tanks acting as artillery, British storming parties worked their way up to our defense posts, suddenly to force their way into our trenches and positions at the point of the bayonet. Everything went methodically and according to a drill. Each separate action was executed with a concentration of superior strength. The artillery followed up close behind the infantry in order to crush any last flickers of resistance. Success was not usually exploited in any depth but was confined to occupation of the conquered positions, into which reinforcements and artillery were then brought up and disposed for defense. Night attacks continued to be a particular specialty of the British.

Was There an Alternative?

As I have already explained at length, our own dispositions at the outset of the battle were guided by the experience we had gained in previous actions. Having once installed our infantry in the Alamein line, we were bound to accept battle there in spite of the enemy's immense superiority in artillery and ammunition. Had we withdrawn immediately, we would have had to abandon all the ammunition we had piled up at Alamein—having no transport to move it back—without having any worthwhile supplies in the rear to replace it. Quite apart from the heavy losses which the nonmotorized infantry would probably have suffered during the retreat, we would also have lost the advantage of prepared positions, for no defenses had yet been constructed at Fuka. As it was, the British suffered considerable losses in our minefields and we managed to shoot off at them almost all the ammunition we had stored in the Alamein line.

Our tactical reactions during the battle were guided by the needs of the situation and the extent of our material resources, which were small enough.

After the battle, with all the experience it had brought us, I had an idea for a plan which might have enabled us to put up a more successful defense of Western Egypt against an enemy with the material strength of Montgomery's army, attacking from Alexandria. Not that we, of course, could ever have put the plan into effect; our petrol shortage would have seen to that. Moreover, we had tied up too much of our material—material which was now irreplaceable—in the construction of the Alamein line. However, I mention the plan here because it contains one or two points of substance.

It would first have been necessary to establish the nonmotorized infantry in the Fuka line, using the maximum possible number of mines and with positions constructed similarly to those at El Alamein. The line at Fuka, like that at El Alamein, rested in the south on the Qattara depression and thus could not be turned. It had the additional advantage that steep declivities rendered some 12 miles of it in the south impassable to tanks and vehicles.

The El Alamein line would have been held by motorized formations and reconnaissance units, while the motorized forces located between Alamein and Fuka would have been grouped for a mobile defense.

On the British launching their attack, the action would probably have developed on something like the following lines: The British motorized forces would have thrust forward into open country, following up our reconnaissance and motorized forces, which would have withdrawn from the Alamein line. Then, in a position favorable to ourselves, battle would have been joined between our mobile forces and the British, who would now have been without the protection of their artillery regiments. In this battle, which would have been fought in front of the Fuka line, our armor would not, of course, have been capable of standing up to the powerful British striking groups for long. However, experience indicated that we would probably have been able to force the overcautious British into more than one difficult tactical situation and to inflict considerable losses on their striking forces. When the moment came, as it was bound to come, that the British had concentrated their forces on the battlefield and were threatening to get the upper hand—in other words, when there was a danger that a continuation of the mobile battle would work more to their advantage than to ours—we would have had to extricate our motorized forces from the battle and bring them back behind the German-Italian line before their losses had become too great. The sole purpose of this mobile fighting in front of the Fuka line would have been to soak up some of the British striking power.

In the absence of their massive artillery support, a British attack at Fuka against a line similarly constructed to that at El Alamein would have met with a bloody rebuff. They would have been forced to bring up their artillery, and this would have meant moving all their installations forward. Thus we would have been given a reprieve during which many things could have happened. The Nebelwerfer regiment might have come across, we might indeed have actually received our "Tigers"—at the very least, somebody might have done something to improve the supply situation. Even so, it is still very doubtful whether we could have held out in the African theater any longer than we actually did. I only include these notes because several of my later plans and actions in Tripolitania and Tunisia were based on principles which had been formed out of our experience at El Alamein.

I have said that our defense plan was a compromise. There was no real redress either for our inferiority in the air or for the supply situation; nor was it possible to motorize the infantry. It was left to the command in Africa to cope with these problems as best it could.

Such a compromise can be no ideal solution. We simply did what we could, with our very meager resources, to come to terms with the unalterable disadvantages under which we suffered. It was a matter of getting the best out of a hopeless situation. Armed with a pitchfork, the finest fighting man can do little against an opponent with a tommy-gun in his hands.

No one can say that we had not given warning, months before the British offensive, that the army would be unable to fight a successful defense, unless a minimum specific build-up was created in Africa and unless certain specific quantities of reinforcements and replacement material reached African soil. That this was not done was very well known to the people who later flung the most mud. To quote only one example—instead of the thirty issues of petrol I had demanded, we had had three. The figure I had given for our material requirements had been based on the anticipated increase in British strength. I could not of course have foreseen just how great the strength of the British was actually to be.

In these circumstances, there was never any chance of the army achieving success at El Alamein. Our sole advantage, compared with the many afforded to the enemy, was the possession of prepared positions; but these were soon stormed, after a terrible artillery and air bombardment, by British infantry, who gnawed their way yard by yard into our defense system. One sector after another of the northern front fell into British hands, until finally the Axis troops lost the whole of the northern part of their line. A further stand at El Alamein was then senseless, for not only were the defending forces exposed to the full weight of the enemy's nonstop air attacks in roughly improvised positions, but also the vehicle assemblies were being obliterated by the torrential British artillery fire. That way lay destruction.

Our counterattacks early in the battle could not be made with a concentration of strength, as British assembly areas in the southern sector gave us good cause to fear that if we drew off all the motorized forces they would attack there as well. And the shortage of petrol would never have allowed us to move the Ariete and 21st Panzer Division back there again. At that stage of the battle, therefore, it was too great a risk to draw off all our motorized forces from the southern front to the north.

There is another very important point to be taken into account. Any formation we employed on the northern front was ground away by the British bombing and drum-fire far more quickly than were the attacking British by our defensive fire. The units which remained in their starting positions mostly had their vehicles dug in and were comparatively seldom attacked. But the northern sector was like a mill. Everything that went into it, regardless of quantity, was ground down to dust.

The bravery of the German and of many of the Italian troops in this battle, even in the hour of disaster, was admirable. The army had behind it a record of 18 magnificent months, such as has seldom been equalled, and every one of my soldiers who fought at Alamein was defending not only his homeland, but also the tradition of the Panzer Army "Afrika." The struggle of my army, despite its defeat, will be a glorious page in the annals of the German and Italian peoples.

Sorties by the German Luftwaffe during the Battle of El Alamein[1]

Date	Total Sorties	Fighter Sorties	Tons of Bombs Dropped
24/10/42	107	69	5.0
25/10/42	140	49	22.0
26/10/42	113	63	28.1
27/10/42	147	78	29.1
28/10/42	163	106	20.2
29/10/42	196	129	29.1
30/10/42	200[2]	125	30.5[2]
31/10/42	242	128	43.3
1/11/42	141	80	12.8
2/11/42	175	111	20.7

[1]These figures were given to Rommel by General Seidemann, Commander of the Luftwaffe in Africa.
[2]Figures for 30/10/42 are estimates only.

Battle Strength, According to Returns, of German-Italian Armored Formations during the Battle of El Alamein

Nature of Action	Date	No. of Tanks held by German and Italian Formations		
		Panzer II, III, IV	M-Tank	L-Tank
	24/10/42	219	318	21
	25/10/42	154	270	21
	26/10/42	162	221	21
Defense	27/10/42	137	210	21
and counter-	28/10/42	81	197	21
attacks	29/10/42	109	190	21
with	30/10/42	116	201	21
limited objective	31/10/42	106	198	21
	1/11/42	109	189	21
	2/11/42	32	140[1]	15[1]
	3/11/42	24	120[1]	0[1]
Decisive break-through	4/11/42	12	0	0

[1]Estimates only.

CHAPTER X

THE BATTLE
FOR LEYTE, 1944

Four major sea battles took place at Leyte Gulf and the surrounding Pacific waters between the fleets of the U.S. Navy and those of Japan. It was the road back to the Philippines—and the U.S. Sixth Army was landing.

General of the Army Douglas MacArthur was to write:

There was Tacloban. It had changed little since I had known it forty-one years before on my first assignment after leaving West Point. It was a full moment for me. Shortly after this, we reached our appointed position offshore. The captain carefully hove into line and dropped anchor. Our initial vantage point was 2 miles from the beaches, but I could clearly see the sandstrips with the pounding surf beating down upon the shore, and in the morning sunlight, the jungle-clad hills rising behind the town. . . . Rocket vapor trails crisscrossed the sky and black, ugly, ominous pillars of smoke began to rise. High overhead, swarms of airplanes darted into the maelstrom. And across what would ordinarily have been a glinting, untroubled blue sea, the black dots of the landing craft churned toward the beaches.

But what was taking place at sea?

Considered the greatest series of sea battles according to naval and military historians, Captain B. H. Liddell Hart, the British historian, relates the events leading up and to the invasion of Leyte Gulf. His is the historian's view after the battles; the errors made by the U.S. and Japanese commanders; the uncertainties, guesses, plans—discarded, and new plans made; the enormous destruction that U.S. planes and ships brought upon the Japanese fleets attempting to choke off ships landing the invading U.S. forces in the Philippines.

In the second part of this chapter on Leyte is Fleet Admiral William (Bull) Halsey's own story of the Third Fleet. Between Halsey's pithy comments and historian Liddell Hart's studied views, is the reckoning, *dead ahead.*

The Liberation of the South-West Pacific
by
B. H. Liddell Hart

At this stage of the war it might well have been possible for the United States forces to bypass the Philippines, and move on in their next bound to Formosa, or to Iwo Jima and Okinawa, as Fleet Admiral King and several other naval chiefs urged. But political considerations, and MacArthur's natural desire for a triumphant return to the Philippines, prevailed against such arguments for bypassing these great islands.

There were several small objectives whose capture had been considered necessary prior to the invasion of the Philippines. The original scheme had been to capture Morotai Island near the Halmaheras (west of New Guinea), the Palau Islands, Yap Island, the Talaud Islands, and then Mindanao—the great southern island of the Philippines—building advance air and naval bases to aid the main attack on the Philippines. Early in September, however, Admiral Halsey's 3rd Fleet (called the 5th Fleet when Spruance controlled it) found that the defenses of the Philippine coast were very weak, and he accordingly proposed that the intermediate stages should be dropped. However, the early parts of this original plan were retained as they were almost under way, and felt to be an extra insurance.

A detachment from MacArthur's forces landed on Morotai Island on September 15, meeting little opposition, and by October 4 American aircraft were operating from the newly built air base there. On September 15, also, the Palau Islands were invaded by Admiral Halsey's Central Pacific forces, and were mostly occupied within a few days. That provided them with advanced airfields only 500 miles from Mindanao, more than halfway from Guam.

The two main lines of advance across the Pacific, MacArthur's and Nimitz's, had now converged, and were within direct supporting distance of one another—ready and able to attempt the reconquest of the Philippines.

The Japanese plan for the defense of the Philippines, known as "SHO-I," was two-fold. On land, it was entrusted to the 14th Area Army under General Yamashita, the conqueror of Malaya in 1941–42, who had for the purpose nine infantry divisions, one armored division, and three independent brigades, plus the 4th Air Army. His command included in addition the naval forces around Manila, which numbered some 25,000 men capable of land fighting. The key part of the plan, however, was the intended action at sea, and on this the Japanese High Command was now disposed to stake everything. As soon as the location of the American landings was known, the Japanese carrier forces were to lure the American fleet northward, while the American landing forces were to be pinned by Yamashita's troops and "pincered" by the two Japanese battleship groups. Toyoda calculated that the Americans, who had come to value the carriers above all, would be the more likely to rush after their opposite numbers as they themselves had always used battleships as the decoy, and carriers as the striking force.

The plan was influenced by Japan's growing weakness in the air, but buttressed by continued faith in battleships. The admirals' pride and confidence had been unduly heightened by the completion of two colossal battleships, much the biggest in the world— the *Yamato* and *Musashi*. These had a displacement of over 70,- 000 tons and mounted nine 18-inch guns—they were the only warships in the world to mount so many guns of that size. By comparison the Japanese had done little, far too little, to develop their carrier-force and the aircraft it required. As so often happens in history, they had been slower than their opponents to apply the lesson of their own great successes at the outset of the war.

Accelerating the planned program by two months, the Americans made their next big bound, to the Philippines, in October. These islands stretch a thousand miles—from Mindanao in the south, as big as Ireland, to Luzon in the north, nearly as big as England. The first thrust was delivered against Leyte, one of the smaller central islands, thus splitting the defense. MacArthur's troops—four divisions of Lieutenant-General Walter Krueger's Sixth Army—began to be landed there on the morning of October 20 by Admiral Kinkaid's 7th Fleet—a convoy and support fleet composed of old battleships and small escort carriers. It was backed and covered by Admiral Halsey's 3rd Fleet—which took up its station, in three groups, a little east of the Philippines. This was the main battle fleet, composed of the newer battleships and of large carriers, all fast.

The invasion had been preceded by a series of air strikes from October 10 on for a week by Mitscher's carrier forces (of Halsey's 3rd Fleet) against Formosa, and to a lesser extent against Luzon and Okinawa, that were of devastating effect and proved of great importance in their influence on subsequent events. On the other hand, the Japanese pilots made such exaggerated claims that their government in official communiqués and broadcasts claimed to have sunk eleven carriers, two battleships, and three cruisers. Actually these American carrier strikes had destroyed over 500 Japanese planes, while losing only 79 of their own—and none of the ships that the Japanese had claimed. Momentary belief in the truth of these claims led the Imperial G.H.Q. to move forward the rest of the forces for the "SHO-I" operation. The naval forces soon discovered the absurdity of these claims, and withdrew, but the army's plans were permanently changed in consequence—three of Suzuki's four divisions in the southern part of the Philippines being ordered to stand there instead of being kept ready for use in the north, in Luzon, as Yamashita had intended.

As already mentioned, the Japanese High Command had planned a crushing counterstroke with all available naval forces when and where the thrust came. Two days before the landing on Leyte Island, an uncoded message sent out from one of the American chiefs provided the Japanese with the vital information they required as a guide for their counterstroke.

Toyoda realized that it was a gamble, but the Japanese Navy depended for its fuel supplies on the oil from the captured East Indies, and if the Americans established themselves in the East Indies that line of supply would be cut. When questioned after the war, Toyoda explained his calculations thus:

> If the worst should happen there was a chance that we would lose the entire fleet; but I felt that that chance had to be taken . . . should we lose in the Philippine operations, even though the fleet should be left, the shipping lane to the south would be completely cut off so that the fleet, if it should come back to Japanese waters, could not obtain its fuel supply. If it should remain in southern waters, it could not receive supplies of ammunition and arms. There would be no sense in saving the fleet at the expense of the loss of the Philippines.

The decoy was to be provided by Admiral Ozawa's force, coming south from Japan. It included the four aircraft-carriers that remained serviceable and two battleships converted to carriers, but could not act as much more than a decoy since its total of aircraft was down to barely a hundred and most of the pilots lacked experience.

So in this great gamble for victory the Japanese relied on an old-fashioned fleet—of seven battleships, thirteen cruisers, and three light cruisers—which came up from the Singapore area. The commander, Admiral Kurita, sent a detachment to push into Leyte Gulf from the southwest via the Surigao Strait, while he came in with the main force from the northwest, through the San Bernardino Strait. He hoped to crush MacArthur's transports and their escorting warships between his two jaws.

He thought the *Yamato* and *Musashi,* with their 18-inch guns, easily able to pulverize the older American battleships and believed them to be almost unsinkable owing to their armored decks and much subdivided hulls. Moreover, air attack should not be heavy if Halsey's carrier-force was off the scene. It was hoped that this would have been lured away by the time that Kurita broke into the Leyte Gulf—a stroke timed for delivery on October 25.

But the decoy did not work. On the night of the 23rd Kurita bumped into a couple of American submarines, the *Darter* and the *Dace,* which had been cruising off the coast of Borneo. These promptly hurried northward, keeping ahead of the Japanese fleet by running full speed on the surface under cover of the dark. When first light came they submerged to periscope depth, awaited the oncoming fleet, and then fired their torpedoes at close range —sinking two of the Japanese cruisers and crippling another. Kurita himself was in the leading cruiser, and although he was rescued before it sank—and later transferred to the *Yamato*—it was a shaking experience. Moreover the American admirals had been made aware of the enemy's approach and strength.

When Ozawa heard of Kurita's clash with the submarines, he made haste to reveal his own approach from the north, sending out uncoded signals repeatedly to catch Halsey's attention. But his signals were not picked up by the Americans. Nor was he spotted by any of their reconnaissance planes—as all of them were sent westward to watch for Kurita's approach!

Soon Halsey's carriers launched their bombers and torpedo-bombers in waves against Kurita's fleet. The only interruption to their onslaught came from the relieving attacks of Japanese land-based aircraft from the islands, and also from Ozawa's carriers. These were beaten off and more than 50 per cent of the attacking planes shot down, though the carrier *Princeton* was badly hit and had to be abandoned.

The American naval planes achieved a greater success in their attacks on Kurita's fleet. For the Goliath-like *Musashi* capsized and sank after the fifth attack, in the afternoon—after a total of 19 hits by torpedoes and 17 hits by bombs. Although the American pilots reported that three other battleships and three heavy cruisers had been heavily hit, actually only one ship, a heavy cruiser, was too badly damaged to continue. After the fifth on-slaught and the sinking of the *Musashi,* however, the Japanese fleet turned about and steamed away to the west.

On getting these reports from his air observers it appeared to Admiral Halsey that Kurita was definitely in retreat. But the fact that no aircraft carriers had been seen in either part of Kurita's fleet had led Halsey to send out reconnaissance planes on a wider search for them, and about 5:00 P.M. Ozawa's force was spotted on its way southward. Thereupon Halsey decided to dash north and smash it at dawn, following his motto "Whatever we do, we do fast." To make sure of annihilating Ozawa's force he took the whole of his available fleet, leaving nothing behind to guard San Bernardino Strait.

A quarter of an hour after announcing his decision in a signal to Kinkaid, a report was received from a night reconnaissance plane that Kurita had turned round again and was steaming at high speed towards the Strait. Halsey discounted the report. Now that he saw the opportunity of playing the kind of bold and dashing game he loved he became blind to other possibilities. Early in the war he had been aptly nicknamed "The Bull."

Kurita's retreat had been only a temporary expedient to get out of reach of air attack while daylight lasted, with the intention of returning under the cloak of darkness. Apart from the sinking of the *Musashi* none of his bigger ships had been seriously damaged —contrary to what the American pilots had optimistically reported.

At 11:00 P.M., when Halsey had gone 160 miles northward, Kurita's fleet was again spotted by reconnaissance planes—still heading for San Bernardino Strait and now only 40 miles away. Halsey could no longer ignore its advance, but discounted the seriousness of the threat, regarding the renewed advance as merely a sacrificial effort on traditional Japanese lines by a badly crippled fleet. He pushed on northward, confidently assuming that Kinkaid's fleet would easily be able to beat off what he supposed to be a much weakened attacker.

So the Japanese bait, though it had not been taken at the intended time, was swallowed in the end.

The situation of Kinkaid's fleet was the more dangerous because he was misled in a double way. The appearance of Kurita's southern detachment, heading for Surigao Strait, had focused Kinkaid's attention in that direction, and he concentrated most of his force there to meet this threat. He assumed that part of Halsey's battle fleet was still covering the more northerly approach through San Bernardino Strait, as it had not been made clear that Halsey had sailed away with the whole fleet. Worse still, Kinkaid did not take the precaution of sending out any reconnaissance to see if any enemy was approaching from that direction.

The attack by the Japanese southern detachment was defeated after a tense night battle—thanks largely to the "night-sight" provided by the Americans' radar, which was much superior to that of the Japanese Navy. Another Japanese disadvantage was that as their ships came in line ahead through the narrow Surigao Strait, they were exposed to the concentrated fire of Admiral Oldendorf's battleships—which could thus "cross the T." The detachment included two battleships, and both were sunk. Almost the whole of the attacking force was wiped out. When daylight came the Strait was empty of the enemy except for bits of floating wreckage and streaks of oil.

But a few minutes after Kinkaid had signalled his congratulations on the victory, another signal came to say that a much larger Japanese force—Kurita's main fleet—had come down from the northwest, through San Bernardino Strait, and was off the east coast of Samar Island assailing the smaller portion of Kinkaid's fleet that had been left there to cover General MacArthur's landing points on Leyte.

This small force, supporting the army's invasion of Leyte Island, comprised six escort-carriers—converted merchant ships—and a handful of destroyers. They fled southward under a hail of heavy shells from the giant *Yamato* and the other three battleships.

After getting this alarming news, Kinkaid sent a signal to Halsey, at 8:30 A.M.: "Urgently need fast battleships Leyte Gulf at once." At 9:00 A.M. Kinkaid made another pressing appeal, and this time, in clear, instead of in code. But Halsey continued to steam northward, determined to fulfill his aim of destroying Ozawa's carrier force. He persisted on this course despite Kinkaid's repeated appeals for help—feeling that Kinkaid's carrier-borne aircraft should be able to hold off Kurita's attack until the bulk of Kinkaid's fleet, with its six battleships, came up to the rescue. He did, however, order a small detached force of carriers and cruisers under Admiral John McCain, then in the Caroline Islands, to hasten to Kinkaid's help. But it was 400 miles away—50 miles farther than he was.

Meantime a brake was put on Kurita's southward onrush by the gallant efforts of the handful of American destroyers that were covering the retreat of the six escort-carriers, as well as of such planes as these still had available. One escort-carrier and three destroyers were sunk, but the rest escaped, though battered.

Just after 9:00 A.M. Kurita broke off the chase and turned towards Leyte Gulf, where a mass of American transports and landing craft now lay open to attack. He was then less than 30 miles from the entrance.

Before striking he paused to concentrate his ships, which had become dispersed in the running fight. The turn and pause again created the mistaken idea on the Americans' side that he was retiring—under pressure of their air and destroyer attacks. They were soon disillusioned, and Kinkaid sent another urgent call for Halsey's help: "Situation again very serious. Escort-carriers again threatened by enemy surface forces. Your assistance badly needed. Escort-carriers retiring to Leyte Gulf."

This time Halsey responded to the appeal. By now, 11:15 A.M., his planes had severely mauled Ozawa's force, and although he dearly wanted to finish it off with his battleships' guns, he curbed his desire and came racing back with his six fast battleships and one of his three carrier groups. But he had gone so far north in pursuit of Ozawa that he could not possibly reach Leyte Gulf until the next morning. Even McCain's carrier force would not arrive near enough to intervene with its planes for several hours still. So the situation at Leyte looked very grim at midday as Kurita's fleet bore in towards the Gulf.

But suddenly Kurita turned back north—and this time for good. What was the cause? A combination of intercepted messages and their effect on his mind. The first was a radio call telling the aircraft of the American escort-carriers to land on Leyte Island. He imagined that this was preparatory to a land-based and more concentrated attack on his ships, whereas it was merely an emergency measure to save them from being sunk with the carriers. A few minutes later he received an intercept report of Kinkaid's 9:00 A.M. signal in clear to Halsey. From this he jumped to the mistaken conclusion that Halsey must have been racing south for more than three hours, for Kurita was out of touch with Ozawa and did not know how far north Halsey had gone. Also, he was worried about his lack of air cover.

The crowning effect came from a confused intercept which gave him the impression that part of the American relieving force was only 70 miles north of him and already close to his line of retreat through the San Bernardino Strait. So he decided to abandon his attack on Leyte Gulf and hurry north to tackle this threat before it was reinforced and his line of retreat blocked.

It was one more of the many cases in history which show that battles are apt to be decided more by fancies than by facts. The impression made on the commander's mind often counts much more than any actual blow and its physical effect.

When Kurita reached San Bernardino Strait he found no enemy there, and slipped away through it to the westward. Although he did not reach this bolt-hole until nearly 10:00 P.M.—delayed in the process by having to dodge repeated air attacks—that was three hours before Halsey's leading ships arrived there in their race southward.

But the escape of the Japanese battleships, which had achieved so little, was amply compensated by the sinking of all the four Japanese carriers—one, the *Chitose,* about 9:30 A.M. by Mitscher's first strike, and the other three *(Chiyoda, Zuikaku,* and *Zuiho)* in the afternoon, after Halsey with the bulk of his fleet had departed on his belated southward dash.

Regarding as a whole its four separate and distinct actions, the Battle of Leyte Gulf, as it is collectively called, was the largest naval battle of all time. A total of 282 ships was engaged as well as hundreds of aircraft, compared with 250 (with five seaplanes) in the 1916 Battle of Jutland. If the June battle of the Philippine Sea had been in a sense more decisive, through its devastating effects on Japanese naval air strength, the four-piece Battle of Leyte Gulf reaped the harvest and settled the issue. The Japanese ship losses in it were four carriers, three battleships, six heavy cruisers, three light cruisers, and eight destroyers—whereas the Americans lost only one light carrier, two escort carriers, and three destroyers.

It is worth mention that this battle also saw the inauguration of a new form of tactics, difficult to counter. For after the American escort-carriers of Kinkaid's 7th Fleet had succeeded in surviving the unexpected and overwhelmingly powerful onslaught of Kurita's "Center Force" until Kurita was led to turn about and withdraw through the San Bernardino Strait, they were then subjected to the first organized "Kamikaze" attack—carried out by pilots who had volunteered for a special air corps dedicated to the sacrificial, suicidal mission of crash-diving their planes on to an enemy ship, setting it on fire with their burst fuel-tanks and the explosion of their bombs. In their first essay, however, only one escort-carrier was sunk, although several were damaged.

The major significance of the battle lay in the sinking of Ozawa's four aircraft-carriers. Without any carriers, the six remaining Japanese battleships were helpless, and they made no further positive contribution in the war. Moreover the Japanese Navy was rendered useless. Thus, while Halsey's northward dash had exposed the rest of the American forces to grave dangers, the outcome provided justification. Moreover it showed the hollowness of the battleship bogey, and exposed the folly of the faith that had been placed in such out-of-date monsters. Their only important value in World War II was for shore bombardment—a role for which, ironically, they had in previous generations been considered unsuitable, and too vulnerable.

I Turn North
by
Fleet Admiral William F. Halsey

. . . The tremendous battle . . . now loomed. . . . We had two fleets in Philippine waters under separate commands: my Third Fleet was under command of Admiral Nimitz; Tom Kinkaid's Seventh Fleet was under command of General MacArthur. If we had been under the same command, with a single system of operational control and intelligence, the Battle for Leyte Gulf might have been fought differently to a different result. It is folly to cry over spilled milk, but it is wisdom to observe the cause, for future avoidance. When blood has been spilled, the obligation becomes vital. In my opinion, it is vital for the navy never to expose itself again to the perils of a divided command in the same area.

The Third and Seventh Fleets also differed in functions and weapons. The Seventh Fleet was defensive; having convoyed MacArthur's transports to Leyte, it stood by to protect them with its cruisers, destroyers, old battleships, and little escort carriers. The Third Fleet was offensive; it prowled the ocean, striking at will with its new battleships and fast carriers. These powerful units were concentrated in Pete Mitscher's Task Force 38, which was made up of four task groups, commanded by Vice Admiral Slew McCain and Rear Admirals Gerald F. Bogan, Ted Sherman, and Ralph E. Davison. The task groups were not uniform, but they averaged a total of twenty-three ships, divided approximately as follows—two large carriers, two light carriers, and two new battleships, with a screen of three cruisers and fourteen destroyers. My flagship, the *New Jersey,* was in Bogan's group; Mitscher's flagship, the *Lexington,* was in Sherman's.

The morning of October 23 found McCain's group on its way to Ulithi for rest and replenishment. The other three were standing eastward of the Philippines, awaiting their turn to retire, and meanwhile preparing further strikes in support of MacArthur. On the basis of the Darter's report, I ordered them to close the islands and to launch search teams next morning in a fan that would cover the western sea approaches for the entire length of the chain. Experience had taught us that if we interfered with a Jap plan before it matured, we stood a good chance of disrupting it. The Jap mind is inelastic; it cannot adapt itself to an altered situation.

The three task groups reached their stations that night—Sherman, off the Polillo Islands; 140 miles southeast of him, Bogan, off San Bernardino Strait; 120 miles southeast of Bogan, Davison, off Surigao Strait. Their search teams flew out at daybreak on the twenty-fourth. At 0820, one of Bogan's teams reported contact with five battleships, nine cruisers, and thirteen destroyers south of Mindoro Island, course 050, speed ten to twelve knots. (This force, the Central Force, was the same that had been dimly sighted by the *Darter;* she and a sister sub, the *Dace,* had already sunk two of its heavy cruisers and damaged a third.)

My log summarizes the events of the next few minutes:

At 0822, I rebroadcast Bogan's report at the top of my radio voice.

At 0827, I ordered Sherman and Davison to close on Bogan at their best speed.

At 0837, I ordered all task groups by TBS, "Strike! Repeat: Strike! Good luck!"

And at 0846, I ordered McCain to reverse course and prepare to fuel at sea. If the battle developed as I expected, we would need him.

Our planes hit the Central Force again and again through the day and reported sinking the battleship *Musashi* (Japan's newest and largest), three more cruisers, and a destroyer, and inflicting severe damage on many other units. These seemed to mill around aimlessly, then withdrew to the west, then turned east again, as if they had suddenly received a do-or-die command from Hirohito himself. (A year later I learned that our guess was close. Vice Admiral Kurita, commanding the Central Force, had strongly considered retiring, but had received this dispatch from Admiral Toyoda, commander in chief of the Japanese Combined Fleet: WITH CONFIDENCE IN HEAVENLY GUIDANCE, THE ENTIRE FORCE WILL ATTACK.)

That they might attempt to transit San Bernardino Strait, despite their fearful mauling, was a possibility I had to recognize. Accordingly, at 1512 I sent a preparatory dispatch to all task-force commanders in the Third Fleet and all task-group commanders in TF 38, designating four of their fast battleships (including the *New Jersey*), with two heavy cruisers, three light cruisers, and fourteen destroyers, and stating that these ships WILL BE FORMED AS TF 34 UNDER VADM (Willis A.), LEE, COMMANDER BATTLE LINE X TF 34 WILL ENGAGE DECISIVELY AT LONG RANGES.

This dispatch, which played a critical part in next day's battle, I intended merely as warning to the ships concerned that *if a surface engagement offered,* I would detach them from TF 38, form them into TF 34, and send them ahead as a battle line. It was definitely *not* an executive dispatch, but a battle plan, and was so marked. To make certain that none of my subordinate commanders misconstrued it, I told them later by TBS, "If the enemy sorties (through San Bernardino), TF 34 will be formed *when directed by me.*"

Meanwhile, at 0943, we had intercepted a message from one of Davison's search teams, reporting that it had sighted the enemy's Southern Force—two old battleships, three heavy cruisers, one light cruiser, and eight destroyers, southwest of Negros Island, course 060, speed fifteen knots—and had scored several damaging hits with bombs and rockets. We did not send a strike against this comparatively weak force for two reasons: it was headed for Surigao Strait, where Kinkaid was waiting with approximately three times its weight of metal—six old battleships, four heavy cruisers, four light cruisers, and twenty-six destroyers, plus thirty PT's; second, Davison's planes, the only ones able to reach it, were more urgently needed at the Central Force, now that Sherman's group was under violent attack by shore-based planes from Luzon. He shot down 110 of them, but they succeeded in bombing the light carrier *Princeton.* The fires reached her magazines and fuel tanks, and late that afternoon he had to order her abandoned and sunk —the first fast carrier that the Navy had lost since the *Hornet* was torpedoed at the Battle of Santa Cruz two years before, almost to the day.

The captain of the *Princeton* was Captain William H. Buracker, who had been my Operations officer at the beginning of the war. He would have been detached in a few days, and his relief was already aboard—Captain John M. Hoskins. The bomb that gave the *Princeton* her deathblow nearly gave Hoskins his; it mangled one foot so badly that the ship's medical officer, himself wounded, cut it off with a sheath knife. Hoskins was then put into a stretcher and carried through the flames to the f'c'sle, but before letting himself be lowered to a whaleboat standing by, he smiled, saluted Bill Buracker, and asked, "Have I your permission to leave the ship, sir?"

(Later, fitted with an artificial foot, he requested command of the new *Princeton* and recommended himself as being "one foot ahead of the other applicants"; further, he said, he could beat them all turning out for general quarters, because he was already wearing a sock and a shoe. I am happy to say that Hoskins put the new *Princeton* in commission and is now a rear admiral.)

The discovery of the Southern Force buttressed my conviction that the Japs were committed to a supreme effort, but the final proof was still lacking—their carriers. Neither our submarines nor search planes had found them yet, but we were dead certain that they would appear; our only doubt was from what direction. Mitscher thought from the China Sea. My staff thought from Empire waters. I agreed with my staff and ordered a thorough search northward. While we waited for a report, Doug Moulton must have pounded the chart 50 times, demanding, "Where the hell *are* they, those goddam carriers?" At 1730 our guess was proved correct. Sherman informed me, 3 CARRIERS 2 LIGHT CRUISERS 3 DESTROYERS 18–32 N 125–28 E COURSE 270 SPEED 15.

This position, 200 miles east of Cape Engano, the northeastern tip of Luzon, was too far for us to reach, even if dusk had not already fallen. But now we had all the pieces of the puzzle. When we put them together, we noticed that the three forces had a common factor: a speed of advance so leisurely—never more than fifteen knots—that it implied a focus of time and place. The crippled Central Force's dogged second approach to San Bernardino, and the weak Southern Force's simultaneous approach to Surigao against overwhelming strength, were comprehensible only if they were under adamant orders to rendezvous with the carriers—the Northern Force—off Samar next day, the twenty-fifth, for a combined attack on the transports at Leyte.

We had no intention of standing by for a test of our theory. Our intention was to join battle as quickly as possible. Three battles offered. The Southern Force I could afford to ignore; it was well within Kinkaid's compass. The Central Force, according to our pilots, had suffered so much topside damage, especially to its guns and fire-control instruments, that it could not win a decision; it, too, could be left to Kinkaid. (The pilots' reports proved dangerously optimistic, but we had no reason to discredit them at the time.) On the other hand, not only was the Northern Force fresh and undamaged, but its carriers gave it a scope several hundred miles wider than the others. Moreover, if we destroyed those carriers, our future operations need fear no threat from the sea.

We had chosen our antagonist. It remained only to choose the best way to meet him. Again I had three alternatives:

1. *I could guard San Bernardino with my whole fleet and wait for the Northern Force to strike me.* Rejected. It yielded to the enemy the double initiative of his carriers and his fields on Luzon and would allow him to use them unmolested.

2. *I could guard San Bernardino with TF 34 while I struck the Northern Force with my carriers.* Rejected. The enemy's potential surface and air strength forbade half-measures; if his shore-based planes joined his carrier planes, together they might inflict far more damage on my half-fleets separately than they could inflict on the fleet intact.

3. *I could leave San Bernardino unguarded and strike the Northern Force with my whole fleet.* Accepted. It preserved my fleet's integrity, it left the initiative with me, and it promised the greatest possibility of surprise. Even if the Central Force meanwhile penetrated San Bernardino and headed for Leyte Gulf, it could hope only to harry the landing operation. It could not consolidate any advantage, because no transports accompanied it and no supply ships. It could merely hit and run.

My decision to strike the Northern Force was a hard one to make, but given the same circumstances and the same information as I had then, I would make it again.

I went into flag plot, put my finger on the Northern Force's charted position, 300 miles away, and said, "Here's where we're going, Mick, start them north."

The time was about 1950. Mick began to scribble a sheaf of dispatches: McCain to close us at his best speed; for Bogan and Davison, COURSE 000 (due north) SPEED 25; Sherman to join us as we dashed by; for Kinkaid, CENTRAL FORCE HEAVILY DAMAGED ACCORDING TO STRIKE REPORTS X AM PROCEEDING NORTH WITH 3 GROUPS TO ATTACK CARRIER FORCE AT DAWN; for the light carrier *Independence,* which was equipped with night fighters, AT 2400 LAUNCH 5 PLANES TO SEARCH SECTORS 320–010 (roughly, from northwest to north-by-east) TO 350 MILES;

finally, at 2330, for Mitscher, SLOW DOWN TO 16 KNOTS X HOLD PRESENT COURSE UNTIL 2400, THEN PROCEED TOWARD LAT 16 LONG 127 (northeastward).

The purpose of this was to avoid overrunning the Northern Force's "daylight circle," the limit which it could reach by dawn from its last known position. If the enemy slipped past my left flank, between me and Luzon, he would have a free crack at the transports. If he slipped past my right flank, he would be able to shuttle-bomb me—fly from his carriers, attack me, continue on to his fields on Luzon for more bombs and fuel, and attack me again on the way back. I had to meet him head-on, and I was trusting the *Independence*'s snoopers to set my course.

They began to report at 0208: CONTACT POSIT 17–10 N 125–31 E X 5 SHIPS 2 LARGE 2 SMALL 1 SIZE UNREPORTED.

At 0214: CORRECTION X 6 SHIPS 3 LARGE 3 SMALL COURSE 110 SPEED 15.

At 0220: ANOTHER GROUP 40 MILES ASTERN OF FIRST.

At 0235: SECOND GROUP 6 LARGE SHIPS.

We had them!

Later sightings, in daylight, established the composition of the Northern Force as one large carrier, three light carriers, two hermaphrodite battleships with flight decks aft (a typical gimcrack Jap makeshift), three light cruisers, and at least eight destroyers.

I ordered TF 34 to form and take station ten miles in advance, and my task-group commanders to arm their first deckload strike at once, launch it at earliest dawn, and launch a second strike as soon afterward as possible. Our next few hours were the most anxious of all. The pilots and aircrewmen knew that a terrific carrier duel was facing them, and the ships' companies were sure that a big-gun action would follow.

The first strike took off at 0630. An hour and a half passed without a word of news. . . . Two hours. . . . Two hours and a quarter. . . . God, what a wait it was! (Mick admitted later, "I chewed my fingernails down to my elbows.") Then, at 0850, a flash report reached me: ONE CARRIER SUNK AFTER TREMENDOUS EXPLOSION X 2 CARRIERS 1 CL (light cruiser)

HIT BADLY OTHER CARRIER UNTOUCHED X FORCE
COURSE 150 SPEED 17.

We had already increased our speed to twenty-five knots. If the
enemy held his course and speed, he would be under our guns
before noon. I rubbed my hands at the prospect of blasting the
cripples that our planes were setting up for us.

Now I come to the part of this narrative that I can hardly bring
myself to write, so painfully does it rankle still. I can reconstruct
it best from a sequence of dispatches in my war diary:

At 0648, I had received a dispatch from Kinkaid: AM NOW
ENGAGING ENEMY SURFACE FORCES SURIGAO
STRAIT X QUESTION IS TF 34 GUARDING SAN BER-
NARDINO STRAIT. To this I replied in some bewilderment,
NEGATIVE X IT IS WITH OUR CARRIERS NOW ENGAG-
ING ENEMY CARRIERS. Here was my first intimation that
Kinkaid had intercepted and misconstrued the preparatory dis-
patch I had sent at 1512 the preceding day. I say "intercepted"
because it was not addressed to him, which fact alone should have
prevented his confusion. I was not alarmed, because at 0802 I
learned from him, ENEMY VESSELS RETIRING SURIGAO
STRAIT X OUR LIGHT FORCES IN PURSUIT.

When the Southern Force pushed into Surigao soon after midnight of the twenty-fourth, it pushed into one of the prettiest
ambushes in naval history. Rear Admiral Jesse B. Oldendorf,
Kinkaid's tactical commander, waited until the enemy line was
well committed to the narrow waters, then struck from both flanks
with his PT's and destroyers, and from dead ahead with his battleships and cruisers. He not only "crossed the T," which is every
naval officer's dearest ambition; he dotted several thousand slant
eyes. Almost before the Japs could open fire, they lost both their
battleships and three destroyers. The rest fled, but Kinkaid's
planes caught and sank a heavy cruiser later in the morning, and
Army B-24's sank the light cruiser the following noon. One of
Oldendorf's PT's was sunk, and one destroyer was damaged.

At 0822, twenty minutes after Kinkaid's second dispatch, I
received his third: ENEMY BBS AND CRUISER REPORTED
FIRING ON TU 77.4.3 FROM 15 MILES ASTERN. Task unit
77.4.3, commanded by Rear Admiral Clifton A. F. Sprague and

comprising six escort carriers, three destroyers, and four destroyer escorts, was the northernmost of three similar task units in the Seventh Fleet's TG 77.4, assigned to guard the eastern approaches to Leyte. The enemy ships were evidently part of the Central Force, which had steamed through San Bernardino during the night. I wondered how Kinkaid had let "Ziggy" Sprague get caught like this, and why Ziggy's search planes had not given him warning, but I still was not alarmed. I figured that the eighteen little carriers had enough planes to protect themselves until Oldendorf could bring up his heavy ships.

Eight minutes later, at 0830, Kinkaid's fourth dispatch reached me: URGENTLY NEED FAST BBS LEYTE GULF AT ONCE. That surprised me. It was not my job to protect the Seventh Fleet. My job was offensive, to strike with the Third Fleet, and we were even then rushing to intercept a force which gravely threatened not only Kinkaid and myself, but the whole Pacific strategy. However, I ordered McCain, who was fueling to the east, STRIKE ENEMY VICINITY 11–20 N 127–00 E AT BEST POSSIBLE SPEED, and so notified Kinkaid.

At 0900 I received his fifth dispatch: OUR CVES (escort carriers) BEING ATTACKED BY 4 BBS 8 CRUISERS PLUS OTHERS X REQUEST LEE (Commanding TF 34, the battle line) COVER LEYTE AT TOP SPEED X REQUEST FAST CARRIERS MAKE IMMEDIATE STRIKE. I had already sent McCain. There was nothing else I could do, except become angrier.

Then came the sixth dispatch, at 0922: CTU 77.4.3 UNDER ATTACK BY CRUISERS AND BBS 0700 11–40 N 126–25 E X REQUEST IMMEDIATE AIR STRIKE X ALSO REQUEST SUPPORT BY HEAVY SHIPS X MY OBBS (old battleships) LOW IN AMMUNITION.

Low in ammunition! Here was a new factor, so astonishing that I could hardly accept it. Why hadn't Kinkaid let me know before? I looked at the date-time group of his dispatch, which told when it was filed. It was "242225," or 0725 local time, an hour and fifty-seven minutes ago! And when I compared it with the date-time groups of the others, I realized that this was actually his *third* dispatch, sent eighteen minutes after he had first informed me that

TU 77.4.3 was under attack. What had delayed it I have never learned.

My message was on its way to him in five minutes: I AM STILL ENGAGING ENEMY CARRIERS X MCCAIN WITH 5 CARRIERS 4 HEAVY CRUISERS HAS BEEN ORDERED ASSIST YOU IMMEDIATELY, and I gave my position, to show him the impossibility of the fast battleships reaching him.

The next two dispatches arrived close to 1000, almost simultaneously. The first was from Kinkaid again: WHERE IS LEE X SEND LEE. I was impressed less by its desperation than by the fact that it had been put on the air "clear," not in code. I was certain that the enemy had intercepted it, and I was speculating on its effect, when the second dispatch drove all other thoughts out of my mind. I can close my eyes and see it today:

From: CINCPAC

To: COM THIRD FLEET

THE WHOLE WORLD WANTS TO KNOW WHERE IS TASK FORCE 34.

I was as stunned as if I had been struck in the face. The paper rattled in my hands. I snatched off my cap, threw it on the deck, and shouted something that I am ashamed to remember. Mick Carney rushed over and grabbed my arm: "Stop it! What the hell's the matter with you? Pull yourself together!"

I gave him the dispatch and turned my back. I was so mad I couldn't talk. It was utterly impossible for me to believe that Chester Nimitz would send me such an insult. He hadn't, of course, but I didn't know the truth for several weeks. It requires an explanation of navy procedure. To increase the difficulty of breaking our codes, most dispatches are padded with gibberish. The decoding officers almost always recognize it as such and delete it from the transcription, but CINCPAC's encoder was either drowsy or smart-alecky, and his padding—"The whole world wants to know"—sounded so infernally plausible that my decoders read it as a valid part of the message. Chester blew up when I told him about it; he tracked down the little squirt and chewed him to bits, but it was too late then; the damage had been done.

The orders I now gave, I gave in rage, and although Ernie King later assured me that they were the right ones, I am convinced that they were not. My flag log for the forenoon watch that day, October 25, gives the bare bones of the story: "At 0835 c/s (changed speed) to 25k to close enemy. At 0919 c/c (changed course) to 000. At 1115 c/c to 180"—or from due north to due south. At that moment the Northern Force, with its two remaining carriers crippled and dead in the water, was exactly forty-two miles from the muzzles of my 16-inch guns, but—I quote from my war diary—

> In view of the urgent request for assistance from Commander Seventh Fleet, Commander Third Fleet directed Task Force 34 (Lee) and Task Group 38.2 (Bogan) to proceed south toward San Bernardino Strait, and directed Commander Task Force 38 (Mitscher) with Task Groups 38.3 (Sherman) and 38.4 (Davison), to continue attacks against the enemy carrier force.

(The period between 1000, when I received CINCPAC's dispatch and 1115, when we changed course, was spent in reshuffling the task force and refueling Bogan's nearly empty destroyers for our high-speed run.)

I turned my back on the opportunity I had dreamed of since my days as a cadet. For me, one of the biggest battles of the war was off, and what has been called "the Battle of Bull's Run" was on. I notified Kinkaid, TG 38.2 PLUS 6 FAST BBS PROCEEDING LEYTE BUT UNABLE ARRIVE BEFORE 0800 TOMORROW.

While I rushed south, Sherman and Davidson struck the Northern Force again and again, and late that afternoon it retired in straggling disorder, with four of our fast light cruisers in pursuit and two wolf packs of our submarines waiting across its course. When the butchery was done, the score for the Northern Force was

Sunk. . . . . 4 carriers, 1 light cruiser, 2 destroyers.
Damaged. . . . . 2 battleships, 2 light cruisers, 4 destroyers.

A curious feature of this engagement is that the air duel never came off. Our strikes found scarcely a handful of planes on the enemy carriers' decks and only fifteen on the wing. We assume that the rest had ferried into Luzon and that our attack had caught them by surprise, because during the morning our radars picked up large groups of bogeys—unidentified planes—approaching from the westward, but they presently reversed course and disappeared. They must have been unarmed, expecting to arm aboard, and when they saw that their mother ships were afire, they could do nothing but fly back to Luzon again.

Meanwhile, Kinkaid had been sending me another series of dispatches: ENEMY RETIRING TO NORTHEASTWARD. Later, CVES AGAIN THREATENED BY ENEMY SURFACE FORCES. Still later, SITUATION AGAIN VERY SERIOUS X YOUR ASSISTANCE BADLY NEEDED X CVS RETIRING LEYTE GULF. Finally, at 1145, ENEMY FORCE OF 3 BB 2 CA 9 DD 11–43 N 126–12 E COURSE 225 SPEED 20.

This position was fifty-five miles northeast of Leyte Gulf, but the course was not toward the entrance. Moreover, the dispatch had been filed two hours before I received it, and I had no clue as to what had happened since then. The strongest probability was that the enemy would eventually retrace his course through San Bernardino Strait, and my best hope of intercepting him was to send my fastest ships in advance. The only two battleships I had that could sustain high speeds were the *New Jersey* and *Iowa*. I threw a screen of light cruisers and destroyers around them, as TG 34.5, and told them on TBS, "Proceed at 28 knots on course 195. Prepare for 30 knots. Be ready for night action," and I notified Kinkaid that we would arrive off San Bernardino at 0100 next morning, seven hours earlier than my original schedule. . . .

CHAPTER XI

THE BATTLE
OF STALINGRAD

At the Battle of Stalingrad, "The hinge of fate had turned," wrote Winston Churchill. It lasted six brutal months, from the heat of the Russian summer to the brutality of a Russian winter. It was, according to many military historians and participants, a battle of wills—Hitler's against Stalin's, for neither would give way at Stalingrad. The capture of the city led to the granary of the Caucasus, to the rich oil fields and the huge industrial plants. It was the old German dream of *Drang nach Osten,* the Push to the East, for Hitler and his generals; and the outcome was, for the Russians, the turning point and the beginning of the end for the invading German armies in Russia.

The German Generals at Stalingrad:

Field Marshal Friedrich von Paulus (1890–1957), born in Kassel, Germany, was 53 years old when he surrendered at Stalingrad. He had served in World War I, joined the War Ministry and later was on the General Staff of the Reichwehr. At the start of World War II he served in France and in Poland. In January 1942 he was in command of a tank corps—and then came his various elevations, at Stalingrad, as the head of the German Sixth Army.

Field Marshal Eric von Mannstein (1887–1973), brought up in the Junker tradition, was considered by his colleagues to be one of the most able of the German generals. As chief of staff to von

Rundstedt, he devised the breakthrough when Belgium and Luxembourg were overrun. Unable to relieve von Paulus at Stalingrad, Mannstein retreated to Poland. Hitler dismissed von Mannstein in 1944. It was General Heinz Guderian who called von Mannstein "Germany's finest operational brains."

Field Marshal Siegmund Wilhelm List (1880–1971) smashed through the French Maginot Line in May 1940. A close associate of Hitler, an expert in blitzkrieg tactics and a ruthless general in the occupied areas, he was sentenced to life imprisonment during the Nuremberg War Crimes Trials in 1948. He served less than five years.

Field Marshal Karl Rudolph Gerd von Runstedt (1875–1953), the traditional Prussian officer, was almost always in disagreement with Hitler's plans of operation. After playing a large role in the invasion of Western Europe, he commanded the Southern Army Group that spearheaded the invasion of Russia. Resigning prior to the battle of Stalingrad, he was shifted to the Low Countries. Before the Normandy breakthrough in July 1944, in a telephone argument with Hitler, von Runstedt is alleged to have told Hitler, "Make peace, you fool!"

The Russian Generals at Stalingrad:

Lieutenant-General Konstantin K. Rokossovski (1896–1968) was commander of the Russian troops on the Don Front, which he shared with Voronov and Lieutenant-General Malinin, chief of the Don Front.

Marshal of the Soviet Army Andrey I. Yeremenko (1892–1970), born in the Ukraine, was one of the leading planners in the battle of Stalingrad. He was minister of defense in 1958.

Colonel-General Georgi K. Zhukov (1896–   ), considered the most celebrated of the Russian generals during the war and rival of Marshal Konev, was entrusted with the defense of Stalingrad.

Colonel-General Nicolai Voronov (1900–1968) was chief of artillery at the Battle of Stalingrad. After the war he was commander of artillery, USSR Armed Forces. Though only 68 when he died, Marshal Voronov had spent 50 of those years in the army. He participated in command roles in the Spanish Civil War and in the Russian-Finnish War.

General Vasili I. Chuikov was the Russian tactical commander in Stalingrad, and to round out the story of one of the greatest battles of World War II, I quote pertinent portions from his book, *The Battle For Stalingrad,* in the second part of this chapter.

Hanson W. Baldwin, who opens the chapter, was formerly the *New York Times* military analyst. He is the author of many military studies, including *Battles Won and Lost,* from which the first selection is taken.

Stalingrad—Point of No Return
June 28, 1942–February 2, 1943
by
Hanson W. Baldwin

The field marshal sat waiting in cataleptic stillness, his face waxen, in the dark, deserted basement beneath the ruins of the Univermag department store.

History, he had said, had already judged him. Now he was to disappear from its stage.

The Russians moved into the bunker; mute, the field marshal stood up and followed them—into captivity and oblivion.

The scene: Stalingrad, January 31, 1943.

The man: Field Marshal Friedrich Paulus, commanding the German Sixth Army, first to break a long tradition that no German field marshal had ever surrendered to an enemy.

With him went into captivity more than 100,000 prisoners; with his surrender disappeared the myth of Nazi invincibility and the hope of German victory. Stalingrad, an epic four-month battle, marked the high-water mark of German conquest in World War II.

Stalingrad (until 1925 it was named Tsaritsyn) was in 1942 a provincial Soviet town of about 500,000 that hugged the western bank of the Volga, where the great river makes its sweeping loop to the west. For 30 miles along the high bluffs of the west bank, the city stretched, from tractor and tank factory and Red October steel works in the north through apartment houses and public buildings in the south.

Stalingrad in 1942 was an important part of the Russian war arsenal—the third industrial city of the Soviet Union. In that year of the war red banners and slogans in the streets exhorted the workers to maximum effort, and in the factories the party members and the commissars spurred the laggards, threatened the lazy. Yet, in early 1942, the front was about 250 to 300 miles to the west at its closest point; and though there had been air raids, the war seemed far away. . . .

At the end of June, 1942, Russia was beleaguered. Everywhere, from Leningrad, grim city under siege in the north, to the Crimea in the south, German armies stood deep on Soviet soil. A year of war had resulted in what seemed almost mortal blows. In the summer and fall of 1941 perhaps 2,000,000 to 3,000,000 Red Army soldiers had surrendered to the Nazis. Hundreds of thousands had been killed; at the beginning of 1942 the Red Army had reached its lowest strength—2,300,000. Most of Russia's iron and coal areas were occupied. Kerch was captured; the fortress of Sebastopol was falling. . . .

German divisions on the Russian front were below strength and were particularly short in transportation; 75,000 vehicles had been lost in the winter battles, and 180,000 horses had been killed or "had died from hunger and exposure."

And Germany's strategic position was far different than it had been in the summer of 1941. The United States, with all its immense potential, had entered the war; England's isolation had ended; the Reich had commenced to feel the fury from the skies; the fruits of the North African victory were still unrealized; and Hitler faced the specter that even he dreaded—war on many fronts.

But the Fuehrer had sounded the tocsin of alarm in the capitals of all his allies; 69 satellite divisions—27 Rumanian, 9 Italian, 13 Hungarian, 17 Finnish, 1 Spanish and 2 Slovak—had bolstered the 171 understrength German divisions on the Eastern Front.

Hitler thought it was enough; his plans were grandiose, untrammeled by advice or objections from the General Staff. The recuperative powers of the Russians he dismissed; when a statement was read to him stressing the tremendous numbers of men (2,000,000) the Russians had massed on the Central Front and in the Caucasus, Hitler called it (according to General Franz Halder) "idiotic twaddle" and "flew at the man who was reading with clenched fists and foam in the corners of his mouth."

"Der Russe ist tod," he said.

For the 1942 campaigns, the German and Axis forces on the 2,300-mile Eastern Front were organized in four great army groups. Army Groups North and Center—the Leningrad-Moscow fronts—were to remain on the defensive (except for pressure against Leningrad). Army Groups A and B, formed out of Army Group South, were to march to new Germanic glories. . . .

In Directive No. 41, dated April 5, personally dictated by Hitler, the objectives of "Operation Blau" were outlined as the destruction of enemy forces in the Don bend, to be followed by seizure of "the oil resources of the Caucasus" and penetration of the mountain barrier. The Russians, he thought, would have to defend their principal oil fields and would thus be forced to stand and fight. His objective was "the destruction of the last remaining human defensive strength of the Soviet Union." As a step toward this objective, "every attempt was to be made to seize Stalingrad or at least bring the city within reach of German artillery so that the Soviets would be deprived of its production and transportation facilities." Stalingrad was to be a by-product, a steppingstone; the Caucasus was the goal.

Army Group A—Field Marshal Wilhelm List commanding— was entrusted with the Caucasian operation; Army Group B— Field Marshal Maximilian Freiherr von Weichs commanding— was to clear the banks of the Don of all Russian forces and to hold the long northern flank of the deep Caucasian salient. About 100 of the Axis divisions and 1,500 of the 2,750 German aircraft on the Eastern Front were concentrated in the south to carry out these grandiose designs.

Opposite them Marshal Semyon Timoshenko commanded the southwest, south and Caucasus fronts, with a grand total of at least 120 to 140 divisions. The Soviet strategic reserve had been concentrated in the Central Front between Moscow and Voronezh, where the Russians anticipated the main German blow.

Both General Alfred Jodl, chief of Armed Forces Operations Staff, OKW, and General Franz Halder, chief of staff of the OKH, had expressed some misgivings about Operation Blau, based mainly on the inadequacy of the forces and their shortages. But they do not appear to have raised any strenuous objections; their criticisms of Hitler's strategy—as in the case of so many of the German generals—were retroactive. Hitler's propensity for relieving from command anyone who disagreed with him did not encourage objections. The dictator had, in any case, usurped the functions of the OKH (the Army High Command) on December 19, 1941, and after dismissing Field Marshal Walter von Brauchitsch had assumed direct command of the army.

German timing was seriously affected, as it had been a year before, by the enemy and by weather. Marshal Semyon K. Timoshenko launched a massive counteroffensive in the Kharkov area on May 9, and made major initial penetrations. Paulus and the Sixth Army played a key role in stemming the Russian onslaught and in turning it into crushing defeat for the U.S.S.R. By the end of May, when the battle ended, the Germans had captured 215,-000 Russian prisoners, 1,812 guns, 1,270 tanks and 542 aircraft, and had annihilated 2 Soviet armies totaling more than 22 divisions. But as Walter Görlitz has written, "The Soviet counteroffensive . . . completely wrecked all the original German plans for May." . . .

On June 28 the first of the hammer blows fell. The Fourth Panzer Army broke through the Russian lines in the Kursk area and by July 6 had taken Voronezh on the Don, which was to be the pivot point for the whole operation. The Sixth Army jumped off on June 30. Soon the whole Southern Front was fluid; masses of tanks, men, trucks, horses, guns pushed eastward across the wheat fields and the steppes into the fertile black-dirt area where the Don makes its great sweeping loop to the east. . . .

In the first three weeks of July the fruits of conquest seemed so easily won that Hitler, from his temporary command post at Vinnitsa in the Ukraine, ordered List to start his drive into the Caucasus. But—fatal error—on July 17 he diverted the bulk of the Fourth Panzer Army from Army Group B to Army Group A—from the middle to the lower Don—in order to help List seize the river crossings between Rostov and Kalach. This left the Sixth Army, then meeting little resistance, unsupported in its drive toward Stalingrad; it soon bogged down, west of the Don, in "wild battle."

Halder protested, but was overruled; within six days (he noted in his diary on July 23) as a result of the diversion

it is becoming obvious even to the layman that the Rostov area is crammed with armor which has nothing to do, while the critical outer wing at Tsimlyanskaya is starving for it. . . .

Now that the result is so palpable he [Hitler] explodes in a fit of insane rage and hurls the gravest reproaches against the General Staff.

This chronic tendency to underrate enemy capabilities is gradually assuming grotesque proportions and develops into a positive danger. The situation is getting more and more intolerable. There is no room for any serious work. This "leadership," so-called, is characterized by a pathological reacting to the impressions of the moment and a total lack of any understanding of the command machinery and its possibilities.

Mistake Number One.

And already the German Army was outrunning its logistics; drenching downpours turned the roadless steppes into mud, and ammunition and fuel lagged far behind the armored spearheads. The First Panzer Army, driving toward the Don crossings east and north of Rostov, had only one tank battalion in each division; it had started the offensive at 40 percent war strength; by mid-July it was down to 30 percent.

But still the Panzers rumbled east and south. On July 23 Rostov fell. The Sixth Army, without the diverted Panzers of the Fourth Panzer Army to help it, was stalled in violent fighting near Kalach.

But units of Army Group A poured across the Kerch Strait, fanned out from Rostov, cut the last rail links from central Russia, and pushed deep into the Caucasus. Russia's Southern Front was gaping and rent. Hitler's confidence was illimitable, his strategy wavering. He now thought the Caucasus battle won; in late July he started transferring troops away from Army Group A. The Fourth Panzer Army (weakened by the detachment of one Panzer corps to Army Group A and its replacement by a weak Rumanian corps) shifted its *"Schwerpunkt"* or main point of attack northward from the Caucasus toward Stalingrad.

Mistake Number Two.

Stalingrad, originally regarded as a by-product, a steppingstone to Caucasian triumphs, now became a prime objective; belatedly Hitler and Jodl realized (in Halder's words) "that the fate of the Caucasus will be decided at Stalingrad." The shift in objectives, the transfer of troops back and forth from Army Group A to Army Group B, plus the overextended supply systems, had made both commands "too little and too late" in both the Caucasus and in the great bends of the Don and the Volga. The Russians were in deep danger, but they had averted major encirclements and final catastrophe. . . .

The German Panzers rumbled ever eastward. "Like destroyers and cruisers at sea, the tank units maneuvered in the sandy ocean of the steppe, fighting for favorable firing positions, cornering the enemy, clinging to villages for a few hours or days, bursting out again, turning back, and again pursuing the enemy." Like water, the German advance sought the weakest channels; inexorably it swept eastward, ever eastward.

In early August the German XIV and XXIV Panzer Corps, and the XI and LI Infantry Corps, closed a *"Kessel"* near Kalach around the remnants of some nine Soviet divisions and nine brigades.

Sixth Army cleared the Don bend, bridged the river and probed toward the Volga, the heart of "Mother Russia." In the Caucasus the front was fluid; Nazi tanks overran the Maikop oil fields; German mountain troops planted the swastika on 18,481-foot Mount Elbrus on August 21. . . .

After a 275-mile advance in two months, on August 23 at 6:35 P.M. tanks and Panzer Grenadiers of the 16th Panzer Division, Sixth Army, reached the Volga in strength in the northern outskirts of Stalingrad, and the trial by fire started.

It was a day of terror. The hot August sun shimmered in merciless heat against the clouds of fine dust stirred up by the tracks of the Panzers. The Luftwaffe heralded the assault on August 23, 24 and 25 with an unending attack against factories, homes, apartments. Buildings collapsed in rubble or burned in unchecked conflagrations; oil tanks by the river blazed in an inferno of leaping flame and towering black smoke; the burning oil spread across the surface of the river "until it seemed that the Volga itself was on fire." The city was chaos. Hundreds of thousands of civilians still lived in Stalingrad when Hitler's legions reached its gates. Thousands died those first few days. Others, the factory workers, downed their tools and took up guns. . . .

On September 7 Stalin issued an order of the day:

"Not another step backward. . . . The Volga has now only one bank."

Field Marshal List of Army Group A was the first of many to feel the Fuehrer's wrath; Hitler blamed others for the mistakes he himself had made. He was displeased because the entire Caucasus had not fallen to the German yoke. List went in early September and Hitler assumed remote command of Army Group A until Field Marshal Ewald von Kleist was assigned in November.

From September until November Hitler wore three hats: commander in chief, Army Group A; commander in chief of the German Army, and commander in chief of the German Armed Forces.

At Hitler's headquarters in early September, Colonel General Alfred Jodl also felt the mania of Hitler's wrath. For a time it appeared several heads might fall and that Paulus, commanding the Sixth Army, might relieve Jodl. But, though Hitler withdrew into himself and "shut himself up in his sunless blockhouse," Jodl had learned his lesson.

"[He] admitted he had been wrong; one should never, he said, try to point out to a dictator where he has gone wrong since this will shake his self-confidence, the main pillar upon which his personality and his actions are based."

But new commanders could not solve the immense problems of an unprecedented front. Kleist's force had been milked away in large numbers for transfer to the north to reinforce the German offensive against Leningrad and, bit by bit, to strengthen the attack on Stalingrad. And behind, his foremost divisions stretched to the bottleneck of Rostov on the Don, 370 miles of distance, serviced only by one dilapidated railroad, and from Rostov to Warsaw, another 1,000 railroad miles—a tenuous supply line, severed intermittently by sabotage and guerrilla attacks. For days on end Kleist's spearheads were immobilized by dry gasoline tanks; to save fuel, camel trains were improvised to transport petrol tins to the front. . . .

The supply lines and facilities were totally inadequate to maintain both the Stalingrad and the Caucasus offensives; as Ziemke has noted, "He could not maintain both and ended up maintaining neither." By mid-September, when Paulus commenced a concentrated assault upon Stalingrad, the area between the Don and the Volga had been cleared of the Russians, and supply dumps and airfields were being completed. But the German divisions, far below strength, were spread thin across an immense and stiffening front, and food, ammunition, spare parts and, above all, fuel were in short supply.

To strengthen the battering ram at Stalingrad, Hitler milked away most of the few German divisions from the vital northern flank. The result: The hinge of the Stalingrad and Caucasian front, the exposed flank upon which the entire offensive depended, was held from Voronezh along the Don to Kletskaya by the Hungarian Second, the Italian Eighth and the Rumanian Third armies —the weakest of the Axis forces in the most important area.

It was Mistake Number Three—a fatal one.

And south of Stalingrad almost to the communications bottleneck at Rostov, there lay an open flank, across the Kalmyk steppes, held only by a single German motorized division which patrolled hundreds of miles of front (reinforced in early November by more weak troops—the Rumanian Fourth Army, transferred from the Crimea and the Caucasus). . . .

It was all too much for Halder, chief of the Army General Staff. Hitler and Halder had differed for months. Arguments, recriminations and a raging spate of words had been the daily fare at Supreme Headquarters. From mid-September on, both Jodl and Field Marshal Wilhelm Keitl, chief of the Armed Forces High Command, were in disgrace; Hitler cut his contacts with his military staff; he sought seclusion in his hut, and refused ostentatiously to shake hands with any general of the OKW. Halder, deeply worried by the overextended German positions, the thin and vulnerable flanks, the mounting opposition in Stalingrad and the reports of the massing of Russian reserves, had urged abandonment of the offensive and a withdrawal to less exposed defensive positions.

On September 24 Halder's diary carried the notation: "After situation conference, farewell by the Fuehrer: My nerves are worn out, also his nerves are no longer fresh. We must part. Necessity for educating the General Staff in fanatical faith in the Idea. He is determined to enforce his will also in the Army."

General Kurt Zeitzler, former chief of staff of Army Group West, was promoted to general of infantry and succeeded Halder. But Zeitzler could work no miracles. He found the atmosphere at Supreme Headquarters "not only weird but positively incredible. It was compounded of mistrust and anger. Nobody had any faith in his colleagues. Hitler distrusted everyone." . . .

But the soldiers at Stalingrad were flesh and blood.

Paulus, ever obedient to Hitler's orders, drove the steel fist of the Sixth Army squarely against the city on the Volga. Just a few weeks before, had the diverted Fourth Panzer Army been available to help Paulus, Stalingrad might have been easily won, for the city, in July and early August, was virtually undefended. Now in September and October, as the days grew shorter and the cold approached, it was a city stripped for siege, grim in resolution, prepared for extinction, ready to fight.

The German attack on the main part of the city started in

mid-September; for more than four months Stalingrad was to die slowly.

Paulus and his Sixth Army, with the Fourth Panzer Army on his southern flank (about five corps—20 divisions in all), held the 40-mile isthmus between the Don and the Volga and opposed in Stalingrad Lieutenant General Vasili Chuikov's Sixty-second Army, originally of about five to eight understrength divisions (later considerably reinforced). Moscow created a special Stalingrad front and elements of the Sixty-fourth Army (Lieutenant General M. S. Shumilov commanding) astride the Volga assisted in the city's defense, and with the Fifty-seventh Army faced major elements of the German Fourth Panzer Army in and to the south of the city.

Stalingrad, an elongated "ribbon city," along the high west bank of the Volga, was dominated by three large groups of factories in the north (which had produced more than a quarter of the U.S.S.R.'s tractors, tanks and mechanical vehicles). Just to the west and south of the southern group was Mamayev Kurgan hill (an old Tartar burial ground), the so-called "Iron Heights." Known as Hill 102 on military maps, it rose 331 feet above the Volga. Factory smokestacks and industrial buildings dominated the high western banks and shut off the residential districts—the strange agglomerate of drab apartments and log houses—from direct access to the river. The high plateau on which the city was built was seamed by seven ravines which tended to canalize and restrict urban life and military movement.

The Germans were handicapped by their own tactics of frontal assault upon a city; their mobility was neutralized; there were no open enemy flanks. Modern cities with masonry structures, steel-beamed factories and a maze of streets make natural fortresses, as the war had shown at Warsaw and Leningrad.

The Russians were handicapped by the Volga. They fought with their backs to the river, in an elongated pattern with no depth for maneuver, and across the Volga had to come the ammunition and supplies which are the lifeblood of any army.

General Chuikov maintained his command post during part of the battle in a deep bunker on the west bank dug into the northern bank of a small tributary of the Volga, the Tsaritsa, which bisected the city. On the west bank of the Volga, soldiers and civilians tunneled into the cliffs in a labyrinthine pattern of shelters and dugouts.

When the major German assault started in mid-September, there had been no general planned evacuation of the city's civilian inhabitants; Stalin had forbidden it; the soldiers, he had said, were more likely "to fight for a live town than an empty" one! Some women and children, fleeing by night, had crossed the Volga after the first heavy bombings; others had wandered westward through German lines. As the siege drew on, and the supply lines across the Volga—rafts and boats and ferries—became strained with military traffic, the civilians either dug underground and were squeezed in little pockets up against the western bank, or they fled westward behind the German lines, across the already devastated land to die by the thousands from exhaustion and starvation. . . .

The initial German assault carried by sheer power deep into the jumbled wreckage of the factory district and to the Iron Heights, but at desperate cost. The Sixth Army faced a battle for every house, for each rubble heap. Counterattack drove the Germans from a shell-pocked part of Hill 102. The Nazis brought up more men and tanks and bombers—milking away still more strength from their flanks—and by day and by night, hour without end, the grim assault continued, house by house, street by street, cellar by cellar, man to man. . . .

In mid-October the Germans commenced a titanic effort to liquidate the Russian bridgeheads across the Volga. Chuikov, commanding the Sixty-second Army, thought it a "battle unequalled in its cruelty and ferocity throughout the whole of the Stalingrad fighting." The tractor plant was surrounded, fighting continued within its shattered walls; casualties on both sides were enormous. Some 3,500 wounded Russians, casualties in one day's fighting, were transported across the Volga the night of October 14.

The fruit of blood was littered rubble, a few square blocks of conquest. The Germans compressed the Soviet bridgeheads, cut the positions in two, pushed their front lines almost, but not quite, to the Volga.

It was a near thing; the situation was, in Chuikov's words, "desperate.". . .

By the end of October about nine-tenths of the city was in German hands. . . .

It became, to both sides, a symbol, a test of wills between Stalin and Hitler, between Germany and Russia, between müzhik and Panzer Grenadier. Stalingrad, once envisaged as a means of an end —the conquest of the Caucasus—had now become an end in itself.

"Where the German soldier sets foot, there he remains. You may rest assured," Hitler told the Germans, "that nobody will ever drive us away from" Stalingrad. . . .

But the Sixth Army, exhausted, cynical, had almost shot its bolt. Already, a few days before the beer hall speech, Paulus had radioed to Hitler's permanent command post, the *"Wulfschanze"* ("Wolf's Lair") near Rastenburg in East Prussia:

"Final occupation of the town with present forces not possible due to high rate of casualties. Army requests assault groups and street-fighting specialists."

Four special engineer battalions, highly trained in house-to-house assault and street fighting—the greatest concentration of these specialists in so small an area during the entire war—were flown to Stalingrad, and on the night of November 9–10 the last German effort began. The objective was the elimination of the final Russian bridgeheads in Stalingrad— *"Der Tennisschläger"* ("the tennis racket"), so named for its shape—a six-square-mile area in the center of the city, and another large bridgehead in the factory district—"a place of huge and awful desolation.". . .

The assault battalions attacked and gained a building here, a block there; they reached the Volga at several points and compressed the Russian bridgeheads into tight perimeters of rubble. But there was no fresh infantry to support them, no follow-up punch; Sixth Army was drained; the last effort petered out by mid-November.

There were ominous indications that the Russians, with remarkable restraint, were feeding in just enough replacements to the ruined city to hold their bridgeheads, while concentrating major forces north and south of Stalingrad opposite the weak and exposed flanks. . . .

In addition to the small bridgeheads in the rubble of Stalingrad, the Russians had succeeded, despite persistent German attacks, in holding several bridgeheads north and south of the city: several across the Don, to the west and *behind* the foremost positions of the Sixth Army; another across the Volga in the Fourth Panzer Army area south of the city.

And here danger loomed.

In early November Paulus urged Hitler to "break off the attack and withdraw the troops to a fortified winter line extending from Kharkov to Rostov."

Hitler's answer was adamant; Stalingrad had become an obsession.

For months the Soviet counterblow was in preparation. It was the conception of the Stavka or Soviet High Command and particularly of General Georgi Zhukov, "savior" of Moscow, aided by Generals Alexander M. Vasilevski (chief of the General Staff) and Nikolai N. Voronov. All during the fall, as the Germans inched ahead in the rubble of Stalingrad, powerful forces had been concentrated in the forests north of the Don bend. Constant attacks were made on the Voronezh "hinge" to pin down the German Second Army, and fords across the Don were seized.

Three army "fronts" were created west of the Volga and north of Stalingrad: the Voronezh (Lieutenant General Filipp I. Golikov), the Southwest (Lieutenant General Nikolai F. Vatutin), and the Don (Lieutenant General Konstantin Rokossovsky). The Stalingrad front (Lieutenant General Andrei Yeremenko) included the city and, south of it, the Ergeni Hills and the northern part of the Kalmyk steppe. A mass of more than half a million Soviet troops and some 900 to 1,500 tanks and 13,500 artillery pieces and mortars had been concentrated on the flanks of the Don and Volga bends until the ground froze and the mud of fall congealed. (The first snow fell on November 16; the bitter wind blew off the steppes, and the ground was hard as iron.)

The objectives were ambitious—to trap the Sixth Army in Stalingrad. Later (it was hoped but not planned) Rostov might be recaptured and parts of Army Group A isolated in the Caucasus. A holding offensive on the Central Front, opposite Moscow, was intended to pin down German divisions and prevent their transfer to the threatened southern areas.

The Germans apparently saw the thunderbolt poised, but Hitler's strategic inflexibility prevented a logical reaction.

On November 19, when the Communists struck, the Nazis were still inching forward in Stalingrad; they had seized Ordzhonikidze in the Caucasus, and their thinly held front was within 75 miles of the Caspian Sea. It was the high-water mark of German conquest; from November 19, 1942, onward for two and a half bitter years it was an ebbing tide for Nazi hopes.

The Russians concentrated their assault against fronts held by Germany's hapless allies—first the Rumanians, later the Italians and the Hungarians.

Rokossovsky and Vatutin struck first—southward toward Kalach—against the Third Rumanian Army, which was thinly holding about a 100-mile sector with battalion frontages averaging one to two miles. Yeremenko (with the Fifty-first and Fifty-seventh Soviet Armies) on November 20 broke through the Fourth Rumanian Army to the south of Stalingrad and drove northward toward Kalach. . . .

For seven and a half hours the Russian massed artillery thundered; then, across terrain which looked as though "cast from molten earth—the surface . . . twisted into weird shapes," thousands of Russian tanks debouched across the ridge lines, with the Twenty-first Soviet Army and Fifth Soviet Tank Army—about 21 divisions in all—in the van.

It was immediate rout. The Soviet troops tore a gap 50 miles wide in the north, 30 miles across in the south. Rumanian divisions disintegrated, fled, fought, died, surrendered. . . . A weak German Panzer division (part of an understrength so-called German corps), ordered only a few days earlier to back up the Rumanian front, arrived piecemeal too little and too late and was engulfed bit by bit. By November 23 Vatutin and Yeremenko had closed their pincers at Sovetskiy near Kalach on the Don bend. A series of green flares heralded the closing of the pincers; the converging Russian units understood their triumph; soldiers hugged and kissed each other. The encirclement cut the railroad to Stalingrad and cut off more than 200,000 soldiers of the Sixth Army, most of the German elements of the Fourth Panzer Army, parts of two Rumanian divisions, Luftwaffe units, a Croat regiment and some 70,000 noncombatants (*"Hiwis,"* prisoners of war and others). Soon the vast Don bend was littered with the flotsam of military disaster—fleeing men, wounded dragging across the snow, blazing tanks, abandoned arms and dumps, a scraggle of isolated battles as small units stood and died—and tried, in vain, to stem the Russian tide.

Back at Rastenburg in East Prussia, where Hitler had returned from his barn-storming political speeches in Bavaria, General Zeitzler, the new army chief of staff, tried to persuade the dictator to order an immediate breakout attempt by the Sixth Army.

Hitler, in a fury, "crashed his fist down on the table, shouting, 'I won't leave the Volga. I won't go back from the Volga.' "

Late on November 22 Paulus knew he was surrounded and so reported to Hitler. Hitler's orders: move army headquarters into the city of Stalingrad; form a hedgehog (all-around defense) and hold fast. Thus, in a pocket of open steppe and little village and shattered city, originally about one-third the size of Connecticut, then reduced to an area about 37 miles wide from east to west, and 23 miles deep from north to south, the Sixth Army stood at bay.

Hitler proudly dubbed them "the troops of Fortress Stalingrad."

It was an ill-prepared "fortress"—its defenders decimated, disorganized, wearied by months of fighting, inadequately supplied and equipped, a "fortress" whose new front lines (to the west) had to be prepared in raging blizzard and icy cold on open steppe.

And its supply lines were severed. . . .

Sixth Army required a minimum of 500 tons of supplies per day to keep fighting—or even living.

In East Prussia Reich Marshal Hermann Göring, the corpulent drug-taker, assured Hitler that the Luftwaffe could supply the Sixth Army's minimum needs by air. He was challenged by Zeitzler, but Hitler believed what he wanted to believe: Sixth Army was to stand fast; the Luftwaffe would deliver its needs; help would come from without.

The airlift started, unpropitiously, about November 25, and on the 27th Field Marshal Fritz Erich von Manstein, shifted from the Northern Front, hurriedly took command of a newly created Army Group Don, composed of the shattered remnants of the

Third and Fourth Rumanian armies, the Fourth Panzer Army and the encircled Sixth Army, plus such few reinforcements as could be spared from the Caucasus and the Northern Front.

The 6th Panzer Division was ordered from faraway Brittany to provide a spearhead of fresh troops. The 80 trains that moved it were delayed by blown bridges, ripped-up rails and guerrilla attacks; it reached the cold steppes and the forlorn prospects somewhat late but with 160 tanks and 40 assault guns. Manstein's task: to break through the Russian encirclement and relieve "Fortress Stalingrad." It was a formidable mission; by the end of November the Russian ring of steel had thickened to some 30 to 60 kilometers.

Manstein, possibly the ablest German commander of World War II, moved with vigor; in an offensive code-named "Winter Storm" he attacked Yeremenko along the Kotelinkovski-Stalingrad railway on December 12, and made major initial gains. The LVII Panzer Corps—initially composed of the 23rd and 6th Panzer divisions, later reinforced by the 17th Panzer Division—spearheaded the attempt to break the ring. By December 21 Manstein's Panzers were some 30 miles from the Sixth Army's outposts; the Germans saw "on the horizon the reflection of the gunfire" at Stalingrad.

But it was already too late. For the Russian offensive broadened; Vatutin and Golikov had crashed through the Italian Eighth Army on the Don ("the entire front fell apart" in complete rout) between the 16th and the 19th, and Manstein's flank was threatened. On December 19 Manstein radioed Paulus to drive south to meet him. But Paulus was never a commander with a "blind eye"; his obedience to orders was literal. He told Manstein he had only 20 miles of fuel for his tanks (Paulus had at this time only 60 operational tanks), yet it was not primarily lack of fuel but Hitler's orders which chained him to impassivity. The attempt at relief had failed; the German debacle was broadening. On Christmas Day the Fourth Army was in full retreat; Paulus was doomed. . . .

The pocket was short of all things—save misery. The airlift had failed. Instead of 500 tons daily—60,000 gallons of fuel; 40 tons of bread; 100 tons of other supplies, including food; 40 tons of ammunition and weapons—the average amount flown in had been less than one-fifth of the bare minimum needed. It was no fault of the pilots or air crews; the vainglorious Göring had promised the impossible. Stalingrad lay in a weather "pocket" at the edge of a "meteorological frontier" which severely restricted flying. There were not enough planes—180 Ju-52's, some Junkers 86's, and less than 100 Heinkel 111's; there were not enough airfields —two main ones at Pitomnik and Gumrak within the pocket (with two alternatives). Two key air resupply fields outside the pocket (Tatsinskaye and Morozovsk) were engulfed in Vatutin's December and January offensives. The planes ran the gantlet of Soviet antiaircraft and fighter opposition; in the whole operation, 500 to 600 transport aircraft were lost, and by the end of December —due in part to transfers to the Mediterranean—there were only 375 single-engined fighters with the swastika on their wings on the entire Eastern Front. . . .

And over the radios, where Christmas carols and messages of hope came from faraway Germany, there intervened, with rasp of static at frequent intervals, the voice of Radio Moscow:

"Every seven seconds a German soldier dies in Russia. Stalingrad—mass grave. One . . . two . . . three . . . four . . . five . . . six . . . seven. . . . Every seven seconds a German soldier dies."

Sixth Army was starving.

The stiff carcasses of frozen horses were hacked to bits for meat; rats, cats and dogs and bits of food scrounged from the wreckage of Stalingrad went into empty bellies. The prisoners suffered, too —even the "tried and trusted" Russian auxiliaries, who collaborated with the Germans. At Voroponov POW Transit Camp No. 204 Russians died by the hundreds. Fifty scrawny horses were sent to the camp, but it was not enough.

Sixth Army was freezing. . . .

The implacable winter held the Germans in its iron grip. Those in the ruins of Stalingrad were lucky; they had some shelter and huddled over fires fueled by rubble. The temperature fell to 20 to 30 below zero. Those on the open steppes froze and died in the awful wind, the impersonal, searching, cruel cold. And the snow soon hid their deaths.

Sixth Army was ill and exhausted.

Dysentery, typhus, spotted fever, frostbite, ravaged the ranks;

dirty, bearded specters stood sentinel and died, too weak to fire a shot.

Sixth Army was wounded.

There were not enough drugs, dressings, doctors, plasma, anesthetic; not enough planes to take the wounded out. Thirty thousand wounded were ready for evacuation long before the end; most of them died. Each wounded man was tagged for air evacuation; "Hans" called these tags "reprieve tickets.". . .

But Sixth Army was still fighting as the New Year dawned—endlessly, ceaselessly, bitterly, hopelessly, by day and by night, until whole units ceased to exist, as the encirclement tightened, as the cold deepened, as hunger knotted the bowels, as the wounded screamed in delirium or unassuaged agony, as the Russians waited. . . . There was never an end to fighting, to shellfire, to mortars, to the staccato of machine guns and the sharp crack of rifles, to the stab in the dark. The Volga was solid now; the Soviet supply problem within the city was eased. The German problem was hopeless.

On New Year's Day, 1943, Hitler radioed to the starving troops in Stalingrad:

"The men of the Sixth Army have my word that everything is being done to extricate them."

About December 28 General Hans V. Hube, a corps commander (XIV Corps) under Paulus, was flown out of the pocket to report to Hitler and to be decorated with a high Nazi medal—the Swords to the Oak Leaves of the Knight's Cross to the Iron Cross. When Hube flew back to Stalingrad on January 8, he brought with him Hitler's message to hold until spring. . . .

And now a greater disaster threatened. For all these weeks, while Sixth Army was fighting for its life, two armies of Kleist's Army Group A in the Caucasus had held their vulnerable and far-flung positions, while the Don flank, on which their safety depended, collapsed behind them. Grudgingly, toward the end of December, Hitler permitted Zeitzler to order their withdrawal. It was the last moment. Manstein, repulsed in his attempt to relieve Stalingrad, was now fighting desperately to hold open the gateway to safety at Rostov, against the onpouring Russian legions of Vatutin, which had smashed the Italian Eighth Army. And thus,

while Sixth Army died, Kleist conducted a brilliant though per-
cipitate retreat from the Caucasian high-water mark of German
conquest, as Manstein held open the Rostov gateway.

But what was going on outside the pocket, few in Sixth Army
knew—or cared.

At the beginning of January, Sixth Army held a shattered area
about 20 miles long by 30 miles deep. It was under constant attack
from Rokossovsky's Don Army front, reinforced now to seven
armies. On January 8 three Russian officers, under a flag of truce,
brought a demand for immediate surrender to Paulus. Sixth Army
transmitted the Soviet ultimatum to Hitler and requested freedom
of action. Hitler refused. There was to be no surrender. It was to
be to the death.

At 0804 on the 10th of January a general assault on the pocket,
with the main effort from the west—or across the open steppes—
started, supported by 7,000 guns and mortars. The Russians expected to finish off the Sixth Army in three to seven days. But the
Germans fought on. It was a grim, relentless battle. Slowly, the
ring compressed; the German lines in the open steppes to the west
of Stalingrad were driven inward. The snowy wastes were littered
with frozen dead, their limbs and features petrified by the cold into
contorted immobility. Those who crossed that eerie landscape
forever remembered it; the track was marked by "the frozen legs
of horses which had been hacked off the dead animals [and] had
been stuck into snow, hooves upward." By the 14th the main
airfield at Pitomnik had been taken; within a few days the western
defense perimeter had been breached; the Germans began to collapse.

Paulus again reported to Hitler that his army was dying, that
his survivors were enduring the unendurable. . . .

By mid-January the Stalingrad pocket was compressed to an
area about 15 miles long by 9 miles deep, with Russian salients and
reentries—bridgeheads across the Volga—thrust into the German
citadel. The airlift was petering out in snow and squall and disaster
as the Russian front lines, pushing both west and east, overran
airfield after airfield. On January 17 a second Russian ultimatum
was rejected.

In the second half of January as the Soviets, driving hard, were chopping the Stalingrad pocket in two, Kleist's Army Group A retreating from the Caucasus found sanctuary in the Taman peninsula bridgehead or reached the Don and crossed it near Rostov—just in time to escape disaster. For the Russian offensive broadened. Golikov's Voronezh Army front struck between January 13 and 16 against the remaining Italians (and captured 17,000 of them) and then broke through the Hungarian Second Army and the German Second Army near the Voronezh hinge on the Don, and turned victory into rout.Within a few days the entire German Don front was, in euphemistic terms, "fluid"; there was no stable front for 200 miles between Manstein at Voroshilovgrad and Voronezh. And all the while the long and bitter frozen miles between the entrapped and dying army at Stalingrad and its nearest allies outside the pocket lengthened. Sixth Army was battered on all sides by elements of seven Soviet armies. . . .

On January 22 the Gumrak airstrip fell. On the next day the last physical link with the outside world—the Stalingradski field—was lost; 150 to 200 miles of frozen, ravaged land now lay between the Stalingrad pocket and the main front. But the loss was anticlimactic; the airlift had averaged only 80 to 90 tons of supplies a day instead of the minimum 500 tons needed and promised.

Again on January 24 a stark message was flashed to Hitler:

TROOPS WITHOUT AMMUNITION OR FOOD. CONTACT MAINTAINED WITH ELEMENTS OF ONLY SIX DIVISIONS. EVIDENCE OF DISINTE-GRATION ON SOUTHERN, NORTHERN AND WESTERN FRONTS. EFFECTIVE COMMAND NO LONGER POSSIBLE. LITTLE CHANGE ON EAST-ERN FRONT: 18,000 WOUNDED WITHOUT ANY SUPPLIES OR DRESSINGS OR DRUGS: 44TH, 76TH, 100TH, 305TH AND 384TH INFANTRY DIVISIONS DESTROYED. FRONT TORN OPEN AS A RESULT OF STRONG BREAK-THROUGHS ON THREE SIDES. STRONG-POINTS AND SHELTER ONLY AVAILABLE IN THE TOWN ITSELF, FURTHER DE-FENSE SENSELESS. COLLAPSE INEVITABLE. ARMY REQUESTS IMMEDIATE PERMISSION TO

SURRENDER IN ORDER TO SAVE LIVES OF RE-
MAINING TROOPS.

SIGNED: PAULUS

The answer was terse:

CAPITULATION IS IMPOSSIBLE. THE SIXTH ARMY
WILL DO ITS HISTORIC DUTY AT STALINGRAD
UNTIL THE LAST MAN, IN ORDER TO MAKE POS-
SIBLE THE RECONSTRUCTION OF THE EASTERN
FRONT. . . .

By January 24, with the pocket split in two, a concerted defense
was impossible. German gunners were firing their last artillery
and mortar shells and destroying their guns; some of the remaining trucks, out of gasoline, were burned or crippled. A Rumanian
unit deserted en masse, with weapons and equipment, to the Russians. Hundreds tried to filter through the Russian encirclement
and started the long and hopeless trek across the frozen, devastated steppe toward German lines 200 miles away. One sergeant
reached sanctuary weeks later, only to die in a front-line dressing
station.

There was no longer, as January ended, a controlled battle—
only a series of individual fire fights: the yammer of the subma-
chine guns, the thrown grenade, the ferocious struggle for a shattered building, the fight of the doomed. . . .

On January 31 Paulus, who believed the first duty of a soldier
was to obey, sat in a state of shock, with blank face and staring
eyes, on his cot. He was in his last command post, deep beneath
the ruins of the Univermag department store in a dead city gutted
by four months of combat. He had been promoted to field marshal;
upon Paulus and his surviving officers and men had been showered
in the final hours radio accolades from Hitler far away, promo-
tions, decorations. . . .

"The Sixth Army," the field marshal had wirelessed, "true to
their oath and conscious of the lofty importance of their mission,
have held their position to the last man and the last round for
Fuehrer and Fatherland unto the end."

At the last, Paulus funked his own "no surrender" orders and left surrender details to his chief of staff.

On January 31, 1943, Sixth Army headquarters sent its last message:

"The Russians stand at the door of our bunker. We are destroying our equipment."

And the operator added: "CL"—"This station will no longer transmit."

It took a few days longer to mop up. The northern pocket, held by the XI Corps, was overrun on February 2, and that day a German reconnaissance pilot reported: "No sign of any firing at Stalingrad."

The German Reich was stunned, numbed with apprehension; the despised *Untermensch* had defeated the Nazi "Supermen." For the first time, in those early days of February, the full dimensions of catastrophe became apparent to the German people. Deliberately, Goebbels emphasized the "glories" of defeat, and the German radio played, over and over again, the Siegfried Funeral March and *"Ich hatt' ein' Kamaraden."* The shock was traumatic, but effective. In place of the arrogant confidence of the past, the Nazis fought in the future with desperation.

With Paulus into captivity went 23 generals, 2,000 to 2,500 officers and almost 90,000 German enlisted men—all that was left of the Sixth Army—some Rumanians and an unknown number (perhaps 30,000 to 40,000) of German noncombatants, and Russian "auxiliaries" and civilians. (An additional 17,000 prisoners had been captured by the Russians between January 10 and 29.)

The statistics of Armageddon will be forever incomplete, but no matter how estimated they are appalling. In mid-October the ration strength of the Sixth Army had been something like 334,-000 men. A segment was separated from the main part of the army, and retreated westward to rejoin the main German forces during the Soviet breakthrough in mid-November. On November 23 Paulus estimated Sixth Army strength in the Stalingrad pocket at 220,000. Between 40,000 and 50,000 wounded and specialists were evacuated from the Stalingrad area by ground and air before and during the siege. Another 60,000 to 100,000 were killed, or died of illness or starvation or cold in and around Stalingrad, or were among the thousands of unfortunates who were suffering in the so-called medical bunkers in Stalingrad when the end came. For many of these wounded survival was not for long; some were entombed alive as bunkers and cellars were sealed by explosives as the victorious Russians mopped up. Others met their ends as grenades or flame throwers sought out the crevices in the ruins.

Those Germans who died in Stalingrad were, perhaps, more fortunate than those who lived. At Beketovka POW camp on the Volga, just south of Stalingrad, thousands of German prisoners—some estimates say 40,000 to 50,000—died of starvation, cold and hardship in the first weeks of captivity. Thousands of others died in the subsequent years. Life was cheap on the Eastern Front. About 5,000 to 6,000 lived throughout the long night of captivity to return to Germany years after the war.

Paulus, castigated by Hitler for his failure to choose death among the ruins rather than life in captivity, lived to testify at Nuremberg. He emerged a shrunken figure, faintly ignoble, ambivalent, with his value judgments shaken, his mind seemingly confused.

Friedrich Paulus—he who was known when a handsome young officer as "The Lord" or "The Major with the Sex Appeal"—was the centerpiece of the Battle of Stalingrad. Upon him and his decisions depended the fate of an army. Walter Görlitz's oversympathetic portrait reveals the man as a painstaking master of minutiae, reserved almost to the point of introversion, with no flair, an experienced and dependable staff officer but with little prior command experience, methodical, slow in decision but stubborn, "a dog in the highly functionalized system of command, completely centralized and controlled by Hitler." Paulus was "the painstaking traditional soldier, who weighed every aspect thrice before reaching a decision."

History will sympathize with Friedrich Paulus; he faced the crucial conflict of any soldier—the conflict of when to disobey. He chose obedience—largely, he later said, because he did not, and could not, know the "big picture." But he won disaster, and in part because he lacked the boldness and the moral courage which are the fundamental requirements of a great commander. He who could have saved an army lives in history as an example of the blind obedience to authoritarianism which has so often been the cause of Germany's downfall. . . .

For Russia, Stalingrad was a tremendous, though costly, victory. Exact Soviet casualties will probably never be known; the Germans could estimate them, but their records were lost with the Sixth Army. Moscow did not compile reliable casualty statistics; then as now, there were no Russian graves registration details; if men did not come home, they were presumed dead or missing. One "guesstimate" of Soviet casualities is 400,000 to 600,000 in the entire Stalingrad campaign (exclusive of the Caucasus), as compared to an Axis overall loss of perhaps 600,000 (exclusive of the Caucasus).

The consequences of Stalingrad were unending.

As Fuller expresses it, "Stalingrad was a second Poltava in which Hitler was as much the architect of his own ruin as was Charles XII in 1709. Into the minds of a hundred million Muscovites flashed the myth of Soviet invincibility, and it forged them into the Turks of the North."

Because, primarily, of its political and psychological effects Fuller saw Stalingrad—with the exception of the Normandy landing—as "the most decisive of all the battles of the war."

Von Senger und Etterlin, who participated as a division commander in the abortive attempt by the Fourth Panzer Army to relieve Stalingrad, saw the battle as "one of the few decisive battles of the Second World War, not merely because it marked the loss of an army . . . but because it represented a culminating point, after which the Axis powers were forced on to the defensive. The war potential of the Allies had clearly proved itself superior."

Stalingrad was a battle whose tortured architecture was carved from many mistakes, where little went according to plan.

The strategy of both sides was faulty. The Germans, under Hitler's command, had, from the beginning, a confused picture of their objective; they violated military principles by shifting from one objective to another in the midst of a campaign. Forces were dispersed instead of concentrated. The Caucasus offensive should never have been started until the exposed flank along the Don and Volga from Voronezh through Stalingrad to Rostov had been completely consolidated and was firmly held. And properly speaking, it should never have been launched at all; the correct German objective was the destruction of the Soviet Army, not the conquest of terrain or economic goals.

Actually—and ironically—Stalingrad itself was not an essential element of the German strategy, but a secure flank along the Don was.

Once the Sixth Army was committed fully to Stalingrad's capture, the Germans should have employed to the full their superior power of maneuver instead of becoming entrapped and pinned down in endless bloody street fighting. Later—at the latest by early November, when Paulus suggested breaking off the battle and withdrawal—the Sixth Army should have been pulled back at least beyond the Don. When the Russian breakthrough of November 19 closed a ring around the Sixth Army, a quick breakout could have saved most of the army and might have restored the front. Even until December 21, when Manstein's relief drive stalled, breakout was probably possible, certainly it should have been attempted. Even the Russians admitted subsequently that such an effort might have succeeded; their military historians, writing a few months later not for public history but for military eyes, stated that "the failure of the encircled enemy to make any determined effort to break out of encirclement saved our troops from a situation which might have been serious."

For most of this Hitler and his rigid centralized system of command were to blame—Hitler and some of the moral cowards of the German Army, who possessed little of the instinct for greatness, and whose obedience was almost subservient. . . .

At the last from Christmas on, when the Sixth Army was dying in its final convulsive agonies, Hitler was correct in forbidding its surrender and Paulus was right in his acquiescence. Hitler was right for the wrong reasons; his own megalomania had sent the First Panzer Army and the Seventeenth Army deep into the Caucasus; their safety hung on what happened at Stalingrad. Had Paulus surrendered in early January, Army Group A—or parts of it—would probably have been doomed in a disaster greater than Stalingrad, for the Rostov gateway and the Kerch Strait were its lifelines to the west. As it was, it was a near thing.

Elements of Army Group A did not cross the lower Don—

where Manstein was fighting desperately to hold the gate—until after January 18, and Kleist's headquarters and much of the Seventeenth Army were not pulled back to a more or less secure bridgehead covering the Kuban and the Taman peninsula until the end of the month. Rostov was finally captured after a desperate defense on February 14. Had the Russian forces around Stalingrad been freed for other operations early in January, Kleist would probably have been doomed. . . .

But the German mistakes were not Hitler's alone. In retrospect German commentators have placed nearly all the blame for the entrapment of Sixth Army and for the success of the initial Russian blow of November 19 upon Hitler and his "no-retreat" orders. But German intelligence, perhaps influenced by Hitlerian policy which kept insisting the Russians were defeated, appears to have been only partially successful in estimating Soviet capabilities and in identifying the areas of maximum Russian build-up. . . .

A fundamental factor in the German defeat was that the Nazis attempted far too much with far too little, and their entire campaign was based on a supply and logistics structure completely incapable of dealing with the vast distances, sparse communications and climatic extremes encountered. A single railway bridge across the Dnieper at Dniepropetrovsk was the tiny funnel through which all supplies for Army Group A and most of Army Group B had to pass. No officer in prewar times who had dared suggest such a logistical solution in the paper wars at the German Kriegsakademie would ever have passed.

The Russians, too, made major mistakes, tactically and strategically.

They early misjudged the German intentions and believed the drive toward Stalingrad portended an attempt to outflank and isolate Moscow from the south. Too many of their troops were massed on the Central Front, far too few in the south.

When Sixth Army was safely trapped in Stalingrad, the last drive to annihilate it required 23 days for completion instead of six. No such offensive was necessary; in fact, it probably prevented a greater Russian triumph. Sixth Army should have been contained and left to wither on the vine; the bulk of the Russian troops, had they been thrown against Manstein holding the Rostov gate, might have slammed it in Kleist's face and accomplished a double victory.

As von Senger und Etterlin notes, "Only weak forces should have contained the besieged German Army . . . while correspondingly strong forces should have been set free for the pursuit and its many alluring strategical prospects."

The Russians were sluggish in exploitation and too inflexible in adapting to opportunity; there was little brilliancy in their strategy; they simply exploited, sluggishly and ponderously, the German mistakes.

Their own view of their own shortcomings, expressed in detail in *Combat Experiences,* reveals many tactical weaknesses.

> The troops were committed to battle unit by unit. . . . The troops went into battle not knowing the system of defense of the enemy. . . . Reconnaissance was conducted in a superficial manner. . . .
>
> The main body of the infantry was inactive on the battlefield. . . .
>
> There was no cooperation between infantry, tanks, artillery and aviation. Each branch of the service operated for itself.
>
> [There were] weaknesses in command of troops and their combat training.

Later, as victory bestows its laurel wreaths, the comments in *Combat Experiences* become more laudatory; it is probably fair to agree that Stalingrad "marked the beginning of a new chapter in Soviet military art," from the massed armed hordes of the past to a better articulated, better trained, more integrated and more skillfully commanded army. Yet the Russian victory was essentially one of mass. Psychologically, the Soviets stimulated their troops by the carrot of Russian nationalism and patriotism and the stick of harsh Communist discipline—literally, death rather than surrender.

On either side two leaders stand out—Marshal Zhukov, the

Russian, who was principal architect of the victorious plan, and Field Marshal Manstein, the German, who almost foiled the plan.

The aftermath of Stalingrad was, for the German Army and its leaders, loyal (on the battlefield) unto death, bitterly ironic. General Walter von Seydlitz-Kurzbach, the commander of the destroyed LI Corps who had repeatedly urged breakout, headed a Soviet-sponsored group of captive German officers (Federation of German Officers) in an attempt to do what the Allies had scorned —separate the German leaders from the German led. Paulus, but particularly Seydlitz and his *Bund Deutscher Offiziers,* part of the "National Committee of Free Germany," bitterly attacked Hitler and his conduct of the war in radio broadcasts to their homeland (after the abortive anti-Hitler plot in the summer of 1944). Paulus lived to testify at Nuremberg against the fellow generals he had once admired, but his honors had tarnished and only in Communist East Germany were Paulus, Seydlitz and their few followers welcome after the war. . . .

At Stalingrad, as Winston Churchill wrote, "The hinge of fate had turned."

Postscript from The Battle for Stalingrad
by
General Vasili I. Chuikov

I arrived at Front H.Q. at exactly 10:00 A.M. on September 12, and was received immediately by A. I. Yeremenko and N. S. Khrushchev.

The conversation was brief. I had been appointed commander of the 62nd Army. Nikita Khrushchev added some more brief comments.

The basic theme was that the Germans had decided to take the city at any cost. We should not and could not surrender it to them, we could not retreat any further, there was nowhere to retreat to.

The 62nd Army's commander, General Lopatin, did not believe that his army could hold the city. Instead of fighting to the death, instead of dying in the attempt to keep the enemy from the Volga, he had been withdrawing units. He had therefore been relieved of his post, and the army had been temporarily put under the command of the chief of staff, General N. I. Krylov. The Front Military Council, with the agreement of G.H.Q., had proposed that I should take over command of the army.

He underlined, in saying this, that he knew of the successful operations of the Southern Group in soundly beating the enemy on the River Aksay, and so protecting our troop movements in the danger area.

I took this as a compliment, a compliment which also meant obligations for me.

Finally, Nikita Khrushchev asked me:

"Comrade Chuikov, how do you interpret your task?"

I had not expected to have to answer such a question, but I did not have to think for long—everything was clear.

"We cannot surrender the city to the enemy," I replied, "because it is extremely valuable to us, to the whole Soviet people. The loss of it would undermine the nation's morale. All possible measures will be taken to prevent the city from falling. I don't ask for anything now, but I would ask the Military Council not to refuse me help when I ask for it, and I swear I shall stand firm. We will defend the city or die in the attempt."

They looked at me and said I had understood my task correctly.

We had finished our business. They invited me to stay for lunch. I declined. We said good-bye. I wanted to be left alone as quickly as possible, to ponder on whether I had not rated myself and my powers too highly. I had for some time been expecting to be sent to take over the defense of the city, was ready to do so, wanted to do so. But now that it had happened, I felt very acutely the full weight of the responsibility placed upon me. I had been honored with a gigantic and extremely difficult task, since the enemy was already on the outskirts of the city.

I left the dug-out of the Military Council and called in to see General T. F. Zakharov, front chief of staff, to find out where the command post of the 62nd Army H.Q. was. . . .

October 14 dawned—a day which saw the beginning of fighting of unprecedented ferocity. Three of the enemy's infantry divisions and two panzer divisions, deployed on a three-mile front, were thrown against our units.

Those of us who had already been through a great deal will remember this enemy attack all our lives.

We recorded some 3,000 sorties by enemy aircraft on that day! German airplanes bombed and machine-gunned our troops without stop. The enemy's artillery and mortars bombarded the whole battlefield from morning to night. It was a sunny day, but the smoke and dust cut visibility down to a hundred yards. Our dugouts shook and caved in like houses of cards.

The enemy's main attack was levelled against units of Zholudev's 37th, Gorishny's 95th and Gurtiev's 308th Divisions and the 84th Armored Brigade in the general direction of the Tractor and Barrikady factories. At 11:30 A.M. some 180 tanks broke through the lines of Zholudev's division. . . .

General Hans Doerr describes the attack on the Tractor factory in the following words:

On October 14 began the biggest operation so far: an attack by several divisions (including the 14th Panzer, 305th and 389th Infantry) on the Dzerzhinski Tractor factory, on the eastern outskirts of which was the Russian 62nd Army H.Q. From all ends of the front, even from the army's flanks on the Don and in the Kalmyk steppe, engineering and anti-tank units were brought up as reinforcements, though they were needed just as much where they had been brought from. Five engineering battalions were brought into the fighting area from Germany by plane. The attack was supported by the entire 8th Air Corps.

The troops which attacked advanced 1¼ miles, but could not overcome the resistance of the three Russian divisions defending the factory and occupying the sheer bank of the Volga. During the day our troops did succeed at some points in reaching the bank, but at night they were forced to retreat, as the Russians in the gullies were cutting them off from the rear. . . .

On November 19 the armies of the Southwestern and Don fronts attacked, and on November 20 the armies of the Stalingrad front did likewise. With bated breath we watched the progress of the gigantic battle. At the same time the troops of the 62nd Army counterattacked even more vigorously, with the aim of pinning down the enemy forces in the city, giving him no room for maneuver, or opportunity to transfer troops to other sectors of the front where the main attacks were being delivered.

I am convinced that the Germans did not expect to be attacked simultaneously on three fronts; they had failed to notice the concentration of our shock groups. Beginning their last offensive against the 62nd Army on November 11, the Germans themselves had crawled into the trap which shut behind them on November 23 in the region of Kalach. On November 24, the 62nd Army's isolated northern group under Colonel Gorokhov joined up with the 99th Infantry Division of the Don Front. Our joy knew no bounds. . . .

The Rout

The Fortress on the Volga had held out, and the news ran round the world: twenty-two of Hitler's divisions were encircled in the great cauldron of Stalingrad.

As we know, the Germans always tried to encircle the enemy facing them. And as they had been successful in doing this, the German generals considered themselves unrivalled practitioners of the encirclement maneuver. Now they themselves were inside an iron ring of Soviet troops. This was the first time it had happened to the German Wehrmacht, and it had not happened somewhere in the West, but on the territory of Soviet Russia, which they believed to be broken and almost under their heel. It happened by the Russian River Volga, some 1,250 miles from Germany. And when, with some delay, the German population found out about it, to judge only by the newspapers of the period, many Germans realized that something irreparable had happened to Nazi strategy. . . .

We knew that the encircled enemy forces amounted to not less than twenty divisions. In fact, there were twenty-two of them, in all about 300,000 men. This powerful group was encircled and held in an iron ring by seven armies, those under A. S. Zhadov, I. V. Galanin, P. I. Batov, I. M. Chistyakov, F. I. Tolbukhin, M. S. Shumilov, and the 62nd Army.

Of the twenty-two enemy divisions facing the seven armies of the Don Front, six divisions remained against the 62nd Army (the 79th, 94th, 100th, 295th, 305th and 389th Infantry Divisions). These divisions had been reinforced with five engineering battalions (the 50th, 162nd, 294th, 366th and 672nd), which Hitler had sent in to storm the city in October. . . .

Only after von Manstein's group was defeated, and our armies had driven the Germans back to Kharkov, Lugansk and Rostov-on-Don, did the morale of the encircled troops become noticeably worse. Not only the rank and file, but also the officers and generals, stopped believing in a breakthrough and release from encirclement.

Soon our men began to take even officers as prisoners, which showed the steep drop in the morale and strength of Paulus's army. . . .

Many German officers and men at the front kept diaries. Why they did so, I do not know, but from the diaries which fell into our hands one can see how the morale of the German armies, which reached its peak in July and August, began to fall, until in January 1943 it had virtually disappeared altogether.

I have in front of me the diary of Wilhelm Hoffman. The notes show that Hoffman served in a company and then in a battalion office of the 267th Regiment of the 94th Infantry Division. The diary begins in May 1942. It looks impressive, with stout binding. I have the diary in my personal files. My quotations from the diary begin with the first mention of the word "Stalingrad."

July 27. After long marches across the Don steppe, we finally reached the Don and took the big village of Tsimlyanskaya almost without a battle. Hot, extremely hot, and how pleased we all were when we saw the Don. How pleasant it was to bathe in the fresh Don water and wash our sweat-soaked clothes.

They say that first-class wine is made in this village. I'll have to send ten bottles home to father—a present from Willi. How pleased he'll be. . . .

August 2. We occupied some station or other, came to the River Sal. The River Sal is not the Don, its water is warm, hardly makes you feel any fresher. . . .

What great spaces the Soviets occupy, what rich fields there are to be had here after the war's over! Only let's get it over with quickly. I believe that the Führer will carry the thing through to a successful end.

August 12. We are advancing towards Stalingrad along the railway line. Yesterday Russian "katyushi" and then tanks halted our regiment. "The Russians are throwing in their last forces," Captain Werner explained to me. Large-scale help is coming up for us, and the Russians will be beaten.

This morning outstanding soldiers were presented with decorations for the fighting near Kantemirovka. Will I really go back to Elsa without a decoration? I believe that for Stalingrad the Führer will decorate even me. . . .

September 8. Two days of nonstop fighting. The Russians are defending themselves with insane stubbornness. Our regiment has lost many men from the "katyushi," which belch out terrible fire. I have been sent to work at battalion H.Q. It must be mother's prayers that have taken me away from the company's trenches. . . .

September 11. Our battalion is fighting in the suburbs of Stalingrad. We can already see the Volga; firing is going on all the time. Wherever you look is fire and flames. . . . Russian cannon and machine-guns are firing out of the burning city. Fanatics. . . .

September 28. Our regiment, and the whole division, are today celebrating victory. Together with our tank crews we have taken the southern part of the city and reached the Volga. We paid dearly for our victory. In three weeks we have occupied about five and a half square miles. The commander has congratulated us on our victory. . . .

November 21. The Russians have gone over to the offensive along the whole front. Fierce fighting is going on. So,

there it is—the Volga, victory and soon home to our families!
We shall obviously be seeing them next in the other world.

November 29. We are encircled. It was announced this
morning that the Führer has said: "The army can trust me
to do everything necessary to ensure supplies and rapidly
break the encirclement."

December 3. We are on hunger rations and waiting for the
rescue that the Führer promised.

I send letters home, but there is no reply.

December 7. Rations have been cut to such an extent that
the soldiers are suffering terribly from hunger; they are issu-
ing one loaf of stale bread for five men.

December 26. The horses have already been eaten. I would
eat a cat; they say its meat is also tasty. The soldiers look like
corpses or lunatics, looking for something to put in their
mouths. They no longer take cover from Russian shells; they
haven't the strength to walk, run away and hide. A curse on
this war! . . .

That was the end of the diary, and presumably of its author.

At the beginning of January we were visited at our command
post by the commander of the Don Front, Lieutenant-General
Konstantin Konstantinovich Rokossovski, the member of the
Front Military Council, Major-General Konstantin Fedorovich
Telegin, and the front artillery commander, Major-General Vasili
Ivanovich Kazakov. They crossed the Volga on the ice.

Leaving their vehicle near the Army H.Q. dug-out, Rokossovski and Telegin asked us questions for a long time, where and in
what conditions we spent the period of heavy fighting and the fires,
how we breathed when the Germans, during their advance, scattered thousands and thousands of bombs on the city.

Entering the dug-out, and sitting down on the bench of earth
at the table of earth, the front commander briefly outlined the plan
for the destruction of the encircled enemy group, and set the army
its tasks. The crux of the plan was that the main attack would be
delivered from the west, by the armies of Generals Batov and

Chistyakov, with the aim of splitting the encircled enemy group. A simultaneous attack would be delivered from the north by the armies of Generals Zhadov and Galanin, and from the south by the armies of Generals Shumilov and Tolbukhin. The 62nd Army had the job of "carrying out active operations from the east, so as to attract more enemy forces in its direction, preventing them from reaching the Volga if they try to break out of encirclement across the frozen Volga."

The task was clear enough, and I assured the front commander that it would be carried out, and that until the main attack was launched by the front armies, Paulus would not withdraw a single division from the city.

On February 2, Stalin received the following dispatch:

Carrying out your order, the troops of the Don Front at 4 P.M. on February 2, 1943, completed the rout and destruction of the encircled group of enemy forces at Stalingrad. Twenty-two divisions have been destroyed or taken prisoner. . . . The prisoners number 91,000, including 2,500 officers and 24 generals, among them 1 field-marshal, 2 colonel-generals, the rest lieutenant-generals and major-generals. . . . As a result of this final liquidation of the enemy, the military operations in the city and area of Stalingrad have ceased.

Lieutenant-General Rokossovsky,
Commander of the Don Front.
Lieutenant-General Malinin,
Chief of Staff of the Don Front.

CHAPTER XII

NORMANDY:
JUNE 6–JULY 25, 1944

Called Operation OVERLORD, all the accumulated military powers of the Allies carried the assaults to the selected beachhead landings. The Allied naval fleets raked the German defenses and protected the transports landing the men; the air force went after the German airfields and selected targets, in advance; the paratroops jumped for other targets. The soldiers landed on the beachheads.

The assaulting armies included:

21st British Army Group (Montgomery)

British Second Army (Dempsey)

U.S. First Army (Bradley)

The Allied invaders spread over beaches symbolically named Omaha, Utah, Gold Note—from La Madeliene to Luc-sur-Mer on the Normandy coast. The soldiers soon spread towards Caen, Cherbourg—and inland, to swamp the German defenders. It was the greatest invasion in the history of all wars.

The four years of Allied planning for this invasion depended, in the last few days, on the turn of the weather in the English Channel. The German High Command, with four years to prepare the defenses of their Atlantic Wall, were taken by complete surprise. Field Marshal Rommel, in charge of the Atlantic Wall, was asleep in his German hometown. German intelligence agents in Great Britain knew that the projected invasion had a flexible dateline—but June 6 was hardly the weather for D day.

From General of the Army Omar N. Bradley's book, *A Soldier's Story*, I have picked the pertinent sequences detailing the anguished preparations for D day—and the final decision to land in Normandy. From Cornelius Ryan's book, *The Longest Day*, I have chosen a selection describing the German reaction to the Allied invasion. Together, both selections encapsulate the dramatic event-on-events of D day; the battle for France and the eventual crushing of the German armies.

Literally every great general on both sides engaged, soon enough, in the battles that followed the landings on the Normandy coast. The number of Allied casualties for the 24-hour period following D day has been put between 10,000 and 12,000; for the German defenders of the Atlantic Wall, between 4000 and 9000; but before a month had gone, the Germans lost 250,000 men, 354 commanders and 28 generals.

General of the Army Omar N. Bradley (1890–   ) was born in Missouri. He graduated from the U.S. Military Academy in 1915. At the start of World War II he was commandant of the Infantry School and later commanded the 82nd Division. In 1943 he led the Second Corps in North Africa and through the Sicilian campaign. Later he commanded the U.S. Army in the United Kingdom and helped plan the invasion of Normandy, leading the 1st Army landings in Normandy. Later he led the 1st, 3rd and 15th Armies, the largest ever placed under one commander, to carry on operations in France, Belgium, the Netherlands and Germany.

General of the Army Dwight D. Eisenhower (1890–1969) was born in Texas and entered West Point in 1911. During his early career he trained troops at the Tank School, graduated from the Army College, worked in the office of the assistant secretary of war and was later assigned to General MacArthur to serve as assistant military advisor to the Commonwealth of the Philippines. When World War II broke out, he became executive officer of the 15th Division and was promoted to a full colonel. He worked with General Marshal in 1942 as assistant chief of staff in charge of planning. In 1942 he was also promoted to the rank of major general and was soon head of the Eastern Theater of Operations to lead the unified command of British and American forces in England preparing for the invasion of North Africa and the Continent. General of the Army Dwight D. Eisenhower was elected president of the United States in 1952.

General George Patton (1885–1945) was born in California and graduated from the U.S. Military Academy in 1909, specializing in the cavalry leaders of the American Civil War. Later he espoused the cause of tank warfare. He participated in the North African campaign in 1942 and commanded the U.S. 7th Army in Sicily. The heart of his career was the great sweep of his army across France in the summer of 1944.

General Bartley S. Hodges (1887–   ) was born in Georgia and enlisted in the army in 1906. He served in Mexico during the period 1916–1917 and in France in 1918. He headed the Infantry School in 1940–1941 and was chief of infantry from 1941–1943. In 1943 he commanded the 3rd Army and served as deputy commander of the 1st Army during the invasion of Normandy, bearing the brunt of the Ardennes counterattack.

Field Marshal Bernard Montgomery (1887–   ) was educated at Sandhurst Royal Military Academy and served with great distinction during World War I. He commanded a division in France at the outbreak of World War II. During the African campaigns he was the most effective campaigner against General Rommel. He invaded Sicily after the German defeat in North Africa and was under the command of General Eisenhower during the invasion of Normandy. He led the 21st Army Group of British and Canadians through France and to the Rhine, to receive the German surrender on May 4, 1945.

Air Marshal Arthur William Tedder (1890–   ) went to Magdalene College, Cambridge. Commissioned in the British Army in 1913, he served in France during World War I in the Royal Flying Corps. In 1941 he was appointed air officer commander in chief in the Middle East and played a notable part in expelling the Axis armies in the Middle East. In 1944 he was appointed deputy commander of the Allied Expeditionary Force under General Eisenhower and worked in the planning and landing of the Allied troops in Normandy.

Admiral Ernest Joseph King (1878–1956) was born in Ohio and entered the U.S. Naval Academy in 1897. During the Spanish-American War he served as a midshipman on the *U.S.S. San Francisco*. During World War I he was the commander of a destroyer division and later served as chief of staff to Admiral Mayo, commander of the Atlantic Fleet. He became a rear admiral in 1933 and the chief of the Bureau of Aeronautics the same year. By 1938 he was commanding the aircraft battle forces and was promoted to vice admiral. In 1941 he was commander in chief of the Atlantic Fleet annd the commander in chief of the U.S. fleet after World War II broke out, playing an important role in the preparation and completion of the invasion of Normandy.

D Day, Normandy
by
General of the Army Omar N. Bradley

It was 7:15 when I went down to breakfast at my quarters in Bristol on the morning of June 3. We had loitered late over dinner the night before, our last evening together in England. Today we were to board Admiral Kirk's flagship for the invasion. D day had been set for June 5 and the warm summer sun that poured through the leaded glass windows of the Holmes Hotel cheered us with the promise of good weather. . . .

Shortly after eight we turned south from Bristol across the Avon on the road to Plymouth where we were to rendezvous with Collins. Hansen rode with an aluminum tube of TOP SECRET invasion maps between his knees. Kean and Dickson, Thorson, and Wilson followed in a second sedan. It was a Saturday morning and we slowed down through the market at Taunton where British housewives had already formed their patient queues before the shops. Although the sausages were now packed with invasion troops, so quietly had the D day force been assembled that Taunton, like those other southern tier towns, remained blissfully unaware that The Day was at hand.

Collins was waiting at a road junction north of Plymouth. He sped us through the MP check-points to the quay where a barge from the *Augusta* was standing by. For the first time since Sicily I buckled on a pistol and bent my neck under the weight of a steel helmet. I tossed my field pack with its greasy gas-protective coveralls to the deck and jumped aboard.

The *Augusta* waited offshore, a rakish beauty among the snub-nosed LST's. Its curved yachtlike bow and eight-inch turrets pointed toward the Channel. Kirk had gone ashore but Rear Admiral A. D. Struble, his chief of staff, welcomed us aboard. I was assigned the skipper's cabin, the one occupied by President Roosevelt in 1941 when he joined Churchill off the Newfoundland shore to draft the Atlantic Charter. . . .

I glanced at the weather forecast in the G-2 journal: *Mist from Sunday to Wednesday, with low clouds and reduced visibility in the mornings. Winds not to exceed 17 to 22 knots. Choppy water in the channel with five-foot breakers. A four-foot surf on the beaches.*

"Doesn't look good," I said.

Dickson was more emphatic. "It stinks."

Kirk and I had worked together once before on the Sicilian assault. As naval commander of the Western Task Force he was again my opposite number. But my directives came from Montgomery, while his originated with Ramsay, the Allied naval commander-in-chief.

Kirk's fleet was divided into three forces. The first, Force "O" for Omaha, was commanded by Rear Admiral John L. Hall, Jr., another old friend from the Sicilian invasion. The second, Force "U" for Utah, sailed under the flag of Rear Admiral Don P. Moon. Hall was paired with Gerow aboard the *Ancon,* command ship for V Corps; Moon shared the *Bayfield* with Collins's VII Corps. The third mounted a follow-up force, combat-loaded from the Bristol Channel. It contained the 2d Division, bound for Omaha Beach and the 90th Division for Utah.

During spring planning Kirk and I had battled side by side in a strenuous effort to coax additional naval gunfire support from naval operations in Washington. For originally the bombardment fleet assigned the invasion looked woefully inadequate for its task. As late as April, 1944, the U.S. Navy could spare only 2 battleships, 4 cruisers, 12 destroyers, and a variety of small craft to support the American landing. We anticipated little resistance from the hit-and-run German navy but we were apprehensive over the coastal guns. Against those fixed shore batteries I would gladly have swapped a dozen B-17's for each 12-inch gun I could wrangle. As in Sicily the American deficit in naval support was to be made up by the British. But because an American destroyer packed almost the fire-power of a British cruiser, while the American cruiser outgunned her British counterpart, I was anxious that our allotment in naval support be tallied in U.S. ships. . . .

If we were to fail on the OVERLORD invasion, we might never get a second chance. Even at the risk of slowing down its timetable in the Pacific war, I begged the navy to stack the odds more heavily on our side. Eventually Washington agreed and Kirk's bombardment fleet was enlarged to 4 battleships (2 of which were holdovers from World War I), 4 cruisers, and 26 destroyers. It could not be called a formidable force in terms of Pacific naval campaigns, but at least our pinchpenny days were ended. . . .

Despite our disheartening forecast on weather, no word had come from Ike at Portsmouth on the likelihood of postponement. He was to meet at 4:00 A.M. the following morning on June 4 with his weather officer and the combined commanders-in-chief. Not until then would Eisenhower make the momentous decision that only he could make: whether to go ahead in the face of bad weather or wait for improvement.

Later that afternoon I boarded a barge to visit Hodges and the First Army staff. They were headquartered aboard the *Achernar*, a converted cargo ship now draped with the antennae and radio mounts of a command ship. . . .

That evening Kirk asked if I would brief the correspondents aboard the *Augusta* on First Army's assault plans. Only three of them had been accredited to Kirk's staff. I first outlined the missions of the airborne and seaborne troops.

"To help the amphibious get elements ashore," I said, "we're going to soften up each of the beaches with an 800-ton carpet bombing. Ten minutes before the first wave touches down, we'll drench Omaha with 8,000 rockets, put another 5,000 on Utah. These rockets should tear up his wire, detonate his mines, and drive him under cover the instant before we land." I pointed to the detailed beach map. "Then promptly at H hour we'll swim 64 tanks ashore. . . ."

"Swim them ashore?" someone asked.

"They're DD tanks," I explained, forgetting for the moment how closely we had guarded this secret.

Another experimental device of the British, the DD, or dual-drive, tank consisted of a conventional vehicle equipped with canvas water wings and an auxiliary propeller. After sealing the tank's hull and fitting the propeller, ordnance had added a tubular frame over which it stretched a canvas float that completely surrounded the tank. The driver could spread these wings by a simple mechanical device as he walked his steel monster off the ramp of an LCT. When I first saw the invention on the Isle of Wight the previous December, I blinked as a 30-ton-Cromwell tank waded out of the surf and snarled over the beach, her gun in position to fire. A blast from a built-in demolition dropped her water wings on the beach. The rig was easily adapted to our 34-ton Sherman tanks.

Tactically these DD tanks provided the answer to our need for heavy well-aimed fire against the beach defenses at the moment of touch-down. Until the DD tanks were developed, we had been dependent upon the machine guns and mortars the infantry carried ashore.

As soon as possible after breaching the enemy's shore defenses we were to lay down advance fighter bases for our aircraft. By eliminating the 300-mile turnaround from Britain we could almost double the effectiveness of existing fighter craft. By D plus 1 we were to open an evacuation airstrip on each beach. By D plus 14 the schedule called for ten airstrips to base as many fighter groups. And by D plus 35, only five weeks after landing, we expected to have cleared 18 fields through the hedgerows of our American sector. . . .

One of Kirk's correspondents nodded toward the map where the words *Festung Cherbourg* had been heavily ringed by a red crayon.

"How soon do you expect to take Cherbourg?" he asked.

"I'm going to have to stick my neck out," I told him. "But as of this moment, I'd gladly sell out for D plus 15—yes, or even D plus 20. The D plus 8 estimate you see here on the map is probably much better than we can do."

The rosier estimate had been written into the OVERLORD plan long before Rommel began to thicken his Normandy defenses. Originally the invasion coast had been held by only three static divisions. Now three additional field divisions had crowded into that sector. Dickson had estimated the enemy could mount a total of seven against us on D day. . . .

"We're going to face three critical periods in this invasion. The first will come in getting ashore. It'll be difficult—but we're not especially worried about that part of it. The second may come on the sixth or seventh day when the other fellow gets together enough reinforcements for a counteroffensive. This counterattack will probably give us our greatest trouble. Then once we hurdle the counterattack, our third critical period will come when we go to break out of the beachhead." . . .

OVERLORD had already gotten under way for D day on the morning of June 5. Either Eisenhower would halt it early this morning of June 4 or the invasion would have gone too far to be called back.

At midnight I turned in and fell asleep. It was almost six when I was awakened on Sunday, June 4. The weather in Plymouth harbor was soupy and wet; visibility was down and I shivered as I dressed. Kean came in with a copy of the Admiralty radio to Kirk.

"Postponed?" I asked.

"Twenty-four hours."

Just as soon as Eisenhower had reached his decision the navy rushed fast destroyers to head off the units that had put to sea and shepherd them back to ports. Now the sharp edge of those troops would be dulled and seasickness would take its toll in another day on the choppy Channel. We checked the weather forecast that had been posted on our journal. It was even less promising than the one on June 3: five-foot waves in the Channel and no sign of a break in the overcast until June 7 or 8.

But unless we adjusted the H hour, tidal conditions on June 8 would rule out that long a postponement. The rising tide would not reach its halfway high-water mark until long after daylight that morning. And while we had planned a daylight invasion at dawn, we backed off at the thought of a late midmorning attack that would enable the enemy to regain his wits after the heavy night bombing.

Thorson ordered his working staff on the *Achernar* to notify all First Army units of the postponements. The code words went out: HORNPIPE to indicate OVERLORD, BOWSPRIT for the one-day delay. The staff there had already been tipped off in a message from Montgomery's headquarters at 5:15 that morning. G-3 had devised a prearranged signal to circulate news of a postponement. Having declared an initial postponement, Eisenhower was left to struggle with the question of whether to go ahead once more. He scheduled another predawn meeting early on June 5 at Southwick House in Portsmouth. For the second time he was to be cornered alone on the single most important yes or no decision of the war. That choice alone might hold the key to success or failure.

On that Sunday afternoon, June 4, I was to go ashore with Kirk to agree on our recommendations in the event of a second postponement. Meanwhile I shuffled impatiently about my cabin. . . .

Before going ashore I crossed over once more to the *Achernar* for one last session with the army staff. For a conference table we used the air filter room where A-2 would track enemy air attacks during our crossing of the Channel. The huge plotting board was painted with naval force channels from the English coast to France. These channels ran from the British ports in the east of England and the American ports in the west to converge in an assembly area off the Isle of Wight. From there they paralleled each other for 50 miles toward the Normandy coast. Within 30 miles of the shoreline they fanned out again toward the five invasion beaches. . . .

The OVERLORD D day had originally been scheduled by the combined chiefs of staff for the "favorable period of the May moon." Later, on Eisenhower's recommendation, they postponed D day to a "favorable period" in June. The specific date would be

left to the discretion of the supreme commander. But in choosing
the actual D day, Eisenhower was to beat the mercy of the tides.
For the lunar cycle left us with only six days each month when
tidal conditions fulfilled our requirements on the beaches. The first
three fell on June 5, 6, and 7. If bad weather forestalled invasion
on all three days, the assault would have to be put off for two
weeks. If bad weather again prevented our going during that
second June phase of the moon, there was no alternative but to
delay the invasion until July. Meanwhile, after having once been
briefed on the OVERLORD plan and destination, the assault
troops would have to be locked up totally incommunicado. The
prospect was a frightening one: 28 days of keeping a secret known
to more than 140,000 men.

Even more frightening than the problem of security was the
likely effect of a month's delay on Allied operations in France. Not
only would that long a postponement shorten by one-third the
time left for our summer campaign, but it would shove us one
month nearer the deadline for seizing a Channel port before the
advent of stormy weather. We were told that we could not bank
on the Channel for beach unloading after September 1. If the
Germans were to hang on to Cherbourg for 50 or 60 days after
a July D-day landing, we might be seriously pressed for winter-
time maintenance of our troops ashore. The choice of D day had
been limited to six days each month because only during those six
days could we satisfy our requirements on morning light and tides.
Both air and navy insisted upon daylight as essential to the
preliminary bombardment. . . .

But on the question of tides the army had to be insistent, for
there we could not give in. Twice each day the Normandy beach
was flooded by a mountainous Channel tide that rose approximately 19 feet from low to high water. At low tide the beach
defenses lay exposed more than a quarter mile behind a moist
sandy shelf. At high tide the Channel lapped almost to the sea wall
behind Omaha Beach. . . .

The choice, therefore, would have been a simple one in favor of
high tide had it not been for the underwater obstacles Rommel
had planted on those Normandy beaches. For had we sailed in on
a high tide, those obstructions would have pinioned our craft and

torn open their bellies. The assault wave might then have foundered in eight feet of surf. . . .

Of all the days in the month, June 6 would best fit our requirements, for it would have sufficient daylight before the incoming tide would reach the obstacles on Omaha Beach. June 5 would be acceptable with 30 minutes less daylight, June 7 with 30 minutes more. But by June 8 the tide would not reach the obstacles until two and a half hours after daylight. A two and a half hour gap between daylight and touch-down we thought too risky in terms of lost surprise. Ike's first choice for D day had been June 5. For then if weather closed in, he could still choose June 6 or 7. Consequently on May 17 he red-lined June 5 as D day.

By June 4 the weather was such that Ike decided to defer D day to June 6. But in Plymouth on the drizzly afternoon of June 4 there were few signs of a break in the weather. We firmly anticipated a second postponement that night.

But here came the hitch in plan. Ike could not make his decision before the westernmost convoys again weighed anchor on a second start. The first time we had simply turned them back to port. If it became necessary to turn them back once more, they would be forced to put in for fuel. And since refueling called for at least a 48-hour delay, there would be no possibility of getting them off before the morning of June 7.

Consequently in this second go-round on weather Eisenhower could no longer get by with a simple yes or no. The choice had become more complex.

1. He could take a chance on the unpromising weather and go ahead on June 6.

2. He could postpone the assault once more and put it ashore for two weeks to await the next favorable phase of the moon.

3. Or he could accept less favorable tide and daylight conditions and risk June 8 or 9. . . .

At 9:30 on Sunday evening, June 4, Eisenhower gathered his commanders once more at Portsmouth to discuss the weather reports. This time the forecast encouraged a flicker of hope. Rain squalls over the beaches were expected to clear in two or three hours. Visibility, it was thought, might hold up until Tuesday, June 6. Meanwhile the winds were reported slackening, the cloud base lifting. But while the weather report held out hopes for improvement, it did not excite lively enthusiasm for the adventure. Instead it looked barely promising enough to tantalize Ike with the thought of taking a chance. For the clouds that were expected to close in again on June 6 might easily wash out air and spoil spotting for the naval bombardment. Risky though it was, both Eisenhower and Smith welcomed this hazardous break in the weather. Almost anything would have been preferable, they thought, to the ordeal of another delay. Monty was for it. But Leigh-Mallory hung back and Tedder was not sure.

At 9:45 Eisenhower edged reluctantly into a decision. "I'm quite positive we must give the order. . . . I don't like it, but there it is. . . . I don't see how we can possibly do anything else."

The day for OVERLORD was now set, save for one last look at the weather at 4:00 A.M., June 5, to make certain the choice need not be reversed.

Aboard the *Augusta* we awaited a postponement signal. But none came and by midnight we heard that Eisenhower had chosen to go. OVERLORD was under way; The Plan had taken over. For the next 24 hours the fate of the war in Europe was to ride not in the big-hulled command ships but in the wet flat-bottomed craft where many GI's were to be seasick on the slippery steel floors as they groaned through the choppy Channel. . . .

Confirmation came at dawn the following morning when a courier arrived from the *Achernar* with a teletype message from Portsmouth: *D Day stands as is, Tuesday, June 6th.* Soon the waters of Plymouth harbor churned in a tangle of wakes as hundreds of ships turned obediently into line. As the columns uncoiled toward the Channel the *Augusta* put to sea, rapidly overtaking the awkward, slow-moving craft. On the eastern lip of the harbor a weathered pillbox squatted lonesomely on stilts offshore. From the gravelly beach behind it a half-dozen concrete blockhouses faced out across the Channel. They had been constructed as part of Britain's hasty preparations to repel a German invasion in 1940. . . .

At an easy 15 knots the *Augusta* flanked the Utah-bound column out of Plymouth harbor and headed for the Isle of Wight. From the YOKE assembly point there, she would head with the

Omaha forces through a mine-swept Channel to the Normandy coast. There she was to fire in support of the initial landing. As far as we could see both fore and aft, ships crowded the British coastline. Overhead their barrage balloons bucked in the wind. Fast destroyers screened us seaward. . . .

All afternoon, Monday, June 5, the *Augusta* scudded past the Utah-bound convoys, heading for her rendezvous with the Omaha force. High above the cruiser's bridge a radar antenna rotated monotonously under the wooly sky. In the plotting room below, an officer bent before the radar screen searching for the telltale pips that would signify enemy air. But day passed and evening came without a bogey report.

"Seems hard to believe," I said to Kirk, "maybe we're going to have a Sicily all over again." There, too, we had held our breaths in anticipation of air attack against the convoys. Yet in Sicily the enemy had slumbered on until we piled up on his beaches. But in the narrow English Channel we could scarcely count on slipping through the enemy's alert without sounding an alarm. On a clear day, aircraft at 10,000 feet over Le Havre could look clear across to Southampton. Enemy radar fringed the French coast and E-boats patrolled offshore in regular nighttime sorties. All that day we waited for signs of enemy recce from across the Channel. First the recce, then probing attacks. On D day we looked for the Luftwaffe to stage a mighty comeback with an attack against our transports in the crowded anchorages offshore. At no time during the European campaign would Goering find a more congested and remunerative target.

We learned later it was nothing less than this dirty weather that spared us enemy detection and air attack. For the enemy could not believe we would venture into the stormy Channel in the face of those weather forecasts available to him. Lacking the weather stations we had established in Greenland and the North Atlantic, German meteorologists had failed to pick up the prospective break that prompted Ike's decision. Because of the high winds and heavy overcast on June 5, German naval patrols were canceled and mine layers restricted to ports. Even the ordinarily vigilant Luftwaffe recce lay grounded on its fields. In this capricious turn of the weather we had found a Trojan horse. . . .

At eleven that evening I went below, unbuckled my Mae West, and fell into bed with my shoes on. Kirk remained on the bridge, buttoned up in his foul-weather gear, as the *Augusta* slipped quietly past the buoys that marked the mine-swept Channel. Only the lonely wind in the rigging and the wash of water past our sides broke the silence of the night. It was 3:35 A.M. when the clanking bell outside my cabin called the crew to battle stations. I reached for my helmet, scrambled into a Mae West, and hurried to Kirk's bridge. The moon hung misted in an overcast sky and the wind still lashed the Channel. According to the log the breeze had slackened but the change was not yet evident in the seas that washed by the *Augusta*. Off in the Cotentin Peninsula, almost 30 miles to the west, both airborne divisions had already been dropped. In its headquarters near the ancient terraced city of Le Mans, 40 miles behind the Normandy beaches, the German Seventh Army flashed an invasion alarm. But in the comfortable villa that Eisenhower was later to occupy in St. Germain near Paris, von Rundstedt deferred judgment. He feared the airborne drop a diversion preparatory to a main Allied attack against the Pas de Calais.

A faraway roar echoed across the Channel, and off our starboard bow orange fires ignited the sky as more than 1,300 RAF bombers swarmed over the French coastline from the Seine to Cherbourg. An enemy AA battery stabbed blindly through the night. A shower of sparks splintered the darkness and a ribbon of fire peeled out of the sky as a stricken bomber plunged toward the *Augusta*. It leveled off, banked around our stern, and exploded into the Channel. By 5:30, first light had diluted the darkness and three Spits whistled by overhead, the first sign of our air umbrella. High above the overcast, relays of American fighters formed a second layer of air cover.

The *Augusta* closed in at five knots to its firing position offshore. High up on the cruiser's open bridge, I squinted toward the shore where it lay blurred in the morning mist. Zero hour had come for the DD tanks on Omaha Beach. They were to be launched from their mother craft at H minus 50 minutes and make their way ashore through paths cleared by demolition teams through the obstacle line. The infantry would swarm ashore on the heels of these DD tanks and push on inland under the cover of their fire.

Thorson stared at the heaving black Channel and shook his head. "I don't like it, General. The DD's are going to have one helluva time in getting through this sea.". . .

The decision as to whether those tanks would swim or be carted ashore could not be made aboard the *Augusta*. It fell to the commanders of those tank detachments. By now OVERLORD had run beyond the reach of its admirals and generals. For the next few tortured hours we could do little but pace our decks and trust in the men to whom The Plan had been given for execution.

At 5:47 a message appeared on the G-2 journal. Fifteen German E-boats had left the harbor at Cherbourg to engage our fleet. Kean smiled and chewed on a piece of gum. Fifteen E-boats against our armada.

The *Augusta's* eight-inch turrets were turned toward the shore. We plugged our ears with cotton. At 5:50 the ship shuddered as it opened fire upon its predesignated targets among the beach defenses. The salvo coasted over the armada and we followed the pinpoints of fire as they plunged down toward the shore. The targets had been painstakingly picked from thousands of aerial photos, by which each gun, trench, and pillbox was sited on a detailed map.

At 6:15 smoke thickened the mist on the coastline as heavy bombers of the Eighth Air Force rumbled overhead. Not until later did we learn that most of the 13,000 bombs dropped by these heavies had cascaded harmlessly into the hedgerows three miles behind the coast. In bombing through the overcast, air had deliberately delayed its drop to lessen the danger of spill-over on craft approaching the shore. This margin for safety had undermined the effectiveness of the heavy air mission. To the seasick infantry, bailing their craft as they wallowed through the surf, this failure in air bombing was to mean many more casualties upon Omaha Beach.

Meanwhile, of the 32 DD tanks launched off Omaha, 27 had foundered in the heavy surf. Our troops had not yet landed and already two critical supports for the assault had broken down. At 6:45, 15 minutes after H hour, word reached the *Augusta* that the first wave had clambered ashore. It was still too early for news from the beach. I choked down a scalding cup of coffee. By now it was daylight and because the sun was hidden in a haze overhead, a gray panorama opened about us. So far we had drawn no return fire from the enemy's coastal guns. "I don't understand this lack of counterbattery," Kean said. "He's had time to get us in range." . . .

As the morning lengthened, my worries deepened over the alarming and fragmentary reports we picked up on the navy net. From these messages we could piece together only an incoherent account of sinkings, swampings, heavy enemy fire, and chaos on the beaches. By 8:30 the two assault regiments on Omaha had expected to break through the water's-edge defenses and force their way inland to where a road paralleled the coastline a mile behind the beaches. Yet by 8:30, V Corps had not yet confirmed news of the landing. We fought off our fears, attributing the delay to a jam-up in communications. It was almost 10:00 before the first report came in from Gerow. Like the fragments we had already picked up, his message was laconic, neither conclusive nor reassuring. It did nothing more than confirm our worst fears on the DD tanks. *"Obstacles mined, progress slow . . . DD tanks for Fox Green swamped."*

Aboard the *Ancon*, Gerow and Huebner clung to their radios as helplessly as I. There was little else they could do. For at the moment they had no more control than I of the battle on the beaches. Though we could see it dimly through the haze and hear the echo of its guns, the battle belonged that morning to the thin, wet line of khaki that dragged itself ashore on the Channel coast of France. Alarmed over the congestion of craft offshore on Omaha Beach, Kirk ordered his gunnery officer in for a close-up view. I sent Hansen with him aboard a PT boat. They returned an hour later, soaked by the seas, with a discouraging report of conditions on the beach. The 1st Division lay pinned down behind the sea wall while the enemy swept the beaches with small-arms fire. Artillery chased the landing craft where they milled offshore. Much of the difficulty had been caused by the underwater obstructions. Not only had the demolition teams suffered paralyzing casualties, but much of their equipment had been swept away. Only six paths had been blown in that barricade before the rising tide halted their operations. Unable to break through the obstacles that blocked their assigned beaches, craft turned toward Easy Red* where the gaps had been blown. Then as successive waves ran in toward the cluttered beachhead they soon found themselves snarled in a jam offshore.

When V Corps reported at noon that the situation was "still critical" on all four beach exits, I reluctantly contemplated the diversion of Omaha follow-up forces to Utah and the British beaches. Scanty reports from both those sectors indicated the landings there had gone according to plan.

With the Omaha landing falling hours and hours behind schedule, we faced an imminent crisis on the follow-up force. There was due to arrive at noon in the transport area off Omaha Beach a force of 25,000 troops and 4,400 more vehicles to be landed on the second tide. However only a portion of the assault force of 34,000 troops and 3,300 vehicles had as yet gotten ashore. Unless we moved both forces ashore on D day, the whole intricate schedule of build-up would be thrown off balance. Whatever the improvisation, our build-up would have to be maintained if we were to withstand an enemy counteroffensive. Despite the setbacks we had suffered as the result of bad weather and ineffective bombing, I was shaken to find that we had gone against Omaha with so thin a margin of safety. At the time of sailing we had thought ourselves cushioned against such reversals as these.

Not until noon did a radio from Gerow offer a clue to the trouble we had run into on Omaha Beach. Instead of the rag-tag static troops we had expected to find there, the assault had run head-on into one of Rommel's tough field divisions.

In planning the assault, originally we had counted upon a thin enemy crust of two static divisions between Caen and Cherbourg. Rommel was known to have concentrated his better reserves behind the beach. Among them was the 352nd Division which had been assembled at St.-Lô.

Just before boarding the *Augusta* in Plymouth harbor, Dickson

---

*Omaha and Utah beaches were divided into sectors designated by D for Dog, E for Easy, and F for Fox. These sectors were further divided and differentiated by colors, such as Easy Red, Easy Green, Fox Red, and so on.

learned that the 352nd had been moved from St.-Lô to the assault beaches for a defense exercise. He promptly forwarded this information to V Corps and the 1st Division but was unable to give it to the troops already "sealed" aboard their craft.

Had a less experienced division than the 1st Infantry stumbled into this crack resistance, it might easily have been thrown back into the Channel. Unjust though it was, my choice of the 1st to spearhead the invasion probably saved us Omaha Beach and a catastrophe on the landing.

Although the deadlock had been broken several hours sooner, it was almost 1:30 P.M. when V Corps relieved our fears aboard the *Augusta* with the terse message: *"Troops formerly pinned down on beaches Easy Red, Easy Green, Fox Red advancing up heights behind beaches."*

Behind Omaha the ground rose steeply up brush-covered slopes from 100 to 170 feet high. At four points along the 7,000-yard beach, lightly wooded draws indented these bluffs to provide exit routes inland. Here the enemy had concentrated his heaviest fortifications and here he had held out the longest. Only one draw was traveled by an improved road; the others contained nothing but cart tracks. Within days these cart tracks were to become the most heavily trafficked roads in Europe.

Reluctant to bank altogether on the laconic reports that trickled in from V Corps, I instructed Kean to go ashore, size up the beach-front congestion, and check on the advance inland that we might calculate our chances on landing a part of the follow-up force that night. With Hansen he sped off in a TP, closed to a thousand yards offshore, and transferred to an LCVP for the final trip through the obstacles. High water had reached its mark and the tide was rolling out, leaving the LCT's and hundreds of craft dried out on the beaches. The *Augusta* had now closed in to within 4,000 yards of the beach and the waters about us were strewn with flotsam from the invasion.

Kean's report was more hopeful than I had dared wish for. Despite the congestion of vehicles on Omaha Beach, our troops had penetrated the enemy's defenses between the well-guarded draws and to the east of Easy Red had pushed one mile inland to cut the first lateral road. Although the strategic draw at Easy Red had not yet been cleared of small-arms fire, bulldozers were already carving a path up its shoulder to the tableland on top of the bluff. And as the tide withdrew from the beach, engineers trailed after it through the debris, blowing new paths through the obstacles as they were uncovered by the Channel.

Despite the improved situation, however, Omaha had fallen seriously behind schedule. The beach was littered with stove-in craft, drowned-out vehicles, and burned-out tanks. Scores of bodies sprawled wet and shapeless in the shingle where they had fallen. Only the lightly wounded could be removed to hospital ships through the heavy surf. The more seriously wounded had been bedded down in slit trenches under the sea wall. And from one end of the beach to the other the tidal shelf was littered with the water-soaked debris that washes in with the surf in the wake of any invasion.

The enormous equipment losses on landing had left Omaha badly in need of replacements. "What do they need most?" I asked Kean.

"Bulldozers," he answered, "bulldozers and artillery. They're badly pinched for both."

Not only were bulldozers needed to clear the debris and obstacles in time for the second tide, but without them our losses mounted as vehicles, ferried ashore on rhino's from the LST's, mired in the soft, low-water sands. Of the 16 dozers that had been sent ashore that morning, only six reached Omaha Beach. Three of these were immediately knocked out by enemy artillery fire.

Although Omaha had squeezed through a crisis, she was still on the danger list. With neither depth, artillery, nor tanks, we might easily be dislodged from our precarious footing and thrown back into the Channel by counterattack. I hurried off to see Gerow aboard the *Ancon*. . . .

While spashing toward the *Ancon* aboard a PT boat, I anticipated that Gerow and Huebner might have been unnerved by the prolonged struggle that morning. Both had gone under fire as senior commanders for the first time, and although neither could have averted the crisis, both bore an immediate responsibility for it. Thus while I was eager to check on the situation and push the follow-up ashore, I went partly to stiffen their confidence if confidence was what they needed. I found, however, that Gerow's map showed penetrations at five points on the Omaha Beach defenses. The lateral road had been cut at Vierville and again at Colleville on the left. And a force was pushing toward Pointe du Hoe to relieve the Rangers there. With that we hoisted our tails and went ahead with the original plan to land the follow-up force on Omaha Beach and put five regiments ashore by nightfall. . . .

Across the estuary that slashed into the Cotentin neck, our PT rammed through the surf for Utah Beach at full throttle. With two lookouts hugging the deck to warn him of floating mines, the skipper drove his eggshelled craft through blinding spray. Inside the Utah anchorage we located the *Bayfield* by its topside antennae. As the PT boat pitched to the crest of a six-foot wave, I jumped for the rope net of the *Bayfield* and clambered up its high steel sides. In contrast to Omaha where the shadow of catastrophe had hung over our heads all day, the landing on Utah had gone more smoothly than during rehearsal five weeks before. As G-2 had predicted, the beach was held by second-rate static troops. Except for casemated artillery north of Utah, the resistance quickly collapsed. In tallying up G-1's reports almost a week later, I found that Collins had cracked the wall on Utah Beach at a cost of fewer than 350 casualties in his assault force. This was less than half of what he had lost in the rehearsal on Slapton Sands. . . .

By daylight, paratroopers from both the 82d and 101st Divisions were fighting for their lives deep in the treacherous hedgerows and swamplands of the Cotentin.

The drop had gone awry almost as soon as the 432 troop-carrier aircraft of the 101st Division made landfall on the west Cotentin coast after a midnight flight from England. Cloud banks forced the closely packed nighttime formations to disperse. As the planes neared their drop zones now marked by pathfinder parties, enemy flak scattered the formations still farther apart. Although the drop concentration might have been judged remarkable in the light of our Sicilian episode, the 6,600 paratroopers of Taylor's division were scattered widely behind the causeways they had been ordered to secure. More than 60 planeloads were dumped from 8 to 20 miles beyond their drop zones. Others were scattered from Utah

Beach through the lagoons. Nevertheless, remnants of the 101st struck smartly toward the causeways that led from Utah Beach while others headed south to seal off Carentan and block that path of enemy reinforcement.

Two-thirds of the 82d Division was to have been dropped eight miles inland behind the Merderet River where it parallels Utah Beach. Here it could shield Collins's beaches from the west and harry the enemy in his reinforcement of Cherbourg. The remaining drop zone lay east of that river astride the principal route from Cherbourg to the beachhead. Here Ridgway would block from the north and "establish a firm defensive base" in the village of Ste Mère Eglise.

Like the 101st, however, Ridgway's 82d was badly scattered on landing, especially those elements scheduled to drop west of the Merderet. As a consequence, much of the division's effort on that first day was wasted in the difficult task of assembling combat units. However the division did establish a base in Ste Mère Eglise from among the paratroopers who landed near that tiny dairying town. And like the 101st, it panicked the enemy in most rear areas during those first critical hours of the assault.

Shortly after noon on D day, Collins established contact with Taylor's 101st Division on the southernmost end of his beachhead. But the fate of the 82d still lay obscured somewhere behind the miles of hedgerow that separated it from the beaches. . . .

The commander of the 4th Division had gone ashore earlier that afternoon while Collins remained with his VII Corps staff aboard the *Bayfield* to keep a line on communications—and to hold down Admiral Moon. Alarmed over the loss of a few vessels in the assault, Moon had been persuaded by his staff to suspend nighttime unloading on Utah Beach. When Collins learned of Moon's decision, he objected strenuously and the admiral was hastily dissuaded. "Let the navy expend its ships," I told Collins, "if that's what it takes. But we've got to get the build-up ashore even if it means paving the whole damned Channel bottom with ships—" . . .

Despite the confusion that still existed in many of the smaller isolated units, our situation had materially improved by the morning of June 7.

On the other hand, we were not yet out of danger. On the thin five-mile sliver of Omaha Beach, we had fallen far short of D-day objectives. German artillery still pounded the beaches were traffic had congealed in the wreckage. And we had not yet reached the Caen-Carentan road that was to have strung our Allied landings together. Nevertheless we took some comfort in the fact that five regiments had been put ashore on Omaha by dawn, a miraculous achievement in view of the disordered condition of the beach. But to get them ashore we had sacrificed bulk tonnage. Had it not been for the 90 preloaded DUKW's that waded ashore on D day, we might have been hard put for ammunition.

However, the enemy had paid dearly for our delay on Omaha Beach. His 352d Division had been mauled at the water's edge, depriving Rommel of one more field division. Meanwhile, during our first 12 perilous hours ashore, the enemy had failed to mount a single coordinated counterattack against our beachhead. The omens were better than our progress.

On Utah, Collins had fared better than Gerow. Although unable to extend his beach to the north and overrun his D-day objective, Collins had expanded to the south. There he anchored his landing tightly on the neck of the Cotentin where we were to force a junction between both beachheads. During the night he had linked up Ridgway's 82d Airborne Division.

It was still too early to evaluate the success of the airborne drop. The dispersal had so shaken our confidence in nighttime airborne operations that we never again attempted a nighttime drop. In the initial count casualties looked excessively high and some feared Leigh-Mallory might be vindicated in his prediction. But as "lost" units trickled in through our lines, we discovered that airborne losses for the drop and the first day aground did not exceed 20 per cent. Not until we had turned the Utah force north toward Cherbourg did we learn how effectively those airborne troops had paralyzed the enemy's rear.

On the morning of D plus 1 the enemy's high command in Berlin awaited word from Rommel that the Allied landing had been roped off and would soon be flung into the Channel. But with the passing of D day, the enemy had lost his best chance to destroy us. By the morning of D plus 1 we had not only gotten a tight grip on the beachhead, but Allied build-up was already beginning to swell.

I had long ago anticipated that the enemy would dash his Luftwaffe against our landing with every plane Goering could put into the sky. For it was while we were hanging precariously to a slender beachhead that we could have been most critically hurt by enemy air.

Throughout the daylight hours of June 6 only a few enemy *jabos* broke through our cordon of Allied fighter cover for ineffectual passes at the beach. And during the nighttime raid that had stranded us aboard the PT, a meager force was all that the Luftwaffe could muster against us. Not only had the Allied air forces whittled the German down to 400 first-line aircraft in the west on D day, but the concentrated attack on his French fighter bases had driven him back to the German border. To conserve his fast-waning strength, Goering had flinched at the very moment a bold blow might have saved him. . . .

Shortly after 6:00 A.M. on June 7 Montgomery came alongside the *Augusta* aboard a British destroyer. He was anxious that the Allied beaches be joined before Rommel could concentrate his forces against any single beach and there break through. While we perspired through the D-day crisis, the British dashed ashore in their sector and quickly pushed inland for a penetration of seven miles near Bayeux. Their primary objective at Caen, however, had eluded them. Sensitive to the British attack against that vital communications center, the enemy had attacked out of Caen in a panzer counteroffensive.

Eisenhower had signaled that he would arrive in the transport area at eleven. Meanwhile I had slipped ashore on Omaha to prod Gerow on Montgomery's order for an early link-up of the beaches. Gerow was to push Gerhardt's 29th to the right toward a juncture with Collins on the Cotentin neck while Huebner's 1st made contact with the British on their left.

V Corps had hidden its headquarters in a ditch behind the hedgerow on the exit road from Easy Red. I hitched a ride on a truck up a road still under construction. A column of infantrymen trudged up the hill, enveloped in dust from a line of trucks. On the flat top of the bluff engineers were already leveling an airstrip for the evacuation of wounded to England. . . .

As Admiral Ramsay's flagship maneuvered into position abreast of the *Augusta,* the coxswain swung our LCVP under the ship's Jacob's ladder. I jumped for it and climbed aboard. Ike greeted me at the rail.

"Golly, Brad," he exclaimed, grasping me by the hand, "you had us all scared stiff yesterday morning. Why in the devil didn't you let us know what was going on?"

"But we did." I was puzzled. "We radioed you every scrap of information we had. Everything that came in both from Gee and Collins."

Ike shook his head. "Nothing came through until late afternoon —not a damned word. I didn't know what had happened to you."

"But your headquarters acknowledged every message as we asked them to. You check it when you get back and you'll find they all got through."

Aboard the *Augusta* 20 minutes later I double-checked our journals. Not only had the messages been sent but each had been properly acknowledged. Later I heard that the decoding apparatus had broken down at Montgomery's CP. So heavy was the D-day radio traffic that code clerks fell 12 hours behind in deciphering the incoming reports.

However, Ike's vigil could not have been any more agonizing than the one we suffered aboard the *Augusta*. For the reports, if anything, were no less worrisome than the fears that are spun out of silence. A week later I confessed to Monty that I would never admit to Ike just how worried I was that morning we waited in the mist off Omaha Beach. . . .

Collins had established his VII Corps CP inside a walled Norman farmyard. He had gone forward leaving behind his deputy corps commander, Major General Eugene M. Landrum. We checked the situation map in a stall in the barn. The 4th Division was pushing north to clear the beach of fire while the 101st shoved south for its link-up with V Corps. Although Ridgway had collected his 82d east of the Merderet, units west of that river were still reported cut off.

"Heard anything from Matt today?"

Landrum showed me a typewritten situation report from the 82d Division.

"Matt must be in pretty good shape. At any rate he's got a typewriter in action."

Ridgway had organized a strong position north of Ste Mère Eglise. There, firmly astride the Carentan-Cherbourg road, he covered the left flank of the 4th Division. . . .

On Friday, June 9, army headquarters moved ashore from the *Achenar* to establish its first CP in an orchard behind Pointe du Hoe where the Rangers had tracked down the battery of French GPF's. With communications ashore there was no longer need for me to remain aboard the *Augusta,* and Saturday morning when I disembarked we closed down our floating CP. Kirk's bright young army aide, Lieutenant MacGeorge Bundy of Boston, Massachusetts, reverted to his earlier eminence as the ranking army officer aboard the admiral's flagship. He reminded me the day I came aboard that I had usurped his position.

Monty had called a meeting that morning at the fishing village of Port-en-Bessin to coordinate First Army movements with those of the British Second Army. Dempsey had plotted an attack south of the unspoiled town of Bayeux, partly to extend his beachhead and partly to envelop Caen from the west. I found Monty waiting with Dempsey in a field where British MP's had been posted as outguards. He wore a faded gabardine bush jacket, a gray turtleneck sweater, corduroy trousers, and a tanker's black beret. A map case had been spread on the flat hood of his Humber staff car. Two panzer divisions were dug in before Caen and Dempsey sought to outflank them in his attack from Bayeux. We were to parallel this British attack and drive south in the direction of Caumont. There Gerow was to establish a strong defensive outpost for V Corps. An attack on this end of the lodgment, we estimated, might also help divert enemy reinforcements from Collins's attack toward Cherbourg. . . .

By Saturday morning, June 10, Gerow had parlayed his original thin holdings on Omaha into a substantial beachhead. Not only had he linked forces with Dempsey but he had thrust beyond the lateral road that tied their landings together. On his right, the 29th Division had pushed through the burning streets of Isigny to reach the flatlands of the Carentan estuary. A few miles across the estuary, glider infantry maneuvered in a move to outflank Carentan from the northeast. Meanwhile paratroopers of the 101st advanced toward that pivotal city down the highway that led south from Cherbourg to Carentan. The road ran through a vast marshland, flooded by the enemy in an effort to restrict us to the narrow roads. . . .

Later that afternoon word reached army that Omaha and Utah had been joined together over a back country route across the estuary. The company of glider infantry from Utah had forced its way to the village of Auville-sur-le-Vey where reconnaissance troops of the 29th Division waited a few miles beyond Isigny. With Hansen I drove down through Isigny to see if we could get through on this overland route to Collins.

A small dairying town of 2,800 known for its Camembert cheese, Isigny lay charred from its shelling the day before when the 29th called for naval gunfire to drive the enemy out of town. A few villagers searched sorrowfully through the ruins of their homes. From one, an aged man and his wife carried the twisted skeleton of a brass bed. And down the street, a woman carefully removed the curtain from a paneless window in the remaining wall of what had been the village café. For more than four years the people of Isigny had awaited this moment of liberation. Now they stared accusingly on us from the ruins that covered their dead.

Beyond the Vire we pulled up short of Auville-sur-le-Vey. In the intersection ahead an armored car had engaged a sniper with its 37-mm. gun. The ping of his rifle was lost in the crash of the car's cannon.

A jeep pulled up with Brigadier General Edward J. Timberlake, Jr., commander of an AA brigade.

"You're crazy as hell to go through, sir," he said. "The road may be mined. Let me go on in front."

"Nope—but thanks anyhow," I said. "I'm not going to go through."

As my driver wheeled the jeep around I turned back to Hansen.

"Be kinda silly to get killed by a sniper while out sight-seeing," I said. "We'd better stick to the PT boat until Carentan is opened."

By dawn on June 12, Taylor's paratroopers had encircled Carentan in a brilliant pincer movement. At 6:00 A.M. that day they drove into the city's streets to open the main road between Omaha and Utah. On our seventh day ashore we had linked the Allied forces together in a beachhead 42 miles wide.

We would now force our way across the Cotentin, then choke it off and capture the port of Cherbourg.

The Longest Day
June 6, 1944
by
Cornelius Ryan

General Erich Marcks stood at a long table studying the war maps spread out before him. He was surrounded by his staff. They had been with him ever since his birthday party, briefing the 84th Corps commander for the war games in Rennes. Every now and then the general called for another map. It seemed to his intelligence officer, Major Friedrich Hayn, that Marcks was preparing for the *Kriegsspiel* as though it was a real battle, instead of merely a theoretical invasion of Normandy.

In the midst of their discussion, the phone rang. The conversation ceased as Marcks picked up the receiver. Hayn recalls that "as he listened, the General's body seemed to stiffen." Marcks motioned to his chief of staff to pick up the extension phone. The man who was calling was Major General Wilhelm Richter, commander of the 716th Division, holding the coast above Caen. "Parachutists have landed east of the Orne," Richter told Marcks. "The area seems to be around Bréville and Ranville . . . along the northern fringe of Bavent Forest. . . ."

This was the first official report of the Allied attack to reach a major German headquarters. "It struck us," Hayn says, "like lightning." The time was 2:11 A.M. (British Double Summer Time).

Marcks immediately telephoned Major General Max Pemsel, chief of staff of the Seventh Army. At 2:15 A.M. Pemsel placed the Seventh on *Alarmstruffe II*, the highest state of readiness. It was four hours since the second Verlaine message had been intercepted. Now at last the Seventh Army, in whose area the invasion had already begun, had been alerted.

Pemsel was taking no chances. He wakened the Seventh's commanding officer, Colonel General Friedrich Dollmann. "General," said Pemsel, "I believe this is the invasion. Will you please come over immediately?"

As he put down the phone, Pemsel suddenly remembered something. Among a sheaf of intelligence bulletins that had come in during the afternoon, one had been from an agent in Casablanca. He had specifically stated that the invasion would take place in Normandy on June 6.

As Pemsel waited for Dollmann to arrive, the 84th Corps reported again: ". . . Parachute drops near Montebourg and St.-Marcouf [on the Cherbourg peninsula]. . . . Troops partly already engaged in battle."[1] Pemsel promptly called Rommel's chief of staff, Major General Dr. Hans Speidel at Army Group B. It was 2:35 A.M.

At about the same time, General Hans von Salmuth, from his Fifteenth Army headquarters near the Belgian border, was trying to get some first hand information. Although the bulk of his army was far removed from the airborne attacks, one division, Major General Josef Reichert's 711th, held positions east of the Orne River on the boundary line between the Seventh and Fifteenth armies. Several messages had come in from the 711th. One reported that paratroopers actually were landing near the headquarters at Cabourg; a second announced that fighting was going on all around the command post.

Von Salmuth decided to find out for himself. He rang Reichert. "What the devil is going on down there?" Von Salmuth demanded.

---

[1]There has been considerable controversy over the timing of the German reaction to the invasion and over the messages that were passed from one headquarters to another. When I began my research, Colonel General Franz Halder, the former chief of the German General Staff (now attached to the U.S. Army's historical section in Germany) told me to "believe nothing on our side unless it tallies with the official war diaries of each headquarters." I have followed his advice. All times (corrected to British Double Summer Time), reports and telephone calls as they pertain to German activities come from these sources.

"My General," came Reichert's harassed voice on the other end of the wire, "if you'll permit me, I'll let you hear for yourself." There was a pause, and then Von Salmuth could clearly hear the clatter of machine gun fire.

"Thank you," said Von Salmuth, and he hung up. Immediately he too called Army Group B, reporting that at the 711th's headquarters "the din of battle can be heard."

Pemsel's and Von Salmuth's calls, arriving almost simultaneously, gave Rommel's headquarters the first news of the Allied attack. Was it the long-expected invasion? Nobody at Army Group B at this time was prepared to say. In fact, Rommel's naval aide, Vice-Admiral Friedrich Ruge, distinctly remembers that as more reports came in of airborne troops "some said they were only dolls disguised as paratroopers."

Whoever made the observation was partly right. To add to the German confusion, the Allies had dropped hundreds of lifelike rubber dummies, dressed as paratroopers, south of the Normandy invasion area. Attached to each were strings of firecrackers which exploded on landing, giving the impression of a small-arms fight. For more than three hours a few of these dummies were to deceive General Marcks into believing that paratroopers had landed at Lessay some twenty-five miles southwest of his headquarters.

These were strange, confusing minutes for Von Rundstedt's staff at OB West in Paris and for Rommel's officers at La Roche-Guyon. Reports came piling in from everywhere—reports that were often inaccurate, sometimes incomprehensible and always contradictory.

Luftwaffe headquarters in Paris announced that "fifty to sixty two-engined planes are coming in" over the Cherbourg peninsula, and that paratroopers had landed "near Caen." Admiral Theodor Krancke's headquarters—*Marinegruppenkommando West*—confirmed the British paratroop landings, nervously pointed out that the enemy had fallen close to one of their coastal batteries, and then added that "part of the parachute drop consists of straw dummies." Neither report mentioned the Americans on the Cherbourg peninsula—yet at this time one of the naval batteries at St.-Marcouf, just above Utah Beach, had informed Cherbourg headquarters that a dozen Americans had been captured. Within minutes of their first message, the Luftwaffe phoned in another bulletin. Parachutists, they said, were down near Bayeux. Actually none had landed there at all.

At both headquarters men tried desperately to evaluate the rash of red spots sprouting over their maps. Officers at Army Group B rang their opposite numbers at OB West, hashed the situation over and came up with conclusions many of which, in the light of what was actually happening, seem incredible. When OB West's acting intelligence officer, Major Doertenbach, called Army Group B for a report, for example, he was told that "the Chief of Staff views the situation with equanimity" and that "there is a possibility that parachutists who have been reported are merely bailed-out bomber crews."

The Seventh Army didn't think so. By 3:00 A.M. Pemsel was convinced that the *Schwerpunkt*—the main thrust—was driving into Normandy. His maps showed paratroopers at each end of the Seventh's area—on the Cherbourg peninsula and east of the Orne. Now, too, there were alarming reports from naval stations at Cherbourg. Using sound direction apparatus and some radar equipment, the stations were picking up ships maneuvering in the Bay of the Seine.

There was no doubt now in Pemsel's mind—the invasion was on. He called Speidel. "The air landings," Pemsel said, "constitute the first phase of a larger enemy action." Then he added, "Engine noises are audible from out at sea." But Pemsel could not convince Rommel's chief of staff. Speidel's answer, as recorded in the Seventh Army telephone log, was that "the affair is still locally confined." The estimate that he gave Pemsel at this time was summarized in the war diary and reads: "Chief of Staff Army. Group B believes that for the time being this is not to be considered as a large operation."

Even as Pemsel and Speidel talked, the last paratroopers of the 18,000-man airborne assault were floating down over the Cherbourg peninsula. Sixty-nine gliders, carrying men, guns and heavy equipment, were just crossing the coast of France, headed for the British landing areas near Ranville. And twelve miles off Normandy's five invasion beaches, the *Ancon,* headquarters ship of Task Force O, under the command of Rear Admiral John L. Hall, dropped anchor. Lining up behind her were the transports carrying the men who would land in the first wave on Omaha Beach.

But at La Roche-Guyon there was still nothing to indicate the immensity of the Allied attack, and in Paris OB West endorsed Speidel's first estimate of the situation. Rundstedt's able operations chief, Lieutenant General Bodo Zimmermann, informed of Speidel's conversation with Pemsel, sent back a message agreeing with Speidel: "Operations OB West holds that this is not a large-scale airborne operation; all the more because Admiral Channel Coast (Krancke's headquarters) has reported that the enemy has dropped straw dummies."

These officers can hardly be blamed for being so utterly confused. They were miles away from the actual fighting, entirely dependent on the reports coming in. These were so spotty and so misleading that even the most experienced officers found it impossible to gauge the magnitude of the airborne assault—or, for that matter, to see an overall pattern emerging from the Allied attacks. If this was the invasion, was it aimed at Normandy? Only the Seventh Army seemed to think so. Perhaps the paratroop attacks were simply a diversion intended to draw attention from the real invasion—against General Hans von Salmuth's massive Fifteenth Army in the Pas-de-Calais, where nearly everybody thought the Allies would strike. The Fifteenth's chief of staff, Major General Rudolf Hofmann, was so sure the main attack would come in the Fifteenth's area that he called Pemsel and bet him a dinner that he was right. "This is one bet you're going to lose," said Pemsel. Yet at this time neither Army Group B nor OB West had sufficient evidence to draw any conclusions. They alerted the invasion coast and ordered measures taken against the paratroop attacks. Then everybody waited for more information. There was little else they could do.

By now, messages were flooding into command posts all over Normandy. One of the first problems for some of the divisions was to find their own commanders—the generals who had already left for the *Kriegsspiel* in Rennes. Although most of them were located quickly, two—Lieutenant General Karl von Schlieben and Major General Wilhelm Falley, both commanding divisions in the Cherbourg peninsula—couldn't be found. Von Schlieben was asleep in his hotel in Rennes and Falley was still en route there by car.

Admiral Krancke, the naval commander in the west, was on an

inspection trip to Bordeaux. His chief of staff awakened him in his hotel room. "Paratroop landings are taking place near Caen," Krancke was informed. "OB West insists that this is only a diversionary attack and not the real invasion, but we're picking up ships. We think it's the real thing." Krancke immediately alerted the few naval forces he had and then quickly set out for his headquarters in Paris.

One of the men who got his orders at Le Havre was already a legend in the German Navy. Lieutenant Commander Heinrich Hoffmann had made his name as an E-boat commander. Almost from the beginning of the war, his speedy, powerful flotillas of torpedo craft had ranged up and down the English Channel, attacking shipping wherever they found it. Hoffmann also had been in action during the Dieppe raid and had boldly escorted the German battleships *Scharnhorst, Gneisenau* and *Prinz Eugen* in their dramatic dash from Brest to Norway in 1942.

When the message from headquarters came in, Hoffmann was in the cabin of T-28, the lead E-boat of his 5th Flotilla, preparing to go out on a mine-laying operation. Immediately he called together the commanders of the other boats. They were all young men and although Hoffmann told them that "this must be the invasion," it did not surprise them. They had expected it. Only three of his six boats were ready, but Hoffmann could not wait for the others to be loaded with torpedoes. A few minutes later the three small boats left Le Havre. On the bridge of T-28, his white sailor's cap pushed back on his head as usual, the thirty-four-year-old Hoffmann peered out into the darkness. Behind him, the two little boats bounced along in Indian file, following the lead boat's every maneuver. They raced through the night at more than twenty-three knots—blindly heading straight toward the mightiest fleet ever assembled.

At least they were in action. Probably the most baffled men in Normandy this night were the 16,242 seasoned troops of the tough 21st Panzer Division, once a part of Rommel's famed *Afrika Korps.* Clogging every small village, hamlet and wood in the area just twenty-five miles southeast of Caen, these men were sitting almost on the edge of the battlefield, the only panzer division within immediate striking distance of the British airborne assault and the only veteran troops in that area.

Ever since the alert, officers and men had been standing alongside their tanks and vehicles, engines running, waiting for the order to move out. Colonel Hermann von Oppeln-Bronikowski, in command of the division's regiment of tanks, couldn't understand the delay. He had been awakened shortly after 2:00 A.M. by the 21st's commander, Lieutenant General Edgar Feuchtinger. "Oppeln," Feuchtinger had said breathlessly, "imagine! *They* have landed." He had briefed Bronikowski on the situation and told him that as soon as the division got its orders it would "clean out the area between Caen and the coast immediately." But no further word had come. With growing anger and impatience, Bronikowski continued to wait.

Miles away, the most puzzling reports of all were being received by the Luftwaffe's Lieutenant Colonel Priller. He and his wing man, Sergeant Wodarczyk, had stumbled into their beds about 1:00 A.M. at the 26th Fighter Wing's now deserted airfield near Lille. They had succeeded in drowning their anger at the Luftwaffe High Command with several bottles of excellent cognac. Now, in his drunken sleep, Priller heard the phone ring as though from a long way off. He came to slowly, his left hand groping over the bedside table for the phone.

Second Fighter Corps headquarters was on the wire. "Priller," said the operations officer, "it seems that some sort of an invasion is taking place. I suggest you put your wing on the alert."

Sleepy as he was, Pips Priller's temper promptly boiled over again. The 124 planes of his command had been moved away from the Lille area the previous afternoon and now the very thing he had feared was happening. Priller's language, as he remembers the conversation, is unprintable, but after telling his caller what was wrong with corps headquarters and the entire Luftwaffe High Command, the fighter ace roared, "Who in hell am I supposed to alert? *I'm* alert. Wodarczyk is alert! But you fatheads *know* I have only two damned planes!" With that he slammed down the receiver.

A few minutes later the phone rang again. "Now what?" yelled Priller. It was the same officer. "My dear Priller," he said, "I'm awfully sorry. It was all a mistake. We somehow got a wrong report. Everything is fine—there's no invasion." Priller was so furious he couldn't answer. Worse, he couldn't get back to sleep.

Despite the confusion, hesitancy and indecision in the higher levels of command, the German soldiers in actual contact with the enemy were reacting swiftly. Thousands of troops were already on the move and, unlike the generals at Army Group B and OB West, these soldiers had no doubts that the invasion was upon them. Many of them had been fighting it off in isolated, face-to-face skirmishes ever since the first British and Americans had dropped out of the sky. Thousands of other alerted troops waited behind their formidable coastal defenses, ready to repel an invasion no matter where it might come. They were apprehensive, but they were also determined.

At Seventh Army headquarters, the one top commander who was not confused called his staff together. In the brightly lighted map room, General Pemsel stood before his officers. His voice was as calm and quiet as usual. Only his words betrayed the deep concern he felt. "Gentlemen," he told them, "I am convinced the invasion will be upon us by dawn. Our future will depend on how we fight this day. I request of you all the effort and pain that you can give."

In Germany, five hundred miles away, the man who might have agreed with Pemsel—the one officer who had won many a battle by his uncanny ability to see clearly through the most confusing situations—was asleep. At Army Group B the situation was not considered serious enough yet to call Field Marshal Erwin Rommel.

CHAPTER XIII

THE INCHON LANDING, 1950

General of the Army Douglas MacArthur (1880–1964), born in Arkansas, the son of Lieutenant-General Arthur MacArthur, graduated from the United States Military Academy in 1903. Emerging from World War I as a brigadier general, he served as superintendent of the U.S. Military Academy in 1919, became the commanding officer in the Philippine Army, and the field marshal of the Philippine Army in 1936. In 1941 he returned to duty in the American Army to become commander-in-chief of all the forces in the Southwest Pacific. After Japan's surrender in 1945 he was the supreme commander of the Allied Powers (SCAP) in Japan. When the Korean War broke out in 1950, MacArthur became the commander-in-chief of the U.N. forces in Korea, until President Truman removed him late in 1951.

The author of the following selection, Major General Courtney Whitney (1897–1969), was born in Maryland and entered World War I as a private. He rose to become a 2nd lieutenant, studied law and practiced in Manila for 13 years. Commissioned a major in 1940, he worked as the chief of the legal division of the Army Air Forces. He joined General of the Army Douglas MacArthur in 1946 in Japan as chief of the Government Section, helped to rewrite the old Japanese constitution and to purge Japanese considered unfit to hold public office. Major General Whitney resigned in 1951, when MacArthur was removed by President Truman. Major-General Whitney is the author of the book *MacArthur: His Rendezvous With Destiny.*

Inchon—the Great Debate; the Great Victory,

September 15, 1950

by

Major General Courtney Whitney

> Some operations if carried out to their logical end may change the entire aspect of war. . . . The entire movable army strikes at the enemy in the heart of his own country. Such resolutions by great generals are stamped with the mark of true genius.
>
> *Dennis Hart Mahan*

> A swift and vigorous transition to attack—the flashing sword of vengeance—is the most brilliant point of the defensive.
>
> *Von Clausewitz*

MacArthur had just taught the North Koreans the same lesson he had taught the Japanese on Bataan. And, had the Communists known it, they could have forearmed themselves by studying the lesson that MacArthur had taught the Japanese at Hollandia. In that first week of the Korean War, as MacArthur had stood on the hill overlooking Seoul and watched the backwash of defeat stream by him, he had planned not only the series of delaying-actions which had slowed the North Korean advance (as on Bataan) but also a strategic maneuver that would wrest the initiative away from the enemy (as at Hollandia).

Once again he had been handed a military situation that verged on disaster. Once again, with only a handful of troops and virtually no heavy arms, he faced hordes of the enemy who were not only formidably armed but were already on the verge of complete victory. Once again he was committed to a campaign in which it seemed that his only chance lay in massive defense. And once again he determined to defend by attack.

His plan, as he conceived it on that hill and developed the myriad details later at Tokyo headquarters, was for an envelopment that would at one stroke cut behind the enemy's rear, sever his supply lines, and encircle all his forces south of Seoul.

The target MacArthur selected for this landing was Inchon, twenty miles west of Seoul and the second-largest port in South Korea. The target date, because of the great tides at Inchon, had to be the middle of September. This meant that the staging for Inchon would have to be accomplished more rapidly than that of any other large amphibious operation in history. To add to its complexities, MacArthur knew beforehand that he would have considerable difficulty persuading Washington to undertake so daring a counterstroke. The best warning he had that the Joint Chiefs of Staff might disapprove of his plan was contained in a statement made by General Omar Bradley to a Congressional committee on October 19, 1949, in which the JCS chairman had given his opinion that amphibious warfare was outdated and said that he could not foresee its use at any time in the future. Accordingly, MacArthur had to move with great caution in order that the Inchon landing should not be vetoed right at the start and U.N. forces thereby tied down in a hopeless defense or committed to the blood bath of a frontal counteroffensive.

But no such envelopment as he envisaged could be brought off without reinforcements. In Japan MacArthur had organized a "Police Reserve" designed to bring a hundred thousand Japanese under arms to control internal Communist pressures and secure the country against sudden seizure by the Soviets. Thus the U.S. 7th Infantry Division could be assembled as a nucleus for the amphibious force. By means of the U.S.-ROK "buddy system" that MacArthur had developed, the 7th Division was nearly back to the full strength it had had before Washington directives had stripped it nearly bare.

The 7th Division, however, could not do it alone. What was desperately needed was a marine force especially trained and equipped for amphibious operations. In mid-July, when Lieutenant General Lemuel C. Shepherd, then marine chief in the Pacific, visited MacArthur's headquarters, he agreed not only that there were marines available for this landing but that an entire division could be delivered in Korea within six weeks. Therefore, on July 10 MacArthur asked the Joint Chiefs of Staff for the 1st Marine Division. Profiting by his experience with Washington's penchant for skeletonizing his forces, he carefully stipulated a division at full strength. He was turned down flat. He patiently tried again five days later, saying: "I cannot emphasize too strongly my belief in the complete urgency of my request." He was turned down again.

Meanwhile Lieutenant General Walton Walker and his forces in South Korea were fighting with their backs to the sea in what amounted to little more than an extended beachhead around Pusan. Only a miracle—or a brilliant counterstroke such as MacArthur planned—could keep that beachhead from slowly constricting upon Walker and his men. MacArthur had to take the chance of having his plan killed by the preconceived notions of General Bradley on the subject of amphibious warfare. It was now or never.

On July 23 he cabled Washington: "Operation planned mid-September is amphibious landing of a two-division corps in rear of enemy lines for purpose of enveloping and destroying enemy forces in conjunction with attack from south by Eighth Army. I am firmly convinced that early and strong effort behind his front will sever his main lines of communication and enable us to deliver a decisive and crushing blow. . . ." He added the urgent warning: "The alternative is a frontal attack which can only result in a protracted and expensive campaign."

His plea was met with stony silence from the Joint Chiefs of Staff. Not for three weeks did the strategists in the Pentagon deign to discuss this subject with him. . . .

On July 27 the *Bataan* was wheeled out onto the Haneda runway, and MacArthur roared off for another inspection trip. Landing at Taegu, he went directly to Walker's headquarters, where he received a formal briefing.

The military term for orderly retreat is "a retrograde movement." MacArthur found that Walker's staff had planned a whole series of retrograde movements, with details so complete as to establish dates on which successive phaselines in the rear would be reached. I remember watching MacArthur's face as these plans were outlined to him. Minute by minute his expression changed from attentiveness to surprise to amazement and then to consternation. Finally he spoke up, with a decided sharpness in his voice and a withering glance at the briefing officer. "These plans," he ordered, "will be scrapped at once." Future planning would emphasize advances rather than retreats. I cannot recall ever seeing him look as stern as he did when he summed up with: "The present line must be held at all costs."

Within forty-eight hours Walker had issued his now famous rallying-cry to his troops. "There must be no further yielding under pressure of the enemy," his order read. "From now on let every man stand or die." By such things can the tide of battle be reversed. The U.N. line of defense formed an arc that covered an almost unbelievable area. And so slim were Walker's resources that many times he could meet an infiltration or a direct assault only by pulling troops from another area and temporarily leaving that position completely exposed. But the line held.

Operating with thirteen divisions and with complete freedom of action to mass at any selected point for a local penetration, the North Koreans closed in for what they thought was the kill. They had reason to believe so at Chinju, in particular, when a two-pronged attack sliced through the thin line of defenders and drove to within twelve miles of this keystone of the beachhead's left flank. But then, in a suprise counterattack, Walker's forces stopped them in their tracks. These units had decided that they would neither "stand or die"—they would advance. Their counterattack was highly successful. By August 11 the Communists had been driven back fifteen miles. For the time being, at least, the threat to the ports of Masan and Pusan was removed. MacArthur watched this and other such local operations with increasing admiration for Walker's generalship—and with obvious satisfaction; he had just such an operation in mind for "Johnnie" Walker, as he called him, when it came time for Inchon.

By mid-August the defense perimeter in Korea had stabilized, and so, apparently, had public opinion in the United States. Our forces had not, as had so widely been predicted, been driven into the sea. But, while MacArthur's pleas for reinforcements were receiving a little more attention in Washington, he still had not been informed of any definite decision on Inchon. Then, finally, the Joint Chiefs of Staff wired him that General J. Lawton Collins, army chief of staff, and Admiral Forrest Sherman, chief of Naval Operations, were coming to Tokyo to discuss this maneuver with him. It was evident immediately upon their arrival that the actual purpose of their trip was not so much to discuss it with him as to dissuade him from it.

Thus, at a little after 5:30 P.M. on August 23, in the Dai Ichi Building, there occurred one of the most important strategy debates in American military history. It was also the most important strategy debate in the Korean war. The conferees included MacArthur, General Collins, and Admiral Sherman, as well as Marine Chief Shepherd; MacArthur's air commander, Stratemeyer; his chief of staff, Almond, already designated commander of the X Corps in the Inchon landing; Admiral Arthur D. Struble; Admiral C. E. Turner Joy; and a gathering of other staff officers and aides making up a veritable constellation of silver stars.

The conference room adjoined MacArthur's office, and its map-studded walls gave the blown-up geographic details essential to military planning. MacArthur sat at the head of the conference table, leisurely smoking his corncob pipe but missing nothing. Occasionally he jerked the pipe from his mouth and gestured with it as he interjected a question or a comment.

As at the Pearl Harbor conference with Roosevelt and Nimitz in 1944, the navy presented its case first. A naval briefing staff argued that two elements—tide and terrain—made a landing at Inchon extremely hazardous. They referred to navy hydrographic studies which listed the average rise and fall of the tides at Inchon at 20.7 feet—one of the greatest in the world. On the tentative target date for the invasion, the rise and fall would be more than thirty feet because of the position of the moon. When Inchon's tides were at full ebb, the mud banks that had accumulated over the centuries from the Yellow Sea were out of water in some places as far as two miles out into the harbor from the shore. And during ebb and flood these tides raced through "Flying Fish Channel," the best approach to the port, at speeds up to six knots. Even under the most favorable conditions "Flying Fish Channel" was narrow and winding. Not only did it make a perfect location for enemy mines but any ship sunk at a particularly vulnerable point could block the channel to all other ships.

On the target date, the navy experts went on, the first high tide would occur at 6:59 in the morning, and the afternoon high tide would be at 7:19, a full thirty-five minutes after sunset. Within two hours after high tide most of the assault craft would be wallowing in the ooze of Inchon's mud banks, sitting ducks for Communist shore batteries until the next tide came in to float them again. In effect the amphibious forces would have only about two hours in the morning for the complex job of reducing or effectively neutralizing Wolmi-do, the 350-foot-high heavily fortified island which commands the harbor and which is connected with the mainland by a long causeway.

Assuming that this could be done, the afternoon's high tide and approaching darkness would allow only two and a half hours for the troops to land, secure a beachhead for the night, and bring up all the supplies essential to enable forces to withstand enemy counterattacks until morning. The landing craft, after putting the first assault waves ashore, would lie helplessly on the mud banks until the morning tide.

Beyond all this, the navy summed up, the assault landings would have to be made right in the heart of the city itself, where every structure provided a potential strong point of enemy resistance. This was a most unfavorable situation for securing a beachhead, especially with the limited-time factors involved. Reviewing the navy's presentation, Admiral Sherman concluded by saying: "If every possible geographical and naval handicap were listed— Inchon has 'em all."

MacArthur continued to puff on his pipe, saying nothing, as Collins presented his arguments. The army, its chief of staff said, felt that Inchon was too far in the rear of the present battle area to have the necessary immediate effect on the enemy. To accomplish this big maneuver successfully with the limited resources available would require withdrawing the 1st Marine Brigade, which was then holding a sector in Walker's hard-pressed defense line, and would thus further ndanger his position. Collins was not at all sure—in fact, did not believe—that even if MacArthur captured Seoul he could make contact with Walker to the south. And furthermore, the army chief of staff said, MacArthur might well run into overwhelming enemy force in the area of the capital city and suffer complete defeat.

Collins had an alternate proposal: to abandon the plan of the Inchon landing and instead aim for the west-coast port of Kunsan. This port was much farther south and presented few of Inchon's physical obstacles. At this point Sherman spoke up and seconded Collins in urging MacArthur to give up Inchon in favor of the safer plan of landing at Kunsan. . . .

MacArthur started to talk in a casual, conversational tone. The bulk of the Eeds, he said, were committed around Walker's defense perimeter. The enemy, he was convinced, had failed to prepare Inchon properly for defense. "The very arguments you have made as to the impracticabilities involved will tend to ensure for me the element of surprise," he said. "For the enemy commander will reason that no one would be so brash as to make such an attempt." His low, resonant voice rose imperceptibly to a convincing intensity as he added: "Surprise is the most vital element for success in modern war."

Then suddenly he was talking about a campaign that took place almost two centuries ago. The Marquis de Montcalm believed in 1759 that it was impossible for any armed force to scale the precipitous riverbanks south of the then walled city of Quebec, and therefore concentrated his formidable defenses along the more vulnerable banks north of the city. But General James Wolfe and a small force did indeed come up the St. Lawrence River and scale those heights. On the Plains of Abraham, Wolfe won a stunning victory that was made possible almost entirely by surprise. Thus he captured Quebec and in effect ended the French and Indian War. Like Montcalm, the North Koreans would regard an Inchon landing as impossible. Like Wolfe, MacArthur could take them by surprise.

The navy's objections as to tides, hydrography, terrain, and physical handicaps, MacArthur agreed, were indeed substantial and pertinent. But they were not insuperable. MacArthur smiled at his old friend Forrest Sherman as he added that his confidence in the navy was complete, and that in fact he seemed to have more confidence in the navy than the navy had in itself. . . .

Then he took up the proposal for a landing at Kunsan. It would indeed eliminate many of the hazards of Inchon, but it would be largely ineffective and indecisive. "It would be an attempted envelopment," he argued, "which would not envelop. It would not sever or destroy the enemy's supply lines or distribution center, and would therefore serve little purpose. It would be a 'short envelopment,' and nothing in war is more futile. Better no flank movement than such a one. The only result would be a hook-up with Walker's troops on his left. Better send the troops direct to Walker than by such an indirect and costly process."

In other words, this would simply be sending more troops to help Walker "hang on"; and hanging on was not good enough. MacArthur's voice rose again in emphasis as he predicted that no decision could be reached by such defensive action in Walker's perimeter. To fight frontally in a breakthrough from Pusan would be bloody and indecisive. The enemy would merely roll back on his lines of supply and communication.

But, he said, stabbing the air with his pipe, seizure of Inchon and Seoul would cut the enemy's supply line and seal off the entire southern peninsula. The vulnerability of the enemy was his supply position. Every step southward extended his transport lines and rendered them more frail and subject to dislocation. And the several major lines of enemy supply from the north converged on Seoul; from Seoul they radiated to the several sectors of the front. By seizing Seoul he would completely paralyze the enemy supply system—coming and going. This in turn would paralyze the fighting power of the troops that now faced Walker. Without munitions and food they would soon be helpless and disorganized, and could easily be overpowered by our smaller but well-supplied forces.

His voice was low and dramatically resonant as he said: "The only alternative to a stroke such as I propose would be the continuation of the savage sacrifice we are making at Pusan, with no hope of relief in sight. Are you content to let our troops stay in that bloody perimeter like beef cattle in the slaughter house? Who would take the responsibility for such a tragedy? Certainly I will not."

Abruptly he switched to a global level. "The prestige of the Western World hangs in the balance," he said. "Oriental millions are watching the outcome. It is plainly apparent that here in Asia is where the Communist conspirators have elected to make their play for global conquest. The test is not in Berlin or Vienna, in London, Paris or Washington. It is here and now—it is along the Naktong River in South Korea. We have joined the issue on the battlefield. Actually, we here fight Europe's war with arms, while there it is still confined to words. If we lose the war to Communism in Asia, the fate of Europe will be gravely jeopardized. Win it and Europe will probably be saved from war and stay free. Make the wrong decision here—the fatal decision of inertia—and we will be done. I can almost hear the ticking of the second hand of destiny. We must act now or we will die."

He paused for a moment or two and then said: "If my estimate is inaccurate and should I run into a defense with which I cannot cope, I will be there personally and will immediately withdraw our forces before they are committed to a bloody setback. The only loss then," he said with a sardonic smile, "will be my professional reputation."

But Inchon would *not* fail, he reiterated. Inchon would succeed. MacArthur's voice was a strident whisper as he concluded: "—And it will save 100,000 lives."

He had finished. The silence was so complete that across the conference room Admiral Sherman could be heard murmuring in undisguised admiration: "A great voice in a great cause."

MacArthur had talked for more than an hour without letup. Nothing more was said, and the spell was broken as the chairs were pushed back and we all rose to leave the room. Neither Collins nor Sherman made a definite commitment at the time, but on August 29, after their return to Washington, MacArthur received a wire from the Joint Chiefs of Staff: "We concur after reviewing the information brought back by General Collins and Admiral Sherman, in making preparations and executing a turn-

ing movement by amphibious forces on the west coast of Korea
—at Inchon. . . ."

Had MacArthur waited until August 29 to get his preparations
under way, he would have missed the September 15 deadline set
by Inchon's tides. But he had not waited. The 7th Division was
rapidly being assembled, as were the elements of the 1st Marine
Division. Incidentally, MacArthur utilized the Kunsan suggestion
in characteristic fashion: a part of the preliminaries to the actual
assault on Inchon would be a feint at Kunsan, to throw the enemy
off guard.

MacArthur also made a special trip to Korea to discuss his plan
with Walker, who was naturally disturbed at the prospect of losing
the 1st Provisional Marine Brigade from his already thin line.
Walker wished that MacArthur would use the fresh troops to
reinforce his perimeter instead of conducting the Inchon landing.
But he had unlimited faith in MacArthur's strategic judgment,
and as soon as he was convinced that MacArthur was invincibly
determined upon the plan, he cooperated wholeheartedly.

In return, MacArthur reassured him to the extent of providing
a regimental combat team from the 7th Division, to be in floating
reserve off Pusan during the withdrawal of the marine brigade.
This combat team would literally be a floating reserve, waiting in
ships off Pusan. It could rush into the gap of Walker's line, but
only on MacArthur's express orders, if the need arose after the
marine brigade had pulled out. Otherwise it would steam for
Inchon and become the last element to land there. . . .

As delicate an operation was the withdrawal of the 1st Marine
Brigade from the front lines. If it became known to the Communists, they might guess that a new operation was pending, and the
Inchon movement would be imperiled. To help fool the enemy,
the brigade was placed in general reserve for a time before it
embarked from Pusan. But no operation of the size of Inchon
could be performed without taking the chance of disclosure. In
this connection it is to the credit of the many news correspondents
at the front who could not fail to witness these troop dispositions
and surmise the reason for them—as well as to the credit of their
editors back home—that the projected counterattack was a secret
well kept by many persons.

By a week before the target date, all the details of the master plan had been worked out. The troops that had come from Japan, the United States, and even the Mediterranean had virtually all arrived. Each unit had been assigned its separate responsibility, and those marines and soldiers who were not already afloat along Korea's west coast were in the final stages of embarkation. It was at this eleventh hour that MacArthur received a message from the Joint Chiefs of Staff which chilled him to the marrow of his bones.

The message read: "We have noted with considerable concern the recent trend of events in Korea. In the light of the commitment of all the reserves available to the Eighth Army, we desire your estimate as to the feasibility and chance of success of projected operation if initiated on planned schedule. . . ." MacArthur read and reread the message with growing concern. What could have given rise to such a query at such an hour? Had someone in authority in Washington lost his nerve? Could it be the president? Marshall or Bradley? Or was it merely an anticipatory alibi if the operation should run into trouble? Whatever lay behind this mysterious, last-minute hesitancy, it clearly suggested the possibility that even after the millions of man-hours expended on this operation, MacArthur might be ordered to abandon it. He immediately penciled a reply.

"I regard the chance of success of the operation as excellent," he wrote. "I go further in belief that it represents the only hope of wresting the initiative from the enemy and thereby presenting the opportunity for a decisive blow. To do otherwise is to commit us to a war of indefinite duration, of gradual attrition and of doubtful result, as the enemy has potentialities of build-up and reinforcements which exceed those of our own. Our stroke as planned would prevent any material reinforcements in build-up of the enemy in the present combat zone. The situation within the perimeter is not critical. It is possible that there may be some contraction, and defense positions have been selected for this contingency. There is no slightest possibility, however, of our forces being ejected from the Pusan beachhead.

"The envelopment from the north will instantly relieve the pressure upon the south perimeter and, indeed, is the only way that this can be accomplished. The success of the enveloping movement from the north does not depend upon the rapid juncture of the X Corps with the Eighth Army. The seizure of the heart of the enemy's distributing system in the Seoul area will completely dislocate the logistical supply of his forces now operating in South Korea and therefore will ultimately result in their disintegration. . . . The prompt junction of our two forces, while it would be dramatically symbolic of the complete collapse of the enemy, is not a vital part of the operation. . . ."

MacArthur concluded with his clinching argument: "The embarkation of the troops and the preliminary air and naval preparations are proceeding according to schedule. I repeat that I and all of my commanders and staff officers, without exception, are enthusiastic for and confident of the success of the enveloping movement."

After dispatching his reply, he waited with growing impatience and concern. Was it possible, he asked himself, that even now, when it was all but impossible to bring this great movement grinding to a halt, he would be forbidden the opportunity for turning defeat into victory simply because of timidity in some office thousands of miles away? With the target time approaching hour by hour, it seemed to MacArthur that he waited an eternity for the answer from Washington.

Finally a short, cryptic message arrived from the Joint Chiefs of Staff, announcing that in view of his reply they had "approved" the operation and "so informed the President." Did this mean that the president had had a change of heart on Inchon eve? MacArthur did not have time to ponder this one. The threat of a last-minute reversal was removed, and he had only just time to implement the final details of his plan. In fact, he would have to hurry to get to Inchon in time himself.

Inchon—the Great Victory: Operation Chromite

On the afternoon of September 12, 1950, a typhoon was brewing in the Sea of Japan. But despite the backlash of it which was sweeping along the coast, MacArthur took off from Haneda Airport in his new plane, the *SCAP*. He could not wait even for typhoons if he was to meet his new rendezvous with history at Inchon.

Only six of us accompanied him. Our departure was shrouded in the utmost secrecy, and not even written orders were issued until after the Inchon operation was completed. Because of the weather, however, we were forced to change our plans at the last minute, and the *SCAP* landed at Itazuke Airfield on Kyushu instead of at Fukuoka, as we had originally intended. One result was that the commanding officer at Itazuke did not know he had a distinguished visitor until MacArthur stepped down from his plane. But our surprised host was able nevertheless to provide us with transportation for the fifty-mile trip to our destination, the naval base at Sasebo. In fact, the air force even provided two blue military police jeeps to lead the convoy, and a new Chevrolet sedan for MacArthur. The sedan was complete with four stars on the front bumper, which seemed to dismay the sergeant driver of the five-star guest. "That's all we could find," he lamented. MacArthur was amused.

Despite the inconvenience and the tension of the occasion, MacArthur was relaxed throughout the two-hour trip and enjoyed the beautiful countryside of Kyushu. The sky had cleared, providing a blue backdrop for the creamy rose colors of a Japanese sunset. But as darkness descended on Kyushu, the charm of the countryside disappeared and our headlights emphasized the curtains of thick, yellow dust rolling up from Japan's country roads. Everything was coated with it by the time we reached the outskirts of Sasebo. As the convoy paused here, one of the members of the party stuck his head in MacArthur's car and, only half joking, asked him if he didn't think SCAP should inaugurate a road-building program in Japan. MacArthur laughed, and said: "The trouble with you fellows is that you're going soft." . . .

The *Mount McKinley* was to be MacArthur's flagship for Inchon. But she had been delayed by the typhoon, and because of the heavy seas had to be warped into the dock; it would be too dangerous to attempt to board her out in the harbor. We were forced to wait only about three hours, but at a time like this it seemed an eternity. We were all tired and hungry, as no dinner had been prepared for us behind the veil of secrecy and expectation that we would board the *Mount McKinley* immediately upon our arrival at the base. But someone had the bright idea that a ship's store nearby would provide our emergency needs, which it did. MacArthur, however, still appeared to be unperturbed. He waited in the base commandant's office, only occasionally betraying the slightest anxiety or impatience by getting up from his chair and resuming his familiar pacing.

It was nearly midnight before the *Mount McKinley's* lines were made fast to the dock and we could go aboard. We lost no time in doing so, and the *Mount McKinley* quickly cast off.

We steamed out of Sasebo's harbor and were hit with the full force of the typhoon-lashed seas. The storm and the racing mountains of water came at us from the port quarter, giving the *Mount McKinley* a sickening combination of pitch and roll. The less said about that first night out, the better.

All the day of the 13th the storm continued to buffet our ship. By the second day out the seas had smoothed somewhat and we did not roll and pitch so heavily. A brisk breeze blew from starboard, off the Korean coast. As we rounded the tip of the Korean peninsula—where Walker and his men were fighting to hold the Pusan beachhead—our course changed; we swung into the Yellow Sea and steamed north for Inchon. The afternoon of the second day was bright and clear as we headed for our rendezvous with the rest of the assault armada.

That evening, as I stood at the port rail of the *Mount McKinley* and watched the sun go down beyond China over the horizon, I could think of nothing but the next morning, D-Day, when we would be threading our way over the shifting bars of "Flying Fish Channel," under the guns of Wolmi-do and skirting the edges of the deadly mud banks that stretched for as much as two miles across the harbor. All over the ship the tension that had been slowly building since our departure was now approaching its climax. Even the Yellow Sea rushing past the ship's sides seemed to bespeak the urgency of our mission.

Inchon, it happened, would mark my twentieth year in active service, and during that time I had accompanied MacArthur on every landing, including every visit to Korea, since Leyte. Only rarely on these occasions had he shown the slightest emotion. But

Inchon was different. Never before had MacArthur embarked on so intricately complicated an amphibious operation. And never before had an operation been carried out with such reluctant approval by the military leaders in Washington. Even with all other considerations aside, it was impossible to measure the personal catastrophe that MacArthur faced should Inchon fail. . . .

We had retired early in preparation for a dawn rising. I judge that I had been asleep for a few moments when I awoke to the sound of knocking on my door. It was the marine sentry who had been posted at the door of MacArthur's cabin.

"General MacArthur would like to see you, sir," he said. I threw on my bathrobe as I followed the sentry down the passageway to MacArthur's cabin. I entered to find him dressed in his robe, his hands thrust deep in the pockets and his brow wrinkled in meditation as he paced the length of the little cabin. He glanced up at me, said quietly: "Sit down, Court," and continued his pacing in silence.

It was a memorable night. The ship rolled gently beneath us as she entered the channel at the prearranged point and time and glided through the darkness toward the target. Faintly I could hear the muffled sound of her engines and the tread of the ship's crew going about their business. The only sound in the cabin was the familiar creak of a ship at sea and the bell of the ship's clock in the wall as it struck the half-hour. Before me MacArthur continued his silent striding, his carpet slippers whispering on the cabin rug. On my left I could see the framed photographs of his wife and son, his father and mother, and his brother—the same photographs that had surrounded him in his Tokyo bedroom, in his cabin aboard the *Nashville* at Leyte, in his temporary headquarters at Port Moresby, and in his office in Manila. These were the symbols of family which meant so much to him and which always went with him, even to such temporary headquarters as a ship's cabin. But despite them MacArthur, at this troubled hour, was a lonely man. My greatest service to him would be not as an aide or adviser but as a friend—to talk with him, hear him think out loud, or share his silence.

What he wanted most was someone to listen to him as he

weighed his thoughts, as he reviewed once more the infinite details as well as the grand design of Inchon. While I sat and listened, he continued his pacing and carried on a monologue that amounted to a kind of self-debate. On the one hand there were the many hazards that lay ahead; they had been graphically described by the Washington officials who had tried to talk him out of the operation. And on the other hand there was only his own reasoning to refute these objections. But did it? Was it still his best judgment that the element of surprise more than made up for the technical difficulties his men would face at dawn? Try as he would, he could not but conclude as he had a month earlier: the very fact of the difficulties was in his favor, for the reason that Inchon would be the last place in Korea where the enemy would expect him to attempt a landing—if the secret known now to so many had been kept. Had it been kept? . . .

His hands thrust even more deeply into his bathrobe pockets, MacArthur frowned as he felt the physical pain of the memory of so many battlefields on which in fifty years of military service he had been forced to commit his men. And as he continued his remarkable soliloquy, he conjured up the scene of the mangled bodies, the bloody wounds, the shrieks of men who fought to live but were to die. In World War II, despite the disparity between the losses occasioned by his surprise landings and the bloody assaults made by the navy and marines against heavily fortified Japanese islands, MacArthur had had to watch thousands of young soldiers pay the supreme sacrifice for their country. He realized that there would be deaths in the morning, no matter how successful the landings; there is no such thing as a bloodless war. But the thought that he might, by a mistake in judgment, be committing hundreds of soldiers, sailors, and marines to slaughter sickened his soul.

He could not believe that this would happen. The same element of surprise that had saved the lives of so many thousands of MacArthur's men in World War II would, he was convinced, protect most of the thousands who now steamed in their blackened ships toward "Flying Fish Channel" and Wolmi-do.

Then he allowed himself to entertain one final doubt. Suppose he was faced with an alerted and well-prepared enemy with a force superior to his own—what then? He could not expect to extricate his forces without considerable loss. The narrow, treacherous channel, the tides, and the sucking mud of Inchon would all be against him. In fact, the entire assault fleet could be placed in greatest jeopardy, and it was possible that tomorrow, September 15, 1950, could go down in history as one of the great United States military disasters. No, there was no doubt about the risk. It was a tremendous gamble. . . .

Finally he stopped his pacing. He stood before the desk and looked at the pictures of his family while he spoke, still as if to himself: "No," he said, "the decision was a sound one, the risks and hazards must be accepted."

His expression changed. The worried creases disappeared from his brow as he turned to me. I rose and he put a hand on my shoulder. "Thanks, Court," he said. "Thanks for listening to me. Now let's get some sleep." He threw off his robe, climbed into his bunk, and reached to the table alongside to pick up his Bible.

As I swung the cabin door closed, I heard the ship's clock strike five bells; it was 2:30 A.M. I went out and took a turn around the deck. . . .

Then I noticed a flash—a light that winked on and off across the water. I sought out the officer of the deck and from him learned that the channel navigation lights were on. Fearful of decoys, the ship's officers had carefully checked them and determined their authenticity. This was the first good omen. Evidently we *were* taking the enemy by surprise. The lights were not even turned off. I felt much relieved as I went to my cabin and turned in.

I could not have been asleep more than a couple of hours when a sudden thunder woke me. Our guns had opened up on Wolmi-do. This was the island which dominated Inchon harbor, and our landings could not proceed until it was reduced. I was trying to get back to sleep when the warning signal was sounded for enemy air attack.

Hurriedly dressing and going to the bridge, I learned that two enemy planes were attempting to bomb the cruiser just ahead of us. The pale lights of dawn had not yet dispersed enough of the darkness for me to follow the course of the action, but an officer reported that both planes were shot down before they could do any damage. I decided, however, that I had better awaken MacArthur because of this danger. When I went into his cabin and gently shook him, he woke, listened while I recounted the incident of the attack, and then turned over to resume his rest. "Wake me up again, Court," he said, "if they attack this ship." I gave up and went back on deck.

It was not long, however, before the red glow of sunrise and the increasing din of battle penetrated his cabin and woke him. He had a quick bite of breakfast and took his position on the *Mount McKinley*'s bridge. From there, as daylight unfolded the scene before us, he scanned the shorelines of Inchon and Wolmi-do through his field glasses.

The water, which had changed from the deep blue of the open ocean to an olive green near the harbor, now showed shades of the silt-filled yellow from which the Yellow Sea gets its name. The closest streaks of yellow water swirled around Wolmi-do, the harbor island that had once been a peaceful summer resort and was now rocking under the bombardment of naval guns and aerial bombs. As MacArthur watched from the bridge, blue Corsairs swooped down from the clouds and added their bombs to the destruction. Through channels that even Korean pilots would not navigate except in broad daylight, and against tidal currents that raced past at speeds up to three and a half knots, destroyers had steamed up alongside Wolmi-do's guns and were bravely daring the beach defenders to open fire on them point-blank, in order to spot the location of coastal batteries for the bigger-gunned ships farther out in the harbor.

Already the bombardment was having its effect, and wreaths of dirty gray smoke were rising from the island. The naval guns were also scoring hits on Inchon itself, and their success was attested to by pillars of purple smoke that rose as high as 5,000 feet. Against this rolling curtain of smoke the arcing, fiery trails of rockets could be seen as they streaked toward Inchon's beaches. It was a devastating amount of fire power; one statistic I recall was that 2,000 rockets ripped into one beach in only twenty minutes before H-Hour. Even from our position out in the harbor we could see the immense explosions that were erupting all along Inchon's shores.

Now the endless circles of little landing craft started churning around and around the mother assault ships. As they did, MacArthur received the word that the enemy guns at Wolmi-do had been silenced. This was one of the best signs that Inchon was lightly defended and that he had indeed achieved the complete surprise on which he had gambled so much. But we could not relax yet. The first assault waves were now going up to the beaches of Wolmi-do. If the marines, who were leading the invasion, were beaten off or even pinned down on the beaches for too long, that would mean that Inchon was protected by the enemy in force. It would take relatively few Communist defenders to slaughter these first waves of invaders while the rest were held back by the enormous mud banks.

Then, finally, the news came. At 8:00 A.M. an orderly climbed up to the bridge and handed MacArthur a slip of paper. His eyes swept it eagerly and his face broke into a broad grin. The message said that the first wave of marines had landed and secured a beachhead without a single fatality. MacArthur turned to Admiral Doyle, the amphibious commander, and said: "Please send this message to the fleet: 'The Navy and the Marines have never shone more brightly than this morning.' " . . .

By the time the tide had gone out of Inchon's harbor only an hour later, leaving some of the landing craft squatting on the mud banks, Wolmi-do had been fully secured. And late that afternoon, as soon as the tides rolled back in, MacArthur climbed into the gig of Admiral Struble, commander of the naval forces, and went ashore at Wolmi-do. There he made the discovery that the Communists had started an intense fortification of the island. As we studied these guns and dugouts, we realized how well MacArthur had timed his attack. Had he listened to those who wanted to delay the landing until the next high tides, nearly a month later, Wolmi-do would have been an impregnable fortress.

Next morning, on the following tide, MacArthur went ashore at Inchon itself, landing on a beach that actually had not been occupied yet. But the Communists had fled, and to get to the front lines MacArthur had to drive three miles beyond the city of Inchon. There he delighted two marine commanders by awarding them the army's Silver Star. He also inspected some North Korean prisoners of war and a Russian-built tank. By early afternoon he climbed along an improvised bridge to Struble's gig to make another inspection of Wolmi-do, where his jeep nearly ran onto an unexploded Russian shell. As the gig finally headed back to the ship, MacArthur rose and took a last look at the shore, where barges were unloading supplies, trucks and jeeps were moving forward along the coastal road, and troops were swinging confidently down the highway into Inchon. He turned back to Admiral Struble and the marine commander, General Shepherd, and said simply: "Well done."

The force that had gone ashore at Inchon had been given the name of the X Corps and constituted a GHQ reserve under the command of MacArthur's chief of staff, Major General Edward Almond. The marines and soldiers of X Corps immediately moved inland in predetermined directions toward predetermined objectives. One column headed for Seoul, with the more immediate mission to cut communications to the south and to seize Kimpo Airfield, the biggest in all Korea. The other column moved on toward Suwon, its mission being to recapture the air base there and to move on as the northern arm of the pincer movement MacArthur intended to apply against the trapped Communists in all of South Korea.

Events now happened with great rapidity. Kimpo Airfield was captured on the 17th, two days after the Inchon landings. One day after that, C-54's and C-119 "Flying Boxcars" came soaring in at the rate of one every eight minutes during the daylight hours. Only three days later the chain reaction of Inchon was felt all the way to the Pusan beachhead, where Walker noticed for the first time signs of growing weakness in the enemy camp.

He had been waiting for this, and promptly crossed the Naktong River in force. The enemy broke in disorder before his attack. Caught between our two pincers, the North Koreans tried to make an orderly retreat, but quickly broke into a rout. Red divisions and regiments ceased to exist as organized units. They abandoned their arms and equipment; tanks, artillery, trucks, and small arms littered the highways all over South Korea. The total of enemy prisoners of war rose to 130,000. In one brilliant stroke—and against the advice of all his superiors—MacArthur had turned defeat into victory and virtually recaptured South Korea.

About all that remained now was Seoul, which the enemy fought fiercely to defend in a face-saving gesture. But by September 28, less than two weeks after the Inchon landings, Seoul was liberated. . . .

On that day MacArthur flew to the newly opened Kimpo Airfield in the *SCAP*, where a five-starred sedan waited for him. Through the swirling dust of Korea's roads he drove from Kimpo to the Han River. Army engineers who had just completed a new pontoon bridge stood proudly at attention as he crossed it. In Seoul his motorcade rolled down Mapo Boulevard, where the rubble of the war had only just been cleaned away and where ROK soldiers saluted sharply as he went by.

Scarcely a house in Seoul failed to bear the scars of battle, and the sight of unburied dead in the midst of such desolation and destruction was heart-sickening. The tragedy of Seoul was alleviated only by the warm smiles of joy and gratitude on the faces of the South Koreans who recognized their liberator.

At the capitol building MacArthur saw Generals Walker and Almond for the first time since he had planned with them the coordinated operations for the Inchon landing and the great pincer movement. With obvious emotion he pinned the Distinguished Service Cross on both of these senior commanders who had so magnificently exploited the situation MacArthur had provided for them. Then a few moments to confer with Syngman Rhee—and the ceremony of handing back the capital city.

Here was another scene as impressive and stirring as it was historic. In the war-shattered assembly room where the ceremony was held sat row on row of heavily armed officers and men of both the U.N. and ROK armies. On both sides of the room the windows gaped brokenly, and the smell of death drifted through them. As I witnessed this occasion, my memory went back to the similar one in Malacañan Palace in Manila, when MacArthur had handed the seat of the government over to the civil authorities of the Philippines. Here too, as he had been at Malacañan, MacArthur was deeply moved. The mask that he was able to wear at times of danger and the eve of great battles did not serve him now. Emotion was visible on his face as he said:

". . . In humble and devout manifestation of gratitude to Almighty God for bringing this decisive victory to our arms, I ask that all present rise and join me in reciting the Lord's Prayer." The steel helmets and mud-caked fatigue caps came off as everyone rose to his feet. Together they recited the Lord's Prayer, and I remember that particles of glass tinkled down from the shattered roof of the assembly room as MacArthur concluded in a voice packed with deep emotion and the crowd murmured in unison: "Thine is the Kingdom, the Power and the Glory, for ever and ever. Amen."

My memory of Malacañan was even more poignant as MacArthur turned to Syngman Rhee and said virtually the same words he had spoken five years before to Sergio Osmeña: "Mr. President, my officers and I will now resume our military duties and leave you and your government to the discharge of the civil responsibility."

President Rhee seemed as moved by it all as MacArthur. He rose from the seat they had been sharing on the platform and clasped MacArthur's hand. "We admire you," he said with tears flowing down his cheeks. "We love you as the savior of our race." . . .

Many were the congratulatory messages waiting for him at the Dai Ichi Building. The text of some of them is particularly interesting because of what was about to take place.

President Truman had wired: "I know that I speak for the entire American people when I send my warmest congratulations on the victory which has been achieved under your leadership in Korea. Few operations in military history can match either the delaying action where you traded space for time in which to build up your forces, or the brilliant maneuver which has now resulted in the liberation of Seoul. . . . I am particularly impressed by the splendid cooperation of our Army, Navy and Air Force. . . . The unification of our arms established by you . . . has set a shining example."

The Joint Chiefs of Staff had not a word to say about their part in endeavoring to kill Inchon, but conceded the soundness of the plan in a generous message: "The Joint Chiefs of Staff are proud of the great successes you have achieved. We realize that they would have been impossible without brilliant and audacious leadership and without the full coordination and the fighting spirit of all forces and all arms. From the sudden initiation of hostilities you have exploited to the utmost all capabilities and opportunities. Your transition from defensive to offensive operations was magnificently planned, timed and executed. You have given new inspiration to the freedom loving peoples of the world. We remain completely confident that the great task entrusted to you by the United Nations will be carried to a successful conclusion." General Marshall wired: "Accept my personal tribute to the courageous campaign you directed in Korea and the daring and perfect strategical operation which virtually terminates the struggle."

Of interest, too, is the message from the British Chiefs of Staff in London: "We send you our warmest contratulations on your brilliant victory. We have admired not only the skill with which you have conducted an extremely difficult rearguard action against odds over many anxious weeks, but equally the bravery and tenacity with which the forces under your command have responded to your inspiring and indefatigable leadership. We believe that the brilliant conception and masterly execution of the Inchon counterstroke which you planned and launched whilst holding the enemy at bay in the south will rank among the finest strategic achievements in military history."

Warmed and gratified by the unanimity of tone in these and many other similar messages, MacArthur pushed on to continue his exploitation of Inchon. First, on October 1, he broadcast a message to the enemy commander-in-chief, calling upon him to have his command lay down its arms and release all United Nations prisoners of war and civilian internees. "The early and total defeat and complete destruction of your armed forces and warmaking potential is now inevitable," he warned. "In order that the decisions of the United Nations may be carried out with a minimum of further loss of life and destruction of property, I, as United Nations Commander-in-Chief, call upon you and the forces under your command, in whatever part of Korea situated, forthwith to lay down your arms and cease hostilities under such military supervision as I may direct—and I call upon you at once to liberate all United Nations prisoners and civilian internees under your control and to make adequate provision for their protection, care, maintenance and immediate transportation to such places as I indicate. . . . I shall anticipate your early decision upon this opportunity to avoid the further useless shedding of blood and destruction of property."

There was no reply, so MacArthur ordered the movement north to continue. Meanwhile he secured the east-coast port city of Wonsan. Thus he attempted simultaneously to close on the remnants of Communist troops fleeing toward North Korea, safeguard the Eighth Army from any attack by regrouped North Korean forces, and provide another badly needed port of entry for supplies and equipment for the U.N. forces who were rapidly liberating all the rest of the area that the Communists had invaded only a little more than five months before.

Inchon had turned the tide of war decisively. The North Korean forces that had attacked their South Korean neighbors were in full flight, and all that remained was to chase them down and finish them off. Nothing could prevent MacArthur and his U.N. forces from accomplishing this now—nothing, that is, so long as those in Washington and the capitals of the other U.N. nations had really meant what they said in their messages of congratulation, and so long as they too wanted the Korean War to end in victory.

The ships, men and countries participating in D day at Inchon: Admiral Struble's armada of 260 ships included ships and men from Canada, New Zealand, Australia, Holland, France—and the British escort carrier *Triumph*. Seventy thousand men were landed on the beaches. Thirty-seven LSTs were operated by Japanese under SCAP's control. The North Koreans sustained 200,000 casualties. One hundred thirty-five thousand North Korean soldiers were captured. The combined U.N. losses were 3500 men during the Inchon-Seoul campaign.

ABOUT THE AUTHOR

Harry Roskolenko ran off to sea at the age of 13. He was a second officer in the merchant marine during World War II and is the author of many books dealing with the South Pacific, Australia, New Guinea, Indo China. He has made two solo trips—one took him around the world on a scooter, and the second down all of the Nile.